LITERATURE OF PLACE

LITERATURE OF PLACE

Dwelling on the
Land before
Earth Day 1970

MELANIE L. SIMO

UNIVERSITY OF VIRGINIA PRESS
CHARLOTTESVILLE AND LONDON

To the memory of
Louise Goodrich, my great-aunt.

This was her time.

Publication of this volume was assisted by a grant from Furthermore:
a program of the J. M. Kaplan Fund.

University of Virginia Press
Printed in the United States of America on acid-free paper

First published 2005

9 8 7 6 5 4 3 2 1

LIBRARY OF CONGRESS CATALOGING-IN-PUBLICATION DATA

Simo, Melanie Louise, 1949–
  Literature of place : dwelling on the land before Earth Day 1970 / Melanie L. Simo.
    p.   cm.
  Includes bibliographical references and index.
  ISBN 0-8139-2500-2 (acid-free paper)
  1. American literature—History and criticism. 2. Landscape in literature.
3. Place (Philosophy) in literature. 4. United States—In literature. 5. Local color in
literature. 6. Regionalism in literature. 7. Setting (Literature) I. Title.
  PS169.L35S57 2006
  810.9'32—dc22   2005014980

All photographs by the author unless otherwise noted

Frontispiece: The old Goffe Mill, Bedford, New Hampshire, now part of the
Wayfarer Conference Center and Quality Inn

Contents

Illustrations

Preface

"I may not know who I am," Wallace Stegner wrote, "but I know where I am from."[1] Returning to his childhood haunts in southern Saskatchewan, Stegner was struck by how much he had never known about the place—even the fact that, in 1805, the Lewis and Clark expedition had come close to it, unawares. In *Wolf Willow* (1962) he recalled his family's homestead on the plains and the little Canadian frontier town, "bare as a picked bone," where they had lived in winter. Back then, a few books had told him of places far away and long ago, while the town dump had told him something about his own neighbors. As a middle-aged man, Stegner saw a few changes in the old town. Then the pungent odor of a gray-leaved plant, wolf willow, brought him back home.

Why do we read, and reread, books like *Wolf Willow*? For the stories, perhaps, or some contact with a place that's authentic, or the pleasure of the author's company. Stegner was a wise and sometimes angry guide to what the western frontier once was and has since become. And there were many others, including Sarah Orne Jewett, Henry James, Willa Cather, Mary Austin, Celia Thaxter, Robert Frost, Joseph Wood Krutch,

James Still, Marjorie Kinnan Rawlings, John Steinbeck, J. B. Jackson, Henry Beston, Rachel Carson, Loren Eiseley, and Wendell Berry, who have shown us what place once was, in novels, poetry, essays, memoirs, and writings on gardens, cities, communities, designed landscapes, and wildlands. Some of their works are finer or more personally revealing than others, but all these writers developed some kind of attachment to a place, then tried to communicate that experience through the written word. The results may tell us a great deal about a particular place—but are they all works of literature? I believe they are.

A literature of place, even one limited to the United States, is bound to be vast and heterogeneous. This book considers selected American works from about 1890 to 1970, a period bracketed by an awareness of frontiers. In 1893 the historian Frederick Jackson Turner called attention to the closing of the western frontier. In July 1969, as the American astronauts set foot on the moon, they dramatized the prospects of another frontier—in outer space. In April 1970, the first Earth Day celebrations were held. Now the latter two events—the moon landing and the first Earth Day—seem to represent a defining moment in our time. Not that euphoria or love for the earth was evenly shared; there were too many divisive events in those years. Yet before July 1969, people could reflect on recent advances in transportation and communication and blandly remark, "It's a small world." Afterward, as the image of a cloud-streaked blue and green sphere in a black void was reproduced again and again, the perception of the earth as not only small but *precious* began to take hold.

As the 1960s came to a close, some Americans called attention to the planet Earth, where social and physical environments were severely stressed and tensions were mounting. Others were optimistic about tourism in outer space and gardens for growing food on the moon.[2] Meanwhile, yet another frontier was opening. As the architect William J. Mitchell recalls, in the fall of 1969, on the UCLA campus, in a back room not far from the university's mainframe computer, some engineers installed a much smaller machine. It was to serve as the first node of ARPANET, which evolved and came to be known as the Internet.[3] Now that expanding network represents the new digital frontier—or cyber-space.

Today the frontiers of outer space and cyberspace remain open. Opportunities to repair the earth also beckon—as a third frontier, but without the wide recognition of a single, unifying phrase. Instead there are signs of promising directions in whatever seems sustainable, new, or next: Sustainable Communities, the Next Industrial Revolution, the Next American Metropolis, the New Urbanism, and more.[4] Then why examine the writings of an earlier time? Why look back?

Wallace Stegner left a clue, admitting his contradictory yearnings for the inheritance of the Old World and the adventures of the New. Then, too, most pioneers try to bring along some heirloom from their old home. Even in cyberspace we find traces of a traditional small town—community, a bulletin board, a room to chat in, sites to visit, people to serve. But as we communicate faster and faster over long distances, as our awareness of geographical space and real time begins to fade, will the traditional meanings of words like "community" and "place" become archaic? The novelist and observer-at-large James Howard Kunstler has described some of the more devastating—and ludicrous—aspects of our contemporary built landscape as a "geography of nowhere." And the astronomer Clifford Stoll has warned, "For all the promises of virtual communities, it's more important to live a real life in a real neighborhood."[5]

More sanguine about these new promises, William J. Mitchell believes that urban design must now be reinvented; we need to extend the definitions of architecture and urban design to virtual places as well as physical places, all electronically interconnected around the globe. And yet for detailed design of the physical places where we live and work, Mitchell looks back to "old-style small towns and urban neighborhoods"—places that the urban critic Jane Jacobs championed in the 1960s, and that New Urbanist planners and designers are studying once again. Ideally, Mitchell suggests, we will devise new patterns that will re-create what was best in older patterns of living that are now disappearing—if they are not already lost.[6]

But what *was* best? Time passes. Memories grow dim. Why not go back to the source, places that people knew intimately in the past and wrote about with conviction? They may have felt isolated, out of touch, or tied to the farm. For what they found mysterious, we may now have scientific explanations. They may have been a bit too close to their experience to keep it in perspective. Or their memory may have been faulty as they pored over their notes on yellow lined paper, then pounded out paragraphs on a Royal Standard typewriter. Think of all they missed. But see what they made of places that others took for granted or never knew.

Acknowledgments

The journey of writing (and reading) a book may be impossible to re-trace. Landmarks do remain, however, and it is a pleasure to notice some of them here.

A generous grant from Furthermore, a program of the J. M. Kaplan Fund, came to me by way of the University of Virginia Press. For that I am very grateful; without such support, this book would probably not have come into being, at least not at this time and in its present form.

At the 2004 symposium "Nature and Culture in the Northern Forest," organized by Pavel Cenkl, of the Association for the Study of Literature and Environment (ASLE), I was able to present a small portion of this book for discussion. To Pavel and all those who attended our session, I extend my thanks for their insights and suggestions.

The doors of many libraries and collections were open to me, at fine universities, colleges (most often, Dartmouth), and other institutions. My thanks go to the librarians, curators, and administrators for their cordial assistance and advice.

At most libraries, state-of-the-art technologies allowed for quick retrieval of items I sought. With a working title, a table of contents, and a growing bibliography—a road map of sorts—I knew what I was looking for. But I could not know precisely what else I needed—ideas, images, unusual books—that would turn up along the way and, in time, become essential parts of the whole. For those moments of serendipity, I depended on many independent booksellers, around the country and nearby. Members of the New Hampshire Antiquarian Booksellers Association and their colleagues in Vermont and elsewhere continue to keep all kinds of books in circulation. Those booksellers are readers, and some are retired professors, now teaching more than they realize.

Their bookshops have also taught me about place, in cities, towns, and out-of-the-way pockets. I recall one journey, driving north through dark redwood forests, coming out into sunlight, and continuing on to a coastal town, with its wooden-plank sidewalks and a many-paned shopwindow full of books—including one that, in time, I needed. Other journeys, driving southwest through mixed hardwood and conifer woodlands— maple, oak, beech, birch, white pine, hemlock—led to something more than a commercial strip along a two-lane highway. There were gas pumps, a grocery store, a garden center, an antiques and collectibles market, and a shop for rare and secondhand books. From inside the shop, through a north-facing window, we could see people chatting as they lined up to buy hot dogs on a Saturday afternoon. Through a south-facing window came the roar of a brook—or a "river," as it is sometimes known. That was for solitude—the waterside window. The view of people by the hot-dog stand was for company—old friends and strangers, talking about books, paintings, politics, the Indian summer weather. We were standing by a table that held doughnuts, coffee, disposable cups, and a framed poster of Muir Woods National Monument. I will always remember that place.

Other landmarks along the journey included Taliesin, in Spring Green, Wisconsin, where Bryan Walton and his colleagues were excellent guides; and Hope, Illinois, east of Urbana, to which my husband kindly drove miles out of our way to see the hamlet where the writer Carl Van Doren had grown up. And the sign reading "Hope" was still standing.

For reading drafts of portions of this book, I thank Larry Anderson, Kate Barnes, Dave Bean, Charles Beveridge, Grady Clay, Bob Cottrell, Barbara Johnson, and Christopher Johnson. They were often much more knowledgeable than I, and some had lived in a place that I could appreciate only from a distance. For their critiques, encouragement, and splendid advice, I am ever grateful.

At the University of Virginia Press, my thanks go to many people, including two editors in particular: Boyd Zenner, who believed in the project and made some excellent suggestions along the way; and Ellen Satrom, who lightened the burdens of the production process in more ways than one. Colleen Romick Clark copyedited the manuscript with great care and extraordinary attention to fine shades of meaning. For any shortcomings that remain, the responsibility is my own.

My husband, Brian, provided one image in this book—his photograph of Mount Haleakala, on the island of Maui. We are both indebted to our parents and extended families for a great deal, including a sense of where we came from, down through generations. They gave us a good place to live. And, although it may have gone over our heads at the time, they taught us ways of knowing, somehow, where we were.

The raging debate over what we have lost and what we have gained, as we flee the old urban patterns of the nineteenth century for the new ones of the twenty-first, is constant. Are we satisfying our deepest yearnings for the good life with Edge City? Or are we poisoning everything across which we sprawl? Getting to the bottom of those questions leads directly to issues of national character, of what we value.

JOEL GARREAU, Edge City: Life on the New Frontier

Introduction

"Literature of Place," an essay by Walter Prichard Eaton, appeared in the autumn of 1918, just as the Great War in Europe was ending. Without mentioning war, Eaton, a writer and former drama critic, may have had in mind the physical destruction of places he had known as he recalled some places known through literature—Robert Burns's bonnie Doon, Shakespeare's Avon, and the lakes of Wordsworth's childhood rambles, as well as American rivers, lakes, mountains, cities, and towns. The American authors he named were a mixed lot—Washington Irving, Sarah Orne Jewett, Mark Twain, George M. Cohan, Celia Thaxter, Walt Whitman, John Muir, and others—but all had taken the simple facts of a place and made of them the "stuff of poetry."[1]

It's an appealing idea—that a literature of place should be inclusive, bridging high culture and popular culture, and limited to no particular genre or form. In Eaton's view, literature of place was not necessarily the literature of *fiction*, although it might be. It might dwell on a place called "home," but not necessarily. Its authors might be well known or obscure. They could be nature writers, focusing on nonhuman life and natural processes, or on human life and local, social norms. What mattered was that the writer could somehow express the *soul* of a place.

That is essentially what a designer of buildings, cities, gardens, and parks often tries to accomplish: to express the *soul* of a place. Usually the aim is to make the place unique and enduring, timeless.

Yet as the architect Christopher Alexander noted in 1979, the timeless way of building, which was once so serviceable and satisfying, had disappeared—at least in the modern, Western world that he knew. By then, Alexander, previously trained in mathematics and the sciences in England, had spent some fourteen years, working with others in Berkeley, California, to evolve a "pattern language." By that he meant some flexible yet methodical way of creating spaces and structures conducive to a rich, full life. What he sought as a designer was something whole yet not entirely contained, something alive and free, yet without ego, without the mark of some dominating will. In time, to characterize his architectural ideal he simply alluded to "the quality without a name," a quality of soul, perhaps.[2]

That is what Henry Beston seems to have had in mind—soul, or spirit—when, in 1935, he wrote of something missing in the gardens of his time, particularly those in the grand manner that seemed to exist merely for display. Those gardens seemed to seek nothing, find nothing: "They make their effect, they attain a perfection, and they are curiously empty of human feeling or emotional appeal." What Beston looked for in a garden was "the mirror of a mind . . . [,] a place of life, a mystery of green moving to the pulse of the year." Along with lovely plants and fragrant, useful herbs, he sought a sense of permanence, order, human associations, and human meaning. In such a garden he could hope to find beauty, occupation, contentment, peace.[3]

These thoughts of Alexander and Beston have lingered in my mind as I have thought about a literature of place from the past that might be meaningful today—not only for designers but for all those who care about the uniqueness and quality of their environment, local and global. There is no dearth of writing on these issues, but I single out Alexander and Beston because, together, their approaches transcend debates about

LITERATURE OF PLACE

modernism versus traditional design, art versus ecology, or humanism versus science. Together, the architect who delights in intimate, humane spaces and the writer who never ceases to find cause for wonder and joy in a small herb garden might offer clues for a kind of design that is not particularly modern or traditional—but simply, deeply satisfying.

In the pages below, Alexander, Beston, and other writers consider the soul or spirit of a place as any designer would. In chapter 6, "The Small Place and the Little Garden," some design issues surface again and again. Chapters 4 and 9 contain vivid memories of small towns before the First World War. Chapter 8 begins with writings by Jane Jacobs and Wolf Von Eckardt on the city. But more often the writer's feelings for place, or home, or some sense of belonging will be evident, while the implications for design remain elusive, between the lines. Some students and teachers may wonder, "Why bother, then? Why press on, if there's not much about design here?"

My short answer would reflect a statement from the literary critic Van Wyck Brooks in 1918. At that time a leader among the younger generation of critics, Brooks was looking for some direction for American culture beyond the advice of the American Pragmatists, even those he considered the best, William James and John Dewey. "For poets and novelists and critics are the pathfinders of society," he insisted.[4]

Today some may find that point debatable—or irrelevant to their concerns. Others might think of pathfinders as a more inclusive group, open to nature writers, ecologists, and other writers of nonfiction as well. But in recent years, with a growing emphasis on scientific knowledge and information technologies, students of planning and design may not be encouraged to read widely, to read poetry, fiction, or nonfiction that has no immediate pragmatic value. There are exceptions, however. In one recent studio course at Yale, as students explored possibilites for design in the workplace, the New York architect Deborah Berke had them read poetry about work—by Walt Whitman, Billy Collins, and others.[5]

The late J. B. Jackson once drew a wide following in schools of design with his essays about ordinary environments that we tend not to notice. And in those seemingly casual yet closely reasoned essays were often some idiosyncratic, even iconoclastic, views of design, planning, and preservation. Jackson was not a novelist, and not primarily a critic, although he observed American society and culture with a sharp eye. He was a kind of poet-geographer, who came to landscape and environmental studies with only a year of professional training—in architecture, at MIT. Yet he had had a wide range of experience, including study and travel in Europe, sheep ranching in the Southwest, and military intelligence during the Second World War.[6] Later his teaching appointments at the University of California–Berkeley and at Harvard in the 1960s and '70s allowed him to offer students of design something like the cultural criticism that Van Wyck Brooks was calling out for in 1918—although at the time Brooks was not very explicit.

Jackson's *American Space: The Centennial Years, 1865–1876* (1972) is an ancestor of sorts for my *Literature of Place* in that it assumes a continental scope and an audience that would include students of planning and design.[7] In fact, we are all indebted to Jackson for models of lucid, graceful prose and fresh insight into problems too complex—socially, culturally, politically, and economically—to be solved by planning and design alone. And yet Jackson's *American Space* is different from *Literature of Place* in that he dwells on spaces and issues that are, in the end, mainly public, affecting the lives of all Americans and of large, sometimes neglected groups. *Literature of Place* strives for a different balance of public and private concerns, often drawing from memoirs and essays to consider the *private* experience of the Great Depression, say, or the loss of the family farm, as well as the impending loss of public places that we tend to take for granted.

✻ ✻ ✻

Literature of Place, spanning the years from about 1890 to 1970, is a kind of mirror image as well as a companion volume to my earlier *Forest and Garden.* The two-part structure is similar, with a focus on certain regions of the United States and certain *types* of places that might appear anywhere in the country. Some ideas came from the earlier study as well, including Eaton's essay "Literature of Place" and Aldo Leopold's idea of uniting natural science and literary art so as to express "the drama of the

LITERATURE OF PLACE

land's workings."[8] Then, too, some of the writings Eaton mentioned in "Literature of Place" were relevant to *Forest and Garden* and its theme of wildness. Other writings, more appropriate for this book, were concerned with home, belonging, and places that were highly cultivated, layered with human experience, whether in Manhattan or thousands of miles away.

Eaton did not anticipate the pervasive standardization and sameness that global trade, finance, and communications are now spreading rapidly. He did notice that places in the United States seemed vulnerable, often impermanent by design or by happenstance. Within a few decades, the swamps and meadows where Eaton had played as a child in the 1880s were absorbed by the Greater Boston metropolis and turned into suburbs. He and his wife chose a more rural place, then, when they left New York in 1910 and moved to the Berkshires of Massachusetts. Settled there, he began to speak out against billboards, hot-dog stands, and other forms of commercial development that crept into the countryside along two-lane roads, leaving "motor slums." By writing essays in mainstream magazines, speaking at conferences, and serving on commissions to protect open land, Eaton tried to defend places against the forces of business as usual.[9]

Other forces became evident later in the century. By 1934 Malcolm Cowley, a younger colleague of Van Wyck Brooks, had recognized that his own generation of writers born around the late 1890s—Ernest Hemingway, F. Scott Fitzgerald, John Dos Passos, and others—had been uprooted long before they sailed to Europe to drive ambulances or take up arms in Europe's Great War. In western Pennsylvania, where Cowley grew up, classes in school were taught with little reference to anything local. Revered writers and thinkers were foreign or long dead. Art, learning, and literature had nothing to do with daily life. And so his generation was "schooled away and almost wrenched away from its attachment to any region or tradition." Education tended to destroy people's roots in the soil and make them "homeless citizens of the world."[10]

Cowley's book *Exile's Return* (1934), briefly mentioned in *Forest and Garden*, contains a few themes important to the chapters below. He recalled Paris, Greenwich Village, rural Connecticut, and a few other places where he and others of the "lost generation" had lived for a while in the 1920s. He recalled people—certain writers who have shaped and colored our views of the modern world. Unrooted in place and tradition, that world seemed at times incoherent, wasteful, frivolous, alienating, but also exciting, energized. And he recalled retreats from the modern world, little islands in space and time, like the converted barn in northwestern Connecticut where, for a season or two, he and his wife could work at a desk in the morning, putter in the garden in the afternoon, and retire to a chair by the kerosene lamp in the evening. In his revision of *Exile's Return* (1951), Cowley identified several stages of exile and the larger pattern of "exile (if only in spirit) and return from exile, of alienation and reintegration."[11]

The pattern of exile and return will recur in these pages, for much of the literature of place depends upon movement away from a place, if only to get a fresh perspective. Sarah Orne Jewett said as much when she passed on to Willa Cather the now legendary advice, "You must know the world before you can know the village."[12] And in Jewett's best-known work, *The Country of the Pointed Firs* (1896), the fictional village of Dunnet Landing on the coast of Maine is seen through the eyes of a narrator who *does* know the world—a woman who has visited the village while on a cruise, then returns one summer to find a quiet place to write.

Most of the *Pointed Firs* stories are centered on older women whose mutual affinities can be measured by the extent to which they can leave many things unsaid. It is the elderly William Blackett, then, who expresses the strongest feeling of attachment to the place as he stands on the highest ledge of Green Island. "There ain't no such view in the world, I expect," Blackett says of his native place. The narrator, too, admires the view of islands, mainland, and bay, but she is at least twice removed from that scene. Green Island is a retreat from Dunnet Landing, which in turn is a retreat from her own world, some place physically and culturally far away. Here, and in the final scene on the deck of the departing steamer, the theme of exile is barely recognizable, so serene are the language and

LITERATURE OF PLACE

the landscape. There is no hint of permanent exile, but we sense the narrator will always feel some distance from the place.[13]

The Country of the Pointed Firs, with its lingering aura of sadness mingled with delight in a place once known, has a strange counterpart in a book by the anthropologist and paleontologist Loren Eiseley. Toward the end of *The Invisible Pyramid* (1970), he described a sunflower forest that used to sprout after floods along a stream near the town (in Nebraska) where he grew up. After wandering through that forest, he and his friends could look back on it from high ground, but they could never find their way back. Their trail would be lost beneath the waving stalks.[14]

That sunflower forest became Eiseley's poetic image of the world of nature out of which human beings evolved from simpler forms of life. The forest also stood for the earth itself, the "blue jewel" then recently photographed from outer space. After the Apollo 11 astronauts had returned, some observers anxiously awaited more flights in outer space. Eiseley understood their yearnings for escape as extensions of the human journey from the world of nature to a second world, one of culture, society, traditions, tools. But he detected desperation in one statement by an aerospace administrator—that unless man fulfilled his destiny (in further space exploration), "the confines of this planet will destroy him."[15]

Eiseley disagreed. The earth had nourished man. *Man* was the threat, the polluter. If he could no longer return to the sunflower forest, he must still *try* to return, using the knowledge gained from space exploration and other journeys in the world of culture. It was a question of survival. If man succeeds, Eiseley mused, it might be by way of a third world, made up of the first two—the natural and the cultural.[16]

The themes of nature and culture, art and science, word and image, exile and return, continue to surface in the literature of place considered here. Often implicit in these writings is an actual or metaphorical voyage of discovery. It may involve a move across town or across the continent, some "immense journey" that may be impossible to quantify or compare—and that's fine.

One aim of this book is to suspend our conventional gauges of importance, of literary or artistic quality or scientific advance, in order to look more closely at a wide range of places—great cities, small mill towns and frontier towns, as well as farm fields and mountains, islands and gardens—that writers have remembered and reconstructed in words on a printed page. Some places have since been drained or logged or bulldozed and paved, then covered over by yet another Wal-Mart. Some remain fragmented—still recognizable, but surrounded by buildings and infrastructures of a later time.

Another aim is to refocus attention on time itself—a period of time, from 1890 to 1970, that might be called the age of the typewriter. Although never one to keep up with all the latest gadgets, Henry James bought a typewriter and hired a part-time typist in 1897.[17] In 1977, when Christopher Alexander mentioned the "vital role" that sophisticated technology had played in the collaborative writing of *A Pattern Language,* he was referring to a copy machine and a few IBM typewriters.[18] Did the typewriter have much impact on James's writing? Would today's far more sophisticated tools have made a difference to Alexander and his co-authors in 1977? Or to Alexander alone in the 1960s? In one old photograph, he is working on his *Notes on the Synthesis of Form* (1964), writing in longhand while seated at a desk covered with magic markers, a jar of rubber cement, books, and what appears to be an Olivetti portable typewriter.[19]

And what if Henry Beston had put aside his sharp pencils to use a typewriter? As his wife recalled, he felt the noise of the keys "destroyed all natural rhythms of the mind."[20] Would Beston have written differently about the land and creatures of the sea and air had his writing tools changed? Are we writing—and reading—differently because, as the critic Sven Birkerts reminds us, we inhabit an environment saturated with signs, words, and images that are no longer fixed? Continually pulsing, speeding us onward, those little cursors keep us from engaging in the "deeper life of words"—or do they?[21] These questions are worth considering, for places and tools are changing all around us at an accelerating rate. In the 1970s, a city's curbside trash might include well-worn office typewriters. Today, personal computers a few years old are tossed out—

Typewriters by the curb, downtown Pittsburgh

not only in cities but in whatever suburban or remote rural area we choose to live and work in, occasionally or year-round.

Some readers may wonder if there is anything more than nostalgia behind these pages. Why should we care what life was like in southwestern Wisconsin, circa 1895, or in an Upper East Side apartment building during World War II? What insights can be drawn? What generalizations? Frankly, I am often more struck by the particulars—small details that may reveal a great deal about people and places. Years ago I was impressed by Kevin Lynch's book *What Time Is This Place?* (1972), a study of urban and rural places where time could be read in small details—parking meters, shop windows, a frozen pond, an industrial waste heap. And the details mattered; Lynch believed that people's well-being depended, in part, on their ability to see legible, tangible connections between past, present, and future.[22]

Planners, architects, and landscape architects know these connections are important; and they can "read" a great deal in anything visual or spatial. Now *Literature of Place* invites another kind of reading, to make connections through stories.

During the Second World War, the writer and poet Elizabeth Coatsworth (who was married to Henry Beston) retold stories that had been handed down through generations of people living in an area of mid-coastal Maine. She believed that many small, deeply loved places would have to be rendered in music, painting, and stories, and absorbed into our very being, if we were ever to become "at home" in America. "For we are not yet at ease with our land," she wrote, "and it is restive and often sullen with us, like a horse which has been roughly broken to riding, and is left frequently standing uncared for in the sleet."[23]

Two decades later, satellite photos of the planet Earth revealed for the first time a lone blue and green sphere in a black void, still in need of care.

PART ONE

THE REGION

ONE

New England

Coastal Towns
and Upland Trails

The day Louise Dickinson Rich first set foot in the general store by the harbor in Corea, on the Gouldsboro Peninsula, she was not entirely a stranger. The storekeeper knew that a woman and her daughter would be arriving that afternoon to spend the summer in the cabin at the end of Cranberry Point. The three men in hip boots and cloth caps, sitting on the bench opposite the counter, also knew this. And everyone knew that the road to the Point could be treacherous to drive on, but Rich would not wait for one of the caretakers. Given directions and warnings, she finally reached the cabin, an L-shaped shelter built of logs and field-stones that seemed to belong there, growing out of moor and ledge, facing the sea. She fell in love with it. Naturally.

Rich describes this incident in *The Peninsula* (1958), a portrait of what was then a relatively unknown stretch of the coast of Maine.[1] Places farther west—Blue Hill, Deer Isle, Rockland, Nobleboro, Gardiner, Sebascodegan Island, Lisbon Falls, South Berwick—were already known through the prose and poetry of some of Maine's finest writers, native or adopted. As some people on the peninsula preferred anonymity, however, Rich had to make her intentions known early on. She sensed that the peninsula was a last frontier, an outpost of individualism that ought to be studied and described before it disappeared.[2]

Rich was also personally engaged; she wanted to find her place on earth, home, somewhere lost in the past. Admittedly nostalgic, she believed she could learn a great deal from the way people lived on this remote peninsula, seemingly bypassed by the modern world. These people worked hard, often alone. They submitted to the great elemental forces of nature and knew them intimately, as they knew their neighbors. In their communities she sensed a rare degree of contentment, tranquility, stability, and peace of mind. Rare, that is, in the 1950s. "Should we leave the past entirely behind us?" she wondered. "Did the people not possess things that we can't afford to jettison and forget?"[3]

Possession and ownership, a sense of belonging or of being an outsider, are especially critical in this first chapter. New England is still a place where stone walls, fences, boundaries, and a sense of belonging are matters of personal, familial, and civic pride. Boston is said to be a "state of mind." So is the entire state of Maine and a few other favored places.

Walter Prichard Eaton, born in Malden, near Boston, wrote about his adopted homeland in western Massachusetts as "Our Berkshires," where the elaborate formal gardens of the summer people would always seem alien to him.[4] Robert P. Tristram Coffin, born in Brunswick, Maine, grew up on an island in nearby Harpswell. Not the genteel part on the mainland, with its sea-captains' mansions, he would quickly add; but the *island,* which was always threatening to secede from mainland Harpswell. Yet Coffin also recognized some primordial connections among parts of his homeland. "Sink a land of long mountain ranges in the ocean, and there you have Maine," he wrote. "The islands are the serrated spines of mountains." And so Coffin linked coastal Maine to its hinterland. Looking northwest from Casco Bay, he could see Portland as "a mountain of an old city . . . with the Presidential Range standing up behind, clean as cut-glass though seventy miles away." Eaton once described the opposite view. On a clear day, he noted, looking southeast from a summit of the Presidential Range in New Hampshire, you could see the blue waters of Casco Bay.[5]

With these glimpses, a local islander and an outsider on a mountain can be equally perceptive. From either direction, the view can be a revelation. It may also change over time. This chapter begins in the mid-twentieth century, with views of the coast of Maine from two outsiders who came to know the place and its people uncommonly well. Peeling back layers of time, we eventually see the Maine coast through the eyes of Sarah Orne Jewett, then retreat to the hills and mountains and move forward from the 1890s to the 1960s. Some large cities and factories are mentioned, but they are peripheral. At the heart of this chapter are more remote places of work, play, congregation, and solitude that can still be found, somewhat altered, in New England.

❧ ❧ ❧

In *Between Wind and Water* (1966) Gerald Warner Brace never allows us to linger too long under the spell of his dreamlike evocations of the coast of Maine. No matter how pungent the smells of spruce and fir or how ghostly the sight of the lighthouse of Petit Manan, at some point he breaks in and shatters the mood of enchantment. Like the clanging of a bell buoy through a dense gray fog that muffles all other sound, Brace abruptly reminds us of realities. Rivers now carry poisons downstream, he writes. Fish are disappearing from the bays. Starlings and crows thrive while hermit thrushes and bald eagles vanish. Increasingly nature is an invented, cultivated scene.[6]

Even in his youth Brace had not been able to maintain the illusion of exploring the unknown several miles out to sea—for he sailed with charts as well as a compass. Granted, tide and wind and fog tested him as they had tested the early explorers. But to the boy in the lobster boat who once towed Brace's leaking boat into a strange harbor, Brace was clearly a summer sailor, someone without any real business in his waters. "In the long run of life you lose the edge of adventure; you get used to strangeness; you have done it all before," Brace admits. "Some may hold the illusion longer than others, but it seems to me that our times are against it."[7]

Those times were the turbulent 1960s. A professor of English at Boston University from the 1940s through the 1960s, Brace could hardly avoid certain pressures, social, political, and academic. But he published more fiction than scholarly research, and, at a time of countercultural questioning, he defended certain illusions and romantic yearnings. His novels were set among the Down East islands and coastal towns that he had known from infancy in the long, leisurely summers before the First World War; and in the hills and mountains of western Massachusetts and southern Vermont, scenes of his college years just after that war.[8] What appealed to him about those places was not only their beauty and their people but also their remoteness, a quality that would soon disappear.

In the early 1900s the journey from his parents' home in Dobbs Ferry, New York, to one of the islands in Penobscot Bay—first North Haven, later Deer Isle and Mill Island—was long and memorable. It involved a series of trips, by horse cab, railway car, and steamers, including two that rolled on in the night and docked around daybreak. Elsewhere Brace would write of siblings, hired help, trunks, pets, and hours whiled away in Boston, en route. Here, all is compressed to sharpen the transition from a mundane, hot, dusty existence to an ethereal one, cold and pure. He recalls the piercing ship's whistle, the strange voices and intonations, the smells of things wet and salty, views of mysterious channels, and glimpses of breakers flecked with gold at sunrise. "It was a colder and brighter and cleaner world than the one you left yesterday," he recalls. "A new world."[9]

That, too, was an illusion, but by admitting as much, Brace disarms his critics. "Men have always been at their best under the spell of illusion, following out their dreams, playing for mortal stakes," he insists. "And they seem to have been at their happiest in close association with what we call nature."[10] Not only the more benign manifestations of nature, Brace might add—but nature as a powerful force, challenging and tempering a people. He admires the uncommon strength and serenity of coastal people, including fictional characters like the eighty-six-year-old islander Mrs. Blackett in Sarah Orne Jewett's *Country of the Pointed Firs* (1896). He comes to know one stalwart individual, the boatbuilder Roy

Coombs, after tracking him down between projects—painting a church mural, shipping a herd of sheep, dynamiting stumps. The natives of Vinal Haven credit Coombs for crafting the fine boat that Brace designs. It's Roy Coombs's boat, they say, and Brace agrees. Coombs was an artist for whom time was not an issue. The price of timber didn't matter. "The great thing was creation itself."[11]

Some will read *Between Wind and Water* for the fine stories about boats: designing them, building them, sailing them. They were Brace's passion, but not the whole of it, for he was writing to defend the values of a fading world, of which handmade seaworthy crafts were only a part. It was a world inhabited year-round by farming and seafaring people who were attuned to the natural forces that shaped and ruled their lives. They used what was at hand—land, water, wind, weather. They made a modest living, and the center of their universe was wherever they were. Brace and his family were outsiders, of course. So was the family of the elder Frederick Law Olmsted, who had first introduced the Braces to the beauty of Deer Isle one summer. (Gerald's grandfather, Charles Loring Brace, founder of the Children's Aid Society in New York, was a boyhood friend of Olmsted's.)[12] But Gerald Brace recalls that his family and other plain-living, unostentatious people were welcomed on the islands. It is a large generalization, but he makes a good case.

In 1966 Brace anticipated a time when human beings would function more and more "electronically." To some extent, human nature would be designed and controlled; and there would be some loss of old traits like independence, endurance, and sensitivity to natural forces—traits indispensable for those who made their living on the sea or on land affected by its presence. That is why *Between Wind and Water* opens and closes with moods of both farewell and discovery. People of Brace's own generation, reared on Wordsworth, Bryant, Whittier, Thoreau, and Emerson, could read the book as a valedictory. Those of a younger generation might still discover there, between illusion and the more sobering aspects of reality, something fresh and new.

While she was getting to know the people of the Gouldsboro Peninsula, Louise Dickinson Rich told one elderly lobsterman about where she had come from—not the towns in Massachusetts where she was born and reared, but the place in Maine where her two children were born, a beautiful country of forested mountains with a Rapid River worthy of its name and a lovely lake, Umbagog, that lay partly in New Hampshire. She described a series of lakes and the aura of light in the surrounding forests, while the lobsterman gazed at the far horizon. He doubted that he could ever live away from the sea—a remark that startled Rich. She herself was more adaptable, and younger—only middle-aged. Were these people misfits in the modern world, she wondered; or were they alone *not* misfits on this planet?

Rich was of Gerald Warner Brace's generation (he was born in 1901; she, in 1903), but her acquaintance with the coast of Maine began much later in life, in her fifties. The cabin at Cranberry Point was lent to her by strangers, people from Chicago who had enjoyed her previous books set in the Maine woods and thought she might like a change of scene.[14] After two summers at their cabin by the sea, Rich often returned to Corea, to a tiny wooden house on the hill above the harbor.

In *The Peninsula* Rich shows how the people of that remote place go about their daily lives, how they speak, what they eat, how the weather and the seasons affect them and their environment, what they live for. One morning before dawn she goes out to sea with a lobsterman to learn about his normally solitary work. She learns that the whole community has contributed in some way to the enterprise, even the children, who have painted wooden buoys and helped their fathers lay out tarred lines to dry in the sun. She sees that the lobsterman is at home in his world, alone, dependent on his own resources for comfort and survival. Then one night in a storm she watches as all the lobstermen drive down to the harbor and shine headlights and spotlights on their tossing boats. At the first sign of trouble, several punts go to the rescue. "Each boat is everybody's boat on nights like this," she writes.[15]

Rich had no reason to doubt that these conditions of solitude and solidarity would last, but other aspects of life on the coast were changing. When a distant whistle sounded, local women would pause, listen, and perhaps leave wet laundry in a basket or cake batter in the bowl to put in some hours at the packing and canning factory in a nearby town. Then, too, that work was part-time, intermittent. The women still knitted bait bags and trap heads, and sons still looked forward to a life of lobstering. "It's the only work I can do where I can be my own boss," one young fellow explained, then added, "I love it."[16]

It happened that Mary Ellen Chase, a native of Blue Hill, set one of her last novels, *The Edge of Darkness* (1957), in a remote place like Corea, somewhere east of Frenchman's Bay. The main occupation is lobstering. Work in a nearby packing and canning factory is sporadic. Adults work hard, some illegally. Most children adopt the values and prejudices of their parents. Some don't. Then something interrupts the daily rounds: a sea-captain's widow dies. It is the end of an era.

The story is bracketed by scenes of the funeral of ninety-year-old Sarah Holt, who had sailed around the world with her husband, Captain Holt, then outlived her husband by half a century. Changes in her lifetime—a shift from sails to steam, the rise of tourism, the loss of shipbuilding and seafaring around the globe—have dimmed the opportunities for sons and grandsons to maintain the self-mastery and independence of their forebears. In dying, the widow leaves a family and a community, both fragmented. And yet the funeral takes place in scenes of great beauty. Men, women, and children gather together from miles around, on the hill and down by the beach. Towing the coffin on a scow, the lobstermen row out to Shag Island—the birthplace and burial place of Sarah Holt, once a thriving center of shipbuilding, now a bit of land reverting to wilderness. The coffin is covered with wildflowers that the children have gathered in nearby swamps and fields. Lucy Norton, who keeps the general store with her husband, has a vision of unity among all those gathered together, despite some mutual animosities and suspicions, to pay their respects to an esteemed neighbor. If only they could all remain like that, Lucy muses, as an aura of unity lingers for a while.[17]

Like Rich, Chase dwells on elusive things—home, belonging, the meaning of a life. Presenting different points of view in the novel, however, Chase leaves such things as risk, security, wildness, and cultivation open to question. Shag Island, a half-wild place where spruces and firs form a dark, encircling wall above the ledges, may seem lonesome. But Elly Randall, the young girl who knows where the red wood lilies are now blooming, *likes* lonesome places. Sam Parker, a lobsterman who has rowed out to Shag Island one evening in fading light and fog to help dig Mrs. Holt's grave, returns the next morning to clear the enclosed burial ground of rank grasses and small trees. He wants to show that the place is not totally abandoned. The children, too, talk of coming to the island some day on a picnic and placing flowers on Mrs. Holt's grave. Some of the children have often sat in that lady's sitting room, heard her stories, and shown her how well they could read. Now they show signs of overcoming their parents' prejudices and failings—perhaps influenced by Mrs. Holt. Maybe they will learn from Elly, whose father has taught her about wild creatures and plants. In time perhaps they will look upon Shag Island as a precious retreat, a half-humanized, half-wild place of mystery and beauty.

Chase's own feeling for places that are partly maintained by humans, partly wild, is evident in *The White Gate* (1954), a memoir of her childhood in the 1890s, in Blue Hill, Maine. In that small, not yet fashionable harbor town, where her father served as a lawyer and district judge, most families kept a cow and, for a small fee, grazed it in someone's pasture. Chase used to enjoy her job leading the family cow to and from pasture, especially on warm summer days when her path led to high ledges and ripe blueberries, rippling brooks and skimming dragonflies. Here and there a dark grove of tall trees would be too frightful to enter alone but wonderful among friends. Once, an itinerant painter, at work in a high pasture, let Chase see for the first time the beauty of her common landscape. Years later she could read the development of her own early consciousness in those pastures. Then it saddened her to see them overrun by alders and undergrowth, virtually lost.[18]

Pastures and cows also meant a lot to Robert P. Tristram Coffin when he was a boy. At the family farm on Sebascodegan Island in Harpswell, as he led the cows to and from pasture, he would swing one of the "story-sticks" that he kept hidden by a pasture gate. Soon the figures of history and myth that he had read about in the district's one-room school would mingle with imaginary ones, and a story would come. He loved that experience: the way a stick balanced as you swung it, the way you could make up life that was better than the one you lived from day to day. He feared that he would lose this ability in town, where there were too many people around to swing the stick properly. But one fear overwhelmed all others in his lightly fictionalized memoir *Lost Paradise* (1934). It was the impending loss of Lost Paradise Farm, a magical place where work was play and land was never far from water. There you could plow and dig up turnips and swim and fish and shoot game in the marsh, and the only terrifying thing nearby was the abandoned Marriner House, which he'd enter by day—but not alone.

These are thoughts of a precocious boy who, at eleven, has already begun to spend weekdays away from the island farm in order to attend school in "Canaan" (Brunswick). The boy, called "Peter," is the sixth of ten children, a dreamer who longs for the farm, the sea, his dog, and his parents, who are larger than life in his eyes, peers of King Arthur and Merlin and Ysolt. But his parents are getting on in years and thinking of more schooling for their younger children. One night in autumn, before the family leaves the farm for winter quarters in town, Peter imagines the slow, relentless deterioration of his family's house and barn, soon to be abandoned to the rain and snow, wind and wild creatures. It is an illusion; his father says they'll return every summer. But all will be different, for Peter will feel like a visitor. The memoir ends with "wandering steps and slow," the last few lines of Milton's *Paradise Lost,* which Peter knows by heart. "You chose the apples of knowledge," he reflects, "and you had to leave the place where the trees were, and the flowers were, that you loved."[19]

Coffin, born in 1892, and Chase, born in 1887, later traveled, studied abroad, became professors of English, and won their laurels—including a Pulitzer Prize for Coffin's *Strange Holiness* (1935), a book of poetry.[20] Coffin married and had children; Chase remained single. Both were children when Sarah Orne Jewett's *Country of the Pointed Firs* appeared in 1896. In effect, they represented some of the promise of their region at a time when Jewett was writing mainly about older people, men and women rich in experience, whose greatest promise lay in the past. Born and reared in South Berwick, Jewett knew that past and appreciated the traditions of these people. She could tell a story of coastal life from the native's point of view; or her narrator, "from away," might be a good listener. On special occasions, such as the Bowden family reunion in the *Pointed Firs*, people rediscover who they are. "Each heart is warm and every face shines with the ancient light."[21]

Mary Ellen Chase had read *The Country of the Pointed Firs* before she met the author on her thirteenth birthday (Jewett was then fifty years old). Years later Chase identified qualities she admired in the book— subtle humor, sensitivity, the precise ear for local speech, the vision through which people and places become more than material for literature; they become "a part of life itself."[22] Another quality is the graceful self-effacement of Jewett's narrator, who makes people feel at ease. They talk freely and share their treasured stories, while the narrator forgets her own writing projects for a while.

We never learn what those projects are. We do know that Jewett sometimes brought social and environmental issues to the forefront in her fiction—the inadequate wages and layoffs at a textile factory, the shooting of wild birds, the clear-cutting of forests, the preservation of old-growth, "landmark" trees. In "The White Rose Road" (1889), the narrator, her driver, and a friend ride in a horse-drawn carriage along country roads not far from South Berwick. On high ground some farmers still work the land and keep their fields cleared. The lowland pastures and rocky hillsides, reverting to woodland, may be poor for grazing and not yet good for timbering. But the narrator knows that those old pastures harbor small wild creatures, wildflowers, and berries. She shares recollections with an old farmer and notices his orphaned grandchildren. Along the road, her attention is also drawn to other things—a funeral, old shrub roses, a view of Mount Agamenticus and the sea. She recalls an abandoned, once lovingly tended garden in Virginia. Her mood of pleasant rambling is broken, however, by thoughts of wastes from factories and tanneries that pollute New England streams and the loss of smelts, bass, shad, and salmon from an upper branch of the Piscataqua River. "Man has done his best to ruin the world he lives in," the narrator muses, briefly, before her mood shifts. Climbing a hill, she sees green fields and houses that seem comfortable. The cheerful scene suggests that wisdom about fish and other things may come in time. Meanwhile, she has a fresh awareness of the "possibilities of rural life."[23]

✻ ✻ ✻

One evening in January 1890, Jewett returned from the country to the home of her companion, Annie Fields, at 148 Charles Street, Boston—where the two literary women used to receive friends on Saturday afternoons. In Jewett's absence, Bradford Torrey had called and left her a copy of *A Rambler's Lease* (1889), his most recent collection of essays on country matters. Writing to thank him, Jewett admitted that she had already read the book and found it delightful. She appreciated the clarity of his vision and his ability to lead others, less sharp-eyed, to see.[24] Torrey could have returned that compliment—although Jewett's gaze was more often directed toward human life, and his, toward birds, moths, beetles, and their habitats. Jewett's motivations were not mainly sociological, however, and Torrey's were not mainly scientific. "There are times when we go out-of-doors, not after information, but in quest of a mood," he observed.[25]

Within two years Torrey's—and Jewett's—publisher brought out a kindred work, *Land of the Lingering Snow* (1891), by Frank Bolles, previously known to the readers of the *Boston Post* as "O.W.L." In his letters to the *Post,* Bolles had described jaunts from his home in Cambridge to some of the wilder lands nearby—Fresh Pond, the Arnold Arboretum, the heights of Belmont and Arlington—as well as to his beloved Mount Chocorua, a peak in the Sandwich Range of New Hampshire. Slightly altered, Bolles's letters formed the basis of *Land of the Lingering Snow,* a book that embodies something of Torrey's patient, nonscientific approach to observing wild creatures, especially birds.[26]

There was a difference, however, in what these men listened for and heard. Torrey could remember vividly the song of a particular bird at a certain time and place, then convey the essence of that experience long afterward. One morning in late September, walking up the Landaff Valley, south of Franconia, New Hampshire, he paused at the first sound of a hermit thrush. He spotted the bird in a tree by the roadside, and in its voice Torrey sensed a mood of reminiscence. Some years later he recalled that hermit thrush's song as "the soul of a year's music distilled in a few drops of sound." Less concise, Bolles would keep searching for words to express what *he* heard, early one morning in May, as he entered a shady swamp near the base of Mount Chocorua. After several birds had chirped and sung, the music of a winter wren seemed to him "like falling drops of crystal water in which the sunbeams play and give out rainbow tints." Then, again, it sounded "like the music of tiny spheres of silver, falling upon slabs of marble and rebounding only to fall again and again at briefer intervals, until their perfectly clear, ringing notes had run into one high, expiring tone too delicate for the ear of man to follow."[27]

Thirteen years younger than Torrey, Bolles was more outspoken about traces of human carelessness—hillsides denuded of trees, for instance; the foul-smelling Charles River and Alewife Brook, used as open sewers; the polluted Nashua River; and tin cans and broken bottles lying below the summit of Mount Wachusett, near Fitchburg, Massachusetts. Then, too, Bolles was a city dweller, a husband and a father of four little girls. Torrey, a bachelor, lived in the village of Wellesley Hills and went to Boston for business and on errands. Bolles lived in Cambridge, and his administrative job at Harvard kept him in town most weekdays throughout the academic year. All the more refreshing, then, was his *Land of the Lingering Snow,* an invitation to other city dwellers to get out and explore the Boston area's wildlands on foot, with some assistance from trolleys, trains, and rented horse-drawn carriages. Some places have since vanished, including the maple swamps of Alewife Brook and certain marshes in Cambridge. Some places remain—the dunes of Ipswich, those "waves of the sea perpetuated in sand," for instance, and the Middlesex Fells.[28]

The mountains of New Hampshire were then accessible by train from Boston's North Station. To reach the base of Mount Chocorua would

THE REGION

take about seven hours, mainly by rail and along shore—that is, until the Piscataqua River divided Portsmouth, New Hampshire, from Kittery, Maine, and the train veered inland. One day in May 1891, from a train window pelted with rain, Bolles watched the drama of tidal rivers churning, marsh grasses bowing, and haystacks spinning around at different rates of speed, depending on their distance from the train. Farther inland, rivers swelled and mountains lay hidden in clouds. After transferring to a stagecoach, Bolles passed Lake Chocorua and finally arrived at his farmhouse—which until recently had been abandoned to deer, crow, fox, and hedgehog. The farmhouse hadn't changed much. "I have done what I can to maintain the belief among the creatures of the forest that it belongs to them," he explained.[29]

In that regard, Bolles and Torrey were of the same mind; they believed that no legal document could confer the kind of possession that wild creatures of the forests and fields had enjoyed long before humans arrived. The two men also enjoyed a spiritual possession of land, something that was not necessarily shared by holders of deeds. Yet it was there for the taking, accessible to anyone with keen senses, curiosity, patience, and perhaps some scientific grounding like that of Torrey's unnamed botanist friend, an "old Franconian," whose spirit lived on in the mosses, the wildflowers, and a certain willow that he had found intriguing.[30]

South of Mount Chocorua, Bolles's spirit lives on in a pond and a pine forest on the grounds of his old farmhouse. Today, 247 acres of those grounds form the Frank Bolles Nature Preserve, a gift of Evelyn B. Phenix, Bolles's daughter, to the Nature Conservancy in 1969. And a few miles to the west, the Bolles Trail runs north across the Sandwich Range from the site of the old Paugus sawmill to the Swift River and what is now the Kancamagus Highway. In *At the North of Bearcamp Water* (1893) Bolles tells about that formerly "lost" trail and credits those who helped to bring it back, including the local farmer and lumberman Nat Berry, who helped Bolles find the passage and blaze the trail, and the people who came a few days later—the men with axes and hatchets to clear the trail, and the women on horseback to test it for comfort. The trail is now an appealing alternative to the more popular hiking trails in those still

Lake Chocorua and the summit of Mount Chocorua, in the Sandwich Range, New Hampshire

fairly wild mountains. But Bolles had also envisioned the trail as a valuable link with civilization—a post office, a store, a doctor, a minister—for people living at the remote, upper end of the Swift River valley.[31]

That is an issue worth tracking down among the many works that touch on New England's upland trails—civilization, its blessings and its ravages. Both Torrey and Bolles cherished their days spent in wildlands, in part because they knew those days were fleeting and that warm, dry beds and human society awaited them on their return. On balance, Bolles seems to have shown more interest in certain aspects of civilization—the repopulation of the abandoned farm country in northern New England, the living conditions of loggers (some with wives and children), and the functional purposes of trails and roads between settlements. Torrey was alert to the varying *degrees* of civilization favored by living creatures. If he noticed no pileated woodpeckers deep in the northern forests, he knew where to find them—on the outskirts of villages, along the Bethlehem Road, and in the more open woods of the valleys. "They have something of Thoreau's mind," Torrey wrote of those birds; "lovers of the wild, they are yet not quite at home in the wilderness, and prefer the woodman's path to the logger's."[32]

Works by Torrey (who edited Thoreau's journals) and Bolles are rooted in a more leisurely age than ours, a time of long journeys by rail, long letters written in handsome script—often answered within a day or two—and long hours devoted to the business of keeping warm on a winter's day. Like Thoreau, Bolles feels no inclination to count the hours passed in quiet observation, doing what others would think of as nothing at all. In *At the North of Bearcamp Water* he dwells on minute details of wildlife in the orchards and bogs, and on little gusts in a grove that keep the canopy of tall beeches moving and changing, now and then filling the air with golden leaves that will settle on the ground and await the snow. Time slows to a trickle. Bolles returns to a familiar theme of his—the unfathomable qualities of life and death. And there is nothing morbid in these thoughts, only a recurring conviction that all in nature is rhythmic and eternal, its life force like a pendulum in a continual rise and fall. Nothing essential is lost, he concludes. Matter is eternal. Something that was once a part of life has simply been transferred.[33]

Bolles died young. He was not yet thirty-eight when, in 1894, he succumbed to pneumonia. All the more poignant, then, are some of his *Bearcamp Water* essays—close studies of life going on around him, which incidentally reveal a man living his own life intensely. The summer night that Bolles spent alone on Mount Chocorua was not merely an occasion to conquer a summit and overcome the normal human fears of darkness, weariness, thunderstorms, and lightning strikes near granite cliffs. Nor was it simply an opportunity to watch meteor showers from a more exalted spot than a field. As he tells the story, understating and lightly mocking the dangers he faced, the narrow cave beneath the huge Cow Rock becomes more than shelter in a storm. The lights of the Pleiades, Venus, Mars, Jupiter, and the passing meteors are more than a display of sparkling, glowing, changing colors. These are all elements in a cosmic struggle between light and dark, day and night, in which there is ultimately no winner or loser, only alternations between scintillation and repose.

Bolles's ultimate reflection on that solitary experience, however, was not even about these grand adversaries—the infinitely remote, dark night and the bright, task-driven day. Instead he focused on the time of fading night, just before dawn, when first a white-throated sparrow sang, then different birds joined in, fifty or more. "There was ecstasy in those matins," Bolles recalled. To him it seemed a choir of sound in honor of the new day, a joyous affirmation of life: "The birds bear witness to the ability of life to love its surroundings and to be happy. The night bears witness to the eternity of life and to the harmony of its laws."[34]

***

Walter Prichard Eaton mentions Bolles in his essay "Literature of Place" (1918). Allen Chamberlain refers to Bolles's lonely night on Mt. Chocorua in his book *Vacation Tramps in New England Highlands* (1919). A recent edition of the Appalachian Mountain Club's *White Mountain Guide* briefly explains the origins of the Bolles Trail before letting hikers know what to expect along the journey of three or four hours across the Sandwich Range. That may be one of Bolles's most enduring legacies, a trail maintained by some public-spirited, energetic people so that others may come along and explore a bit of rugged country on foot.[35]

And Bolles's writing? Evidently Eaton hoped to carry on the kind of nature writing for which Bolles, Torrey, Thoreau, Enos Mills, and John Muir found ample audiences. In the early twentieth century, a widespread movement toward nature study and life out-of-doors kept the field of nature writing wide open. But sometime after the Great War of 1914–18, Eaton found that readers' (and editors') interests were changing along with the times. The faster pace of modern life, in cities, in industry; the ways people chose to spend their leisure time; even the very idea of "leisure" as something separate from productive work; all would influence a reader's interests and tastes. Here, rather than speculate on the fundamental causes for changing tastes in literature, we might isolate just one factor—transportation—and consider how quickly or slowly people got around from place to place in the hinterlands of New England.

Eaton had his first glimpse of the Berkshire Hills in September 1899. Before entering his senior year in college, he left Boston on a train that ran west through Fitchburg and Greenfield, then up the Deerfield River. From the station at Zoar, he rode north in a stagecoach to the higher ground of Rowe, a village with a church, a general store, a sawmill, and a few houses. There he boarded at a widow's home and set off on daily "tramps," alone or with the local minister. Looking down into a gorge, he saw the Deerfield River flowing south out of Vermont. From a high pasture he saw the peak of Vermont's Haystack Mountain. One day he walked down a steep dirt road into the factory town of North Adams, Massachusetts, then took a trolley to Williamstown, a college town. Returning to Rowe, he rode the night train through the Hoosac Tunnel, then ascended in darkness, on foot, along the swift Pelham Brook. "I felt oddly as if I were going home," he wrote nearly fifty years later.[36]

He was. After leaving college and working as a drama critic and journalist for ten years, mainly in New York, Eaton settled in the Berkshires in 1910. He returned not to the wildly picturesque northern gorges, however, but to the gentler lands farther south: first to a village house in

Stockbridge, where he wrote most of *Green Trails and Upland Pastures* (1917); then to an old farmhouse in Sheffield. There, with views across old fields that hugged the lower slopes of Mount Everett, Eaton wrote several more books, including *In Berkshire Fields* (1920), *On Yankee Hilltops* (1933), and *Wild Gardens of New England* (1936).[37] These were collections of essays about hiking, gardening, birds and other wild creatures, and chores such as chopping wood to feed several fireplaces in the old farmhouse.

In some of those essays, Eaton dwelled on boyhood memories of stone walls, meadows, and marshes along the Ipswich River, north of Boston, and the salt ponds and shores of Old South County, in Rhode Island. Eaton's deepest affection seemed to be reserved for higher ground, however—high pastures along the flanks of Mount Everett; Berkshire County hill towns with cellar holes and bits of usable treasure; trails up Mount Katahdin, in Maine; and, in the White Mountains, Mount Moosilauke, which he had first seen from within a barn as a thunderstorm subsided. He was then a sleepy child, a bit worn out from the long train journey from Boston and the bumpy ride in a horse-drawn wagon. But as rain clouds and mists rose up and vanished, there appeared through the open barn door the flanks, shoulders, and peak of Moosilauke, unforgettable and incomparable. "It came out of the mist of rain; it came framed alone," Eaton recalled.[38]

In time, Eaton would write less about enchanting views and more about environmental issues, such as logging on steep slopes, soil erosion, and intrusive motor roads to a mountain summit. His allusions to blossoming romance along mountain brooks subsided, but his memories of childhood and feelings for the spiritually rewarding aspects of country life would surface again and again. In one essay, "Upland Pastures" (1914), he delights in a Berkshire winter, when the motor cars of the summer people have vanished and the sounds of horses' hoofs and sleigh bells prevail. Then he and his wife can wander afield on snowshoes, oblivious to property lines but alert to the tracks of foxes, pheasants, rabbits, and deer.[39]

In "Nature and the Psalmist" (1915), Eaton let the verse beginning "I will lift up mine eyes unto the hills" initiate a reverie that transcended regional affinities, even a fondness for high places. What Mount Greylock and Mount Moosilauke were to him, the sea, the prairie, the Arctic, and the tropics might be to others. What mattered was the sense of divinity in the lands and waters of one's surroundings. He knew that Native Americans understood those things—the Pemigewassets, who believed that the Great Spirit dwelled on the summit of Moosilauke, and the Narragansetts, who named a beautiful fresh-water pond in Rhode Island "The Lake of the Great White Gull." But the need for a return to "primal wonder" was especially acute in modern life, Eaton observed, "when neither the scientific inquiry of the naturalist nor the summer exodus through the countryside in automobiles is enough to give the world again the quick, poetic, instinctive sense of the divinity of rocks and trees and springing crops."[40]

Perhaps Eaton knew he was fighting a losing battle for those needs of the spirit. If so, he fought harder with all the eloquence he could muster. His fellow enthusiast for high places, Allen Chamberlain, took another tack. In *Vacation Tramps in New England Highlands* he offered practical advice on what to pack, how to get there (by train, stagecoach, or rented autos, then on foot), and where to stay (in summit houses, huts, shelters, and nearby farmhouses). Chamberlain quoted Muir (mountains as fountains of life) and Enos Mills (the trail, a web of joy spreading over wild gardens). Otherwise he avoided anything mystical, poetic, or controversial. His accounts of trails, estimated times, and work accomplished by the Appalachian Mountain Club, the Dartmouth Outing Club, and the Green Mountain Club all seem realistic and reliable—although some of his facts are remarkable. In summer, for instance, three trains a day ran between Boston and the little village of Glencliff, on the edge of the White Mountain National Forest![41]

To find out how people got around among the hills and mountains of New England (increasingly by private auto), we could pore over travel literature such as Louise Closser Hale's *We Discover New England* (1915) and Charles Hanson Towne's *Jogging Around New England* (1939), as well as WPA guides to the states. In *The Friendly Mountains* (1942), a volume in Roderick Peattie's American Mountain Series, Katharine Toll mentions bobsleds as well as rope tows, chairlifts, aerial tramways, and other lifts for skiers in the Adirondacks, the Green Mountains, the White Mountains, and the Berkshires. Before the Second World War, she recalls, "snow trains" used to bring skiers to the mountains on Sundays from Boston and New York, sometimes from Albany, Hartford, and Springfield. But as details of trains, tows, boots, lessons, and lift tickets accumulate, we move further away from personal experience and acute perceptions.[42]

It is rare, but not impossible, to find within those midcentury series of books on American mountains, rivers, regions, and states a voice that seems more suited to the personal essay or to poetry. Eaton's voice is usually like that—more lyrical than factual. The nonfiction writing of his contemporary Dorothy Canfield Fisher may seem detached at times; yet her "Hiker's Philosophy" is one of the more personal contributions to a fine collection of essays on the human and natural history of Vermont's Long Trail, *Footpath in the Wilderness* (1941). A prolific novelist, Fisher was also a Vermonter by inheritance. She grew up in Kansas and Nebraska but spent childhood summers on her grandparents' farm in Arlington, Vermont. In 1907 she returned, newly married, to make Arlington her home—mainly on a Canfield family farm but also along mountain trails. Living out-of-doors "restores to us something we lose with indoor comfort and ease," she writes. It has to do with wholeness, self-reliance. We set aside whatever specialized work we do in the modern world and shape a few raw materials to our basic needs. Then even breakfast can be an event: "when, stirring before dawn, you pause, frying pan in hand perhaps, to gaze, smitten with awe, at the miracle of the daily flooding of our planet with light."[43]

✳ ✳ ✳

Nearing seventy, Eaton was asked to write the introductory chapter of *The Berkshires* (1948), another volume in Roderick Peattie's American Mountain Series. He did so, letting a woman have the last word. Esther Edwards, aged seventeen, daughter of the theologian Jonathan Edwards, was leaving her native Stockbridge to be married. It was June 1752. Heading west, she turned back to see her little town in the valley below. Her diary reads, "On either side stood the hills, lately clothed with new verdure; between them the beautiful intervales; beneath which crept the river, the smooth-gliding Housatonic, and where were feeding the cattle. I shut my eyes if I might fix the picture and make it mine forever, and then rode on with my companions."[44]

More than a century later, in *The Country of the Pointed Firs,* Sarah Orne Jewett's narrator stood on the deck of a steamer and looked back at the harbor town of Dunnet Landing. The language was more flowing than that of Esther Edwards, and the scene cinematic, not still. The narrator saw grazing sheep, not cows. She waved to old Elijah Tilley in his dory. He nodded. She said nothing aloud, yet between the lines we sense the same desire to capture a place and make it one's own, forever.

That is the desire of many writers in these pages. They are seeking what John Hay sought in 1969, when he tried to get beyond the kind of possession that leaves us impoverished. "Possession has thrown place behind, knocked out the ghosts and woodland dreams," he wrote, as traces of careless, mindless possession sprawled about him on a beach at Cape Cod. In the sky was a thin line left by a jet bomber; on the sands, bits of oil; in the grass, litter. Then the thought of fish (alewives) running "like galaxies in the heavens" gave him cause for hope. Among such confident, resourceful living beings he might still belong.[45]

Hay's essays about places in New England make some demands on the reader. "Slow down," he writes in *Nature's Year: The Seasons of Cape Cod* (1961). That calm, quiet study begins with a terrible car crash. Beneath a hot July sun, Hay is one of many drivers forced to pause in their annual migration to the sea; they must witness calamity and death before moving on, picking up speed. Hay ends the book, however, with a slow, gentle rain in June, binding forms of life to one another.[46]

Hay's *In Defense of Nature* (1969) is often harsher in tone, reflecting the times. Signs of violence, poverty, greed, poisoning, and deterioration keep turning up, in a land teeming with technological marvels. People are no longer bound to one place but incredibly mobile, moving faster, living longer. Through genetic manipulation, they may even direct the course of human evolution. Having heard the futurists' predictions, Hay simply asks, "Do we know what we are losing?" His answer lies in a series of meditations on many natural resources that need conserving—not only in his home territory of Cape Cod, and not merely the resources of oil, gas, timber, or uranium, but *inner* natural resources. "The soul still needs to stretch," he writes; "being needs exercise." And so he is patient, peering into a salt-water cove in Maine, watching a great blue heron as it stirs up fish with one slow, deliberate step and then another. Once Hay has climbed above the tide line of that little cove, he knows he is upland. The bit of woods he stands in is merely the fringe of a field, a wooded fringe that is continually being eaten away by chain saws. Still, those woods belong with the great northern forest.[47]

Along with others in these pages, John Hay writes about place, home, and belonging on many levels, local and global. Like Thoreau, he sees humans as a part of nature, not separate from it, dominating and destroying it. And so he moves from minute, concrete details of places by the sea and in the mountains, to something intangible. We can cut down any tree, we can move things, or we can try to belong, he suggests; "the available world, the whole earth with its sea of life, still has its correspondence to a home, somewhere inside us."[48]

The Southern
Highlands

When Horace Kephart first set out to explore the southern highlands, in 1904, he had little to guide him—a few maps, a government report on forestry, some fragments of literature. A former librarian, he knew of one vague reference to the wild mountains of Virginia, in a story by Edgar Allan Poe. He was familiar with popular fiction set in the hills of Kentucky and Tennessee. But the higher mountains of eight contiguous southern states, some 650 miles of the Appalachian Mountain system, were still mysterious and largely unexamined.[1]

Nine years later Kephart brought out *Our Southern Highlanders* (1913), now a classic study. It was not definitive. "The great mountain masses still await their annalist, their artist, and, in some places, even their explorer," he wrote. And yet, having lived in the mountains of western North Carolina and explored much more of Appalachia, he had come to appreciate the mountain people, their conditions, their tacit assumptions. He understood their need for elbow room and solitude, their disdain of charity and luxury, their hospitality to kinfolk and strangers alike. He knew how to dispose of his gun on entering a mountain cabin. He knew the geographical limits of blood feuds and traced their cultural origins to seventeenth-century Scotland and England. Now, as railroads and auto roads brought modern civilization deeper into the mountains, old grudges, old ways were fading. In a new era, would the independence of these mountain people survive? The issues were complex, the writer objective yet sympathetic. Since then, many others have turned to Kephart's book to understand both the place and the people.[2]

One small book that Kephart may have overlooked, however, is Bradford Torrey's *A World of Green Hills: Observations of Nature and Human Nature in the Blue Ridge* (1898). Birds were his main interest during those weeks of April and early May, six or seven years before Kephart came to the southern highlands. Then, too, Torrey never penetrated the dark corners of the Blue Ridge and the Smokies that Kephart sought out. The roughest roads and wildest waters Torrey came across were never far from the hotel that served as his base camp for daily jaunts, mainly on foot. In contrast, Kephart distanced himself from hotels and tourists; he wanted to understand *real* mountaineers, the typical mountain man and his family, whose remoteness from the rest of twentieth-century America seemed to preserve a way of life essentially unchanged from the eighteenth century. Some unforgettable characters stood out, but Kephart's main interest was the typical, and a way of life that might soon disappear.

Torrey observed the rare along with the typical among birds, trees, wildflowers, and humans, young and old, resident and migrant. He also noticed people and things that Kephart did not mention. For instance, from just below the summit of Peak Knob—or "Peach Knob"—Torrey surveyed a sea of mountain peaks on the horizon and spotted the town of Pulaski, Virginia, a thousand feet below, in a valley lying some two thousand feet above sea level. Down there was his hotel, the Pulaski railroad station, an industrial furnace, and another furnace perhaps a mile or two away, with open country in between. About halfway up the mountain, on the knolls, he noticed a hamlet of scattered houses, each with its own garden, orchard, and bushes of currants and gooseberries. African Americans lived there—"black highlanders," he called them. The place seemed "thrifty," and a maze of paths and roads led to the highway below.

On another occasion, walking up a mountain road east of Pulaski, Torrey came upon a group of black children carrying branches of flowering apple trees back to the town. The children seemed happy. Torrey then recalled another black child, down in Florida, who had listened attentively to the cooing of a mourning dove. Were these children unusually susceptible to natural sights and sounds, he wondered, as they lived "nearer to nature than some of us"?[4]

From Pulaski, Virginia, to the small mountain village of Highlands, North Carolina, by the famous Natural Bridge and in isolated hollows, Torrey came across people who seemed remarkably gentle, courteous, happy. He freely admitted that his main interest was in flora and fauna. And yet, in his quest for birds such as the elusive raven, he had to approach more than one passerby for advice and reassurance. Once, an unexpected bird—a female Wilson's phalarope—was flushed from beneath a bridge as a carriage passed overhead, driven by a woman in a large black bonnet. Silently Torrey thanked the woman, then became absorbed by every feature, every motion of this winged straggler, which had been blown off course, perhaps, en route to the upper Mississippi Valley or places farther north and west. Now it was swimming, wading, feeding, and preening in a mountain pond nearly four thousand feet above sea level. This was an artificial pond about a mile from Highlands, its waters held by a dam and its harsh edges not yet softened by rain and wind and wild growth. Still, it was home—or a temporary refuge—for spotted and solitary sandpipers, barn swallows, rough-wings, brown creepers, a phoebe, and the curious phalarope. Torrey could have focused solely on the birds at the pond and along creeks and mountain roads, but he was intrigued by the people as well, coming and going, often on foot.

Approaching the shy mountain children was difficult for Torrey. He had no gift for meeting strangers, he explained. With parents, he might exchange a greeting, then come away unsure of the meaning of a word or two. Later, he was not entirely consistent in his reflections. "The lot of the native mountaineers is hard and pinched," he wrote, recalling a mother and her son of about ten or eleven, running a crosscut saw through a large fallen trunk. He had seen a father, mother, and son trudging up a mountain road, each with a sack of grain or a large bundle to carry. For the children, especially, prospects seemed dim; yet they seemed happy, playing near the cabin door. They and their families lived in poverty, but not the "degrading, squalid poverty" of an urban slum. Here their playground was magnificent, a landscape of great beauty. These people treated him, a stranger, with kindness. Apparently they enjoyed life. In any event, Torrey remained an observer, not a reformer. What strikes us, a century later, is Torrey's impartial eye, alighting on whatever seemed rare, curious, or interesting. "It is one advantage of out-of-the-way places that they encourage human intercourse, as poverty helps people to be generous," he remarked, then resumed his story of the raven.[5]

After rambling for a few weeks in the Blue Ridge, Torrey admitted that his observations were limited (and sporadic). On a train to the Natural Bridge, two elderly men were conversing. Both were African American, old enough to recall the days before the Civil War. Now each addressed the other as "mister" repeatedly: "Mr. Brown" and "Mr. Smith." Torrey noted this token of dignity among men, perhaps former slaves, with the same acute but fleeting attention that he gave the homes of rough-winged swallows: nests within a row of holes in stratified rock by a stream. Water dripped before the holes. Above the nests were ferns, sedges, and arborvitae; below one nest was a doormat of green moss. What links these observations are the eye and ear of a single observer, alert to changes in human time but also in geological time.

Studying panoramas of hazy, forested mountains and the high peaks of Whiteside, in North Carolina, and Rabun Bald, in Georgia, Torrey noticed fleeting shadows cast by little cumulus clouds. He thought of the earth itself as a fleeting shadow, evolving, changing. In geological time, all before him would pass away. Meanwhile he would long remember a small garden on the flanks of Mount Satulah, once Native American territory, now the property of a man named Selleck. In the garden he admired the fine old oaks, chestnuts, and maples, the ferns, the mountain laurel, the azaleas: a landscape of greens, browns, pale pinks, and yellows. The colors of spring would soon change, but Torrey hoped that the landscape garden as a whole would last until his own dying day.

***

That desire, to preserve something of the earth from passing away, is pervasive in *The Carolina Mountains* (1913), by Margaret Warner Morley. The book opens with glimpses of peach trees in bloom, seen from a train heading west to the mountains of North Carolina. With allusions to enchantment and a "Fortress of Dreams" that represents a real place in the Blue Ridge, this could be the beginning of an enticing travel guide. In fact, people may have used it as such, for Morely describes the mountains, lakes, rivers, resort towns, and nearby cities such as Asheville and Hendersonville. But soon it becomes clear that Morley had other intentions as well.

Beyond extolling the beauty of each season in the mountains near Tryon, North Carolina (where she lived for parts of the year and tended a garden), Morley wanted to defend the forests from careless exploitation. She wanted people—especially those not native to the southern mountains—to obey the command of the southern sun and slow down, perhaps cultivate the local art of "settin' around," and discover what it was to be rich in *time*. She wanted readers to appreciate the mountain people's way of life, the product of an old order that was passing. And, as telephone lines, railroads, and auto roads spread farther into the mountains, readers should consider the human and environmental costs of accessibility, material comforts, and other signs of progress. Like Kephart, she welcomed the spread of educational and economic opportunities for mountain people. With her background in biology and teaching, however, along with her interest in both wild terrain and seemingly natural, subtly refined landscapes, Morley looked upon the southern mountains with different eyes and, in some ways, complemented the work of her better-known contemporary Kephart.[6]

Both Kephart and Morley admired the forests of different ranges in the southern Appalachian Mountains. They appreciated the beauty and diversity of the tree species and deplored some wasteful practices of the timber and paper-pulp industries. But Morley gave more attention to this subject as she sketched in the history of human use of American forests, both before and since the arrival of Europeans, and emphasized a balance between humans and forests. Native Americans had maintained that balance, she believed; later it was somewhat disturbed by white people who cleared patches on the mountainsides for farms. Now, however, that balance was more seriously threatened by lumbermen with portable sawmills. Morley touched on the functions of forests in protecting watersheds, maintaining hydrologic cycles, and preventing erosion. She also mentioned the Weeks Bill, of 1911, which had authorized recent land purchases for national forests in the South and the Northeast. That bill, along with the proposed national park in the Great Smokies, was a promising sign of broad public concern that she wanted to sharpen.

"Every one owning land in these mountains should remember that it is also the sacred and inalienable right of the tree to bestow beauty on the landscape," Morley asserted. Having noted the importance of forest products in a civilized world, she could not censure all logging. "The primeval forests must go," she admitted. But she made the case for letting a great monarch of the forest stand while lesser trees around it were cut—as long as it could survive the loss of its neighbors. In time, under proper forestry, young forests would replace the old. Meanwhile, superlative trees and those on the slopes of prominent ridges should be allowed to stand. Her main reason for preserving the trees (apart from environmental protection, mentioned earlier) had to do with beauty and economy—the aesthetic pleasure of the many visitors who would come to the mountains on holiday and thereby enrich the local economy.[7]

Aesthetics, economics, ecology: these are intertwined in Morley's picture of the Carolina mountains. Rather than elevate one consideration above another, she tried to show that each was important to sustaining (and enhancing) the way of life of mountain people. Like Kephart, she hoped to see the best elements of that life preserved, even as the forces of modern civilization were poised to overwhelm it. Independence and self-reliance, qualities both authors admired in the mountain people, might fade as the mountains lost their isolation. People might cease to grow or make what they needed to live, then work for wages in a shop, a mine, a mill, a factory. But this process, under way by 1913, might take

THE REGION

many years to run its course. As Morley put it, "Man is so close to the soil here that he recognizes the relationship. He sees his bread—and molasses—come directly from the earth. He loves the land, and the ambition of every youth is to possess a little farm of his own."[8]

And women? Some of the finest photographs in the book, all taken by Morley, are of a lone woman, walking up a mountain path, crossing a mountain stream, bending over the washtubs, or weaving cloth. Aware that some domestic crafts were dying out, Morley briefly explained *why* (mountain girls preferred machine-made products; many people no longer owned sheep; wool was too expensive to buy) before turning to those who still made things with heart, mind, and hand.

The tradition of weaving was still strong among some mountain women, mainly older women and those in living memory. Telling their composite story, Morley had the legendary Penelope, faithful wife of Odysseus, stand for them all. Some of their work was seasonal, some sporadic. They grew indigo and gathered bark and herbs to make dyes. In winter, especially, they would card, spin, and weave. They also collected old patterns with names like "wheels of time," "rattlesnake trail," "Bonaparte's March," and "Missouri trouble." Some women created new patterns to weave and share. Others freely passed on bits of practical advice. Just as a prized coverlet was passed down from one generation to another, so the loom itself was an heirloom. Weaving was, and to some extent remained, woman's work, "an occupation exclusively her own and which in a peculiar way relates her to a by-gone world," Morley noted.[9]

On the craft of constructing a still and making corn-juice, or whiskey, Morley had less to say than Kephart. She did, however, seek out a mountain potter and watch him at work on his homemade wheel. He was an elderly African American named Rich Williams, a man who dug his own clay from the Tiger River, ground it in a homemade mill powered by a mule, and shaped it into crocks and jugs, which he then glazed and fired in his own brick-and-clay oven. "Rich loves his work," Morley observed. "He says he can make anything he wants to out of clay." But the tin pail that store-bought lard came in was beginning to replace the handmade clay vessel in mountain homes.[10]

Penelope, *a weaver in the southern Appalachians. (Image from Margaret W. Morley,* The Carolina Mountains *[1913]; photograph by Margaret W. Morley)*

Writing about moonshine whiskey, Kephart, too, noted changes in the larger context. Once pure, satisfying, and useful for medicinal purposes, that whiskey was now often adulterated with unseemly ingredients, and the reasons were intertwined with a long, complicated history. Kephart traced it to excise laws of early-eighteenth-century Ireland and late-eighteenth-century Pennsylvania, along with more recent laws on prohibition in the southern mountain states. (North Carolina and Tennessee had been voted dry in 1909.) In the end, having blended scholarly history with anecdotes and stories he had gathered firsthand, Kephart argued that the typical mountain man and his family, mostly of English, Scottish, and Scots-Irish extraction, now living under conditions roughly

THE REGION

comparable to those of eighteenth-century Britain and America, must be given the chance to enter the modern world on fair and reasonable terms. The problem, he argued, was largely an economic one.

Kephart's depiction of modern civilization's arrival in the southern mountains was vivid, with steam whistles shrieking, dynamite booming, forests being leveled, rivers dammed, telephone wires stretched, and a great deal of property bought and sold. In some cases this amounted to an "invasion" by men who had no concern for the people they dispossessed. As one northern lumberman said to Kephart, "All we want here is to get the most we can out of this country, as quick as we can, and then get out."[11] And once a mountain man had sold his homestead to such a lumberman, what then? Kephart pointed to certain needs, including local industries that would require skilled labor, manual training schools, and well-educated native sons and daughters able to lead their own people. That was more or less what Morley hoped for as well. In fact she knew of one place where a bright future was already taking shape.

In the transition from the old order to the new, Morley looked to the "guiding star" of Biltmore, with its good macadam roads, its fine gardens, a stock farm, a dairy, and more than a hundred thousand acres of woodlands managed by trained foresters. This was George W. Vanderbilt's country place, south of Asheville, North Carolina, where thousands of mountain people were learning new skills on the grounds and indoors. Aside from wages, they were gaining an understanding of discipline, punctuality, business methods, and the development of natural resources. At Biltmore Industries, a school of industrial arts, mountain boys, girls, and women were learning wood carving, furniture making, weaving, and embroidery. Meanwhile, visitors to the estate were learning what they, too, could do with a bit of wildland in order to enhance its beauty. Under the general direction of Frederick Law Olmsted (whom Morley identified as "America's greatest landscape gardener"), the grounds beyond the immediate vicinity of the stately home at Biltmore had been so subtly laid out and planted that all seemed natural, apparently wild. Along the winding valley road some visitors might detect subtle touches— a nonnative shrub discreetly planted, a ravine that somehow felt different, more refined, than in the wild. Others, less knowledgeable, might still "feel something that he does not feel in the wilderness," as a sensitive soul would respond to a great picture.[12]

Writing of Biltmore, Morley recognized its environmental significance as a demonstration of large-scale scientific forestry, at a time when forests around the country were being rapidly destroyed. She emphasized Biltmore's social significance as a model of "advanced cultivation of the outer world," brought into being near once-remote mountains by mountain men themselves, as laborers, overseers, and managers. She also saw the landscape and gardens as aesthetically important—a model for the whole region, in blending the beauty of wilderness with the grace of cultivated landscape and civilized life.

Kephart's view of Biltmore can be detected in one brief allusion to it, as a place of luxury and the occasion of a bit of mountain humor. Aside from that, Kephart had little to say about wildland that had been refined and civilized for aesthetic purposes. The landscape improvements he discussed in *Our Southern Highlanders* involved terraced farmland, to replace the typical mountain cornfield, steeply sloping and eroding. In fact it was a model farm for *each* mountain county—not one superlative estate within a region—that Kephart hoped to see created for the education of mountain people.[13]

The wilderness that Kephart had initially sought out in 1904 would have been uninhabited, some unspoiled Eden to explore alone. But the wilderness he actually found near his base camp on Hazel Creek, in the lee of the Great Smokies in North Carolina, was inhabited; and traces of heavy industry remained. With permission, he lived in an abandoned cabin owned by a copper-mining company. And so he came to know mountain people through casual encounters, interviewing, overnight visits, bear hunting, and attending to people's ailments with a first-aid kit (for there was no doctor for miles around). He saw what these people could gain from civilization, as well as much that they should hold on to. "The *independence* of the mountain farm must be preserved," he wrote, "or the fine spirit of the race will vanish and all that is manly in the highlander will wither to the core." The word "highlander," however, identified Kephart as an outlander or "furriner." As he explained, his neighbors would rather be known as mountain people or citizens.[14]

In any event, it is *Kephart's* account of the southern highlanders that has become a treasured classic—not Morley's. His picture of the place and the people was not always flattering, but mountain people thought he had got it just about right.[15] Morley may have found a more appreciative audience among newcomers, permanent or seasonal. A representative woman of *her* place and time—a northern visitor in the Progressive Era—she was confident that the Carolina mountains would be able to withstand invasions and in time regain their beauty through a blend of wilderness and civilized life. "For the whole world is now one population, all knowing each other," Morley wrote in 1913, "and it is incredible that the work of the future will not be in the direction of abolishing war, misery, and ugliness."[16]

❊ ❊ ❊

Two decades passed. War had not yet been abolished, nor were misery and ugliness unknown. A nationwide depression had set in, yet it would be difficult to detect any trace of it in a book that appeared in 1933, *The Traipsin' Woman,* by Jean Thomas.[17] The title refers to the author, a "furriner," who, as a young woman, took up a new job in eastern Kentucky and gradually won the confidence and affection of the mountain people. But the heart of the book lies in the way of life of those mountain people and their rich musical heritage: traditional ballads, songs, and tunes brought over from Europe, mainly from Scotland and England, and rendered with or without the accompaniment of fiddles, banjos, guitars, dulcimers, or other instruments. The story takes place from the late 1890s to the early 1930s, but dates are rarely mentioned. Most incidents seem to occur outside of time, despite talk of a proposed railroad right-of-way. It is as if a gentle haze had settled over the mountains, the people, and the narrative. A wary reader might wonder—is this fact or fiction? Or some kind of ballad, telling of rare beauty, courage, and justice served or thwarted?

Other books by Jean Thomas—hybrid works that combine stories of Kentucky mountain people, transcriptions of their songs and ballads, musical notation, and fragments of Thomas's own life—help to set *The Traipsin' Woman* in context. From one book to another, certain names and situations are altered while a few main incidents remain unchanged—as if they had become legendary. In her most autobiographical work, *The Sun Shines Bright* (1940), Thomas periodically leaves Kentucky for New York, London, and other cities. But *The Traipsin' Woman* is more firmly centered in one place, the mountains of eastern Kentucky, where she apparently felt free to invent and reshape her material, even as her neighbors had made up ballads and sometimes reshaped melodies and lyrics handed down, orally, from across the ocean, over many generations. The result is a balladlike story of a ballad-loving people, and also something more: a glimpse of a possible future for some of those children who used to play near the doors of a mountain cabin.[18]

Jean Thomas, known as Jennie Bell in her childhood, was only a generation or two removed from the mountains. Her father, who had settled in the mill town of Ashland, Kentucky, among the foothills along the Ohio River, still had kinfolk in the Kentucky mountains. Her father's sister lived there and her father's uncle preached there, in a church built of logs. He also led the hymns—haunting, mournful hymns that little Jennie heard, remembered, and later sang for her music teacher in Ashland, unaware of their ancient links with Gregorian chants. That preacher in the mountains, Jennie's great-uncle, quoted chapter and verse of the Bible, yet he could not read or write. Years later she remembered him at his own dinner table, bowing his head in prayer, then inviting his guests, "Thar hit is afore you. Take holt and eat all you're a-mind to!"[19]

After graduating from school in Ashland, in the 1890s, Jennie Bell had few opportunities. As her mother had done before marriage, she could teach in a rural school; or she could take in sewing. Any other form of remunerative work was not considered proper for a young woman of her place and time. Instead, inspired by the example of a local lawyer's secretary—a woman—Jennie borrowed money to attend a business school in Ashland, learned typing and shorthand, and, after a few false starts, took up a job as court stenographer in some mountain counties notorious for blood feuds (known as "war" or "troubles" among mountain people). The job entailed travel from one remote county court-house to another, attending court week with the judge and a "passel of lawyers," then moving on.

The Traipsin' Woman resembles other tales of local color, all marked by strong regional accents and memorable turns of phrase. Yet it may be more compelling than many of them, for Jean Thomas was both profes-sionally distant from and personally close to her subjects. Her job re-quired discipline and strict objectivity; she had to produce an accurate, literal transcription of all that was said under oath in a courtroom and deemed admissible by the judge. Something of that objectivity re-appeared in *The Traipsin' Woman,* then faded as ordinary human emo-tion welled up, barely contained. Once, on hearing the prison sentence of Young Bije Croswite, whose wife and nine children all sat quietly on a front bench, Thomas nearly broke down—but offered no comment. On another occasion she could not sleep the night before a murder trial; the accused was said to be lodged in the next room, in an old house without locks on the doors. Suddenly she lost her fear, for a fine male voice far-ther up the mountainside came echoing down the valley, singing of a man of high degree and a lady fair of beauty bright, a silver knife, and the surging main. Out came the notebook and pencil; Thomas took down the ballad by moonlight—in shorthand.

That ability (or instinct) to forget fear and pursue whatever is haunt-ing, beautiful, or wonderfully human helps to explain how mountain people could accept Jean Thomas as they did, welcoming her into their homes and freely passing on to her whatever songs and ballads they knew. Over a kitchen table lit by oil lamp, she taught some of those peo-ple to read and write. But in between the lines of *The Traipsin' Woman* there is no suggestion of social work, nor any hint that modern civiliza-tion, arriving via railroad and telephone line, would somehow bring these people into the twentieth century. Granted, some of the women made a fuss over her contraption (a portable typewriter), and an elderly man was horrified to see her about to appear in public without a hat. But those are minor differences; Thomas clearly saw herself and mountain people living in the same century, sharing a common sense of human decency along with a love of singing and performing. Among these people were fine craftsmen and artists, and Thomas developed a passion to share their gifts with as wide an audience as possible—even with the British, who had lost the musical traditions that Kentucky mountain people kept alive.

How Jean Thomas established an annual "singin' gatherin'," performed by mountain people of all ages on all kinds of handcrafted instruments, in the foothills south of Ashland, Kentucky, is a story retold in several of her books. The annual event, first held in September 1930, and thereafter on the second Sunday in June, became known as the American Folk Song Festival.[20] In *The Traipsin' Woman* this festival offers a part for nearly everyone in the community and songs to remember many who had passed on. "Down in the Valley," the well-known ballad of a man in jail, was also a reminder of the very place where all were gathered, a real place that seemed better than any stage set that Jean Thomas—or her narrator—had ever seen in Hollywood.[21] The place was in Thomas's home county—Boyd County, Kentucky—along a ravine up Lost Hope Hollow, where a stage was built before a windowless cabin of hand-hewn logs. Whatever liberties Thomas may have taken in the retelling, that festival was a reflection of the whole far-flung mountain community and their way of life, distilled to an essence and raised to the level of performing art. With that, her own little performance, *The Traipsin' Woman*, nearly came to a close. It ended quietly, however, with a death, a hint of new life, and a journey.

River of Earth (1940), by James Still, ends with some of the same elements: death, birth, a journey. On the final page of *The Traipsin' Woman*, Jean Thomas is heading for Breathitt County, Kentucky, just north of Knott County, where Still came to settle in the early 1930s. The two authors knew and loved the same mountainous land, perhaps followed some of the same creek-bed roads, noted the same courtly phrases and idioms, and went through the same stage of initiation from "furriner" to neighbor and friend. Yet they are far removed in some ways, as well as a generation apart in time (Jean Thomas was born in 1881; James Still, in 1906). It is not in Thomas's language, but between the lines and apart from the dialect, that her intense feeling for mountain people and their music shines through. With Still, the feeling and the language are all of a piece, inseparable.

Long known in the southern Appalachian Mountain states as a fine writer, storyteller, and novelist, James Still is becoming better known, nationally, as a poet as well. Shortly after his death in 2001, a collection of all his mature poetry, *From the Mountain, from the Valley,* appeared; and in the preface, the poet Ted Olson recognized Still's poetic voice, "calm, quiet, unmannered, minimalist," along with his wisdom, humor, and understatement. Olson also quoted another poet, James Dickey, who sensed in Still's prose work the vision of a poet.[22]

The vision of an environmentalist, one without labels or ties to any organization, is evident as well. One main character in *River of Earth* can apparently get along without calendars and almanacs, so long as he has eyes and ears. "I saw green rashes yesterday," he says, "but I never figure spring's in for shore till the basket oaks sprout buds. Never spring till a titmouse whistles lonesome."[23]

The speaker is Uncle Jolly, a man known for his pranks, his earthy humor, the shortness of his stays in jail (he knows the ways and means of being pardoned), and the country wisdom at the heart of his transgressions. With dynamite he blows up a neighbor's milldam so that creek waters can flow freely and fish can swim upstream. His brief spell in the county jail cannot make him change his ways; the legality of an action means little to him, but its impact on the larger landscape may trouble him. At his best he is out on the land, plowing the black earth in straight furrows, sweating beneath an April sun, pausing for a long drink of spring water from a jug, and alerting his little nephew to the ways of the world. "Land a-wasting and a-washing. . . . Timber cut off and hills eating down. Hit's alike all over. . . . What's folks going to live on when these hills wear down to a nub?"[24]

Another question echoes now and again, the one intoned by the preacher from Troublesome Creek, Brother Sim Mobberly: "Oh, my children, where air we going on this mighty river of earth, a-borning, begetting, and a-dying—the living and the dead riding the waters?"

There is no answer. Still's narrator, a boy of seven, drifts off to sleep as the preacher's words beat down on him without meaning. The boy's father shakes him awake, and the family walks home. "A great voice walked with me, roaring in my head," recalls the boy, who is known by no Christian name.[25] To his grandmother, he is simply "Chap," one of several little chaps she has known and loved and seen move on.

The central dilemma of the novel is about moving on—or holding fast to one place and settling down. The boy's mother, Alpha, whose people work the land and get by somehow, yearns to settle down, tend her garden and crops, and see that her children learn to figure and "read writing." She and her husband, Brack, cannot read a letter that arrives one day; she recognizes the name of her brother Jolly but knows it's not his handwriting. Brack Baldridge is bemused by all the curlicues—little tails at each end of every word. He is a miner, tall, strong, proud of the calluses on his hand, and unable to breathe freely in summer when the pollen is heavy in the fields and pastures. "I was born to dig coal," he declares. Alpha Baldridge, a loyal mountain woman, defers to him, although it means a life of moving on. Work in the mines is never certain, for a man's hours can be cut without warning, and the mines are always shutting down indefinitely.

What the Baldridge children make of all this moving hither and yon comes through indirectly. For the boy of seven, going on eight and nine, place is mainly a matter of sensations, and so is time. On an April morning among the Middletons, his mother's people, the fences are covered with "a rash of green." Beech and leatherwood are brown in the sunlight, and redbuds are swollen with unopened flower and leaf. The boy climbs up to benchland that lies flat against the air and sky. He hears gold-finches singing *Per-chic-o-ree,* then sees them, like a sudden bloom of yellow flowers, pecking the seed pods of dried stickweeds. July is the time of cornstalks in tassel, bees hovering, groundhogs bold enough to feed in daylight, and Uncle Jolly singing "Rich and Rambling Boy" in a distant field. October comes after the baby's funeral, when the leaves have fallen and the trees look dead. Then the Baldridges move on to the Blackjack mining camp, where the slag heap burns with oily flames, the hills are bare, the waters of the creek run yellow with acid, and no fish swim among the rocks that are "snuffy brown, eaten and crumbly."

The environmental impacts are obvious, but Still makes no overt comment. He simply shows us what his young narrator sees and lets him speak. (The boy refuses to grow up to be a miner; he'd rather be a horse doctor.) Years later, Still reflected on his own impecunious days in Nashville, in 1929 and 1930, when he did graduate work in English at Vanderbilt University. There he heard presentations by some of the poets and writers known as the "Fugitives"—Allen Tate, Robert Penn Warren, John Crowe Ransom, Donald Davidson, and others. At that time they were just about to publish their manifesto, *I'll Take My Stand,* a collective, many-faceted position against industrial society in favor of agrarianism.[26] But again, Still did not explain where he himself stood, back in 1929–30 or thereafter.

Still's position—or inclination not to declare one—is evident in *River of Earth,* where no major character is wholly good or bad. Uncle Jolly, Granny Middleton, Brack and Alpha Baldridge, the children, the foreman at the mine, Uncle Samp, all are seen in three dimensions, as flawed and endearing, against a landscape partly of their own making: the tunneled hillsides; the pungent, root-entangled, furrowed fields; the sapsuckers fleeing from the black birch when the old farmhouse goes up in flames, as planned. Even the narrator steals a penny from inside the clock on the mantle, feels an overwhelming sense of guilt, then finds his crime covered up, effortlessly, by indolent Uncle Samp.

In *River of Earth* the narrator remains a conscientious, somewhat shy boy, small for his age, unable to read (although he knows his letters). His opportunities to learn from books are fleeting, and what he begins to decipher in his primer is not very promising: "Henny Penny found a grain of wheat." But the world he knows through his senses is vivid, full of wonder, danger, uncertainty. He remembers places by some detail or other: the waters of Redbird River, "clear as a goblet-glass"; the martins at Little Angus, a rented farm. Meanwhile, impressions of light, color, sound, and smell move the story onward. "The days shortened," Still writes. "The air grew frosty. Nights were loud with honking geese, and suddenly the leaves were down before gusts of wind. The days were noisy with blowing, and the house filled with the sound of crickets' thighs."[27]

* * *

Out Under the Sky of the Great Smokies, the published journals of Harvey Broome, begin in January 1941. To read them through to the end, in October 1966, is to follow the journeys, physical and intellectual, of a man who craved to be in the mountains. Broome, a founding member and president of the Wilderness Society, also craved the skill to convey the intensity of his experiences to others. "How can people be persuaded," he mused, "that there is something of priceless worth to the human spirit in the very existence of tracts of the primeval, which they have never seen or experienced?"[28]

Good question. In the long run, in any functioning democracy, who but the people could finally call a halt to the relentless cutting up of remnant wilderness with yet another logging road, graded trail, or scenic highway? The next generation, perhaps content with smaller patches of wildland or views from a mountain road, might not protest. But Broome wanted them to see what he had seen, on foot: delicate phacelias, dwarf irises, a scattering of "sarvises" (serviceberry, or *Amelanchier*), a single lady's slipper, a grove of hickories, a stately tulip poplar. He loved to hear the wind soughing through tall pines. In the song of a tiny bird, the winter wren, he heard the story of all life expressed in a single "jetting effusion." Often he wished he could achieve something comparable in words. Whether hiking with his wife, Anne, or with fellow members of the Smoky Mountains Hiking Club, or alone, he could become so completely immersed in the mountains of his native Tennessee—especially when utterly soaked and muddied—that he felt himself a part of the wilderness. For a while, at least, before his thoughts returned to environmental degradation, the atom bomb, population pressures, or the city he had left behind on Friday afternoon.[28]

Broome knew that, to some people, the wilderness movement was an urban issue. Its origins were supposed to lie in the conscience of city people who saw how shabbily the natural world had been treated around them, then looked elsewhere for a bit of nature to protect or restore. But

THE REGION

his own experience ran counter to this notion. From a hill in his "home village" in the eastern part of Knoxville, he could see the Great Smoky Mountains rising on the southern horizon. When he was born, in 1902, Knoxville was a small valley town, where most people walked or rode electric trolleys. Lamps at home burned coal oil or gas. The water in the river was rust-colored before it was treated, cleansed, and raised to a standpipe for use by the town. Across the river, on Cherokee Bluffs, he and his friends found relics from the Civil War. Five miles from town was his grandparents' farm, and beyond that, the country church that served as a social center, like churches back in Knoxville. The places, the people, the pastimes seem typical, but for one detail. One summer Broome, an undersized, frail boy, went with his uncle and three mountain men on a two-week camping trip in the Great Smokies. And it was a revelation: the rain on tin plates, the plunge into wildness, a cliff for a shelter, the summits of Silers Bald and Clingmans Dome—the highest peak in Tennessee. Looking back, Broome insisted that no metropolitan mind-set had made him a defender of wilderness. It was a trek at age fifteen, in his own home state, that had set him on his life's course.[29]

Until now, we have not paid much attention to an author's origins; they did not always seem relevant to what he or she wrote about the southern highlands. We *did* need to know about Jean Thomas's youth in Ashland, Kentucky, and her father's kinsmen in the mountains of Kentucky. But Bradford Torrey's birth in Massachusetts, and the fact that Horace Kephart and Margaret Morley had both lived in Iowa in their youth seemed less significant to *their* writings about mountain people. Ancestry, however, might be relevant. Kephart had thought of his ancestors, including immigrants from Switzerland, when he set out to recapture a semblance of their pioneer experience elsewhere in America. And James Still wrote of *his* pioneer ancestors, the Lindseys and the Stills, who had settled in Virginia, then moved into Georgia, Alabama, and Texas. Some details and incidents in *River of Earth* were drawn from Still's childhood (he was born on a farm near Lafayette, Alabama) and some, from the lives of Still's ancestors.[30]

When Harvey Broome wrote of ancestors, however, he seemed to have in mind more than his English forebears. Writing of a winter hike up Winnesoka in 1953, Broome remembered ice in the streams and the vegetation on northern and southern slopes that seemed to grow in different worlds, different seasons. As he and his friends scaled the steep slopes in the cold air, they seemed half gods, half earthmen. Then sunlight poured in, views opened up, and Broome saw snow and ice on the north face of Mount Le Conte. Down in the valley, leafless hardwoods seemed like so much primordial dust. Sitting on the sunny forest floor, he marveled at that roomlike space, warm, snug—the sort of place where his ancestors had made their homes, he imagined. "Out of such beauty and peace must have been born aspiration," he reflected. One summer in 1943 he wondered, "Can it be that innately we are still primal and that when we return to the woods we are feeling a kind of homesickness?" And he thought of a primordial home and ancient forebears—*our* forebears.[31] Such thoughts run like undercurrents through the journals: Am I—are we—alien in these woods? Do I—do we—belong here? Loren Eiseley posed similar questions some years later, with certain phases of evolution in mind.[32]

Eiseley does not figure in Broome's journals, but many kindred spirits do: Horace Kephart, Sally Carrighar, Joseph Wood Krutch, Justice William O. Douglas, and fellow founders of the Wilderness Society, including Bob Marshall, Aldo Leopold, and Benton MacKaye. The published journals are dedicated to MacKaye, and the ideas most often paraphrased are Leopold's. Broome's own concerns range widely between two poles—his recent hikes in the Great Smokies; and thoughts of the distant past or future. From the occasional mention of indoor confinement, orgies of work, tax accounting, and corporate clients, we gather that Broome, an attorney, derived little inspiration from his livelihood. The great moments all seem to occur outdoors, in rain, snow, fog, wind, sunlight, or the darkness of night. Through them all he kept his faith in life and the vitality of the earth.

In the journals, Broome alluded to only a few of his own efforts to protect wildlands, acting in concert with others. There was the "Save the Smokies" hike of the late 1960s, an ultimately successful protest against a proposed highway. And in 1954 he joined Justice Douglas and others on a now legendary walk along the Chesapeake and Ohio Canal from Cumberland, Maryland, to Washington, D.C. Another success, that walk to protest the impending loss of the canal's towpath to highway construction was well covered by the media. Later Broome, who had walked the whole 185 miles, wondered about the journalists who had walked along with them. Why, he wondered, did those fine journalists defer to America's love of the automobile in the end? And why that love? For power? Or had people grown soft?[33]

To learn more about Broome's environmental activism, we can turn to others, such as the writer Michael Frome, who had hiked with Broome in the Smokies and admired his gentle, sensitive spirit.[34] That spirit comes through in the journals, as Broome responds to his ever-changing, yet enduring, Great Smokies and reflects on a world growing more mechanical. One entry describes two trips that Broome and his wife made in the summer of 1957, each within about twenty-five miles of Knoxville. One day they went west to Oak Ridge, home of the second-oldest atomic pile in the world. Broome noted the thick windows of amberglass and the sparkling deionized water in a pool. The elemental force contained in the reactor was sobering, but not entirely comprehensible. The next day he and Anne and some friends went south into the Smokies, to Ramsay Falls and Drinkwater Pool. The blowdowns, the tangled laurel and rhododendrons, the gnats, the fogged spectacles, rain, thunder, sunlight, all were part of a place they could feel rather than understand. In the end, seen from outside, the "modern wonders of man" at Oak Ridge remained impenetrable to Broome. The "ancient wonders of the wilderness" drew him in with all his senses, showing him the miracle of a mountain pool, its waters filtered through miles of forest.[35]

And so the journals accumulated, joy mingling with foreboding, place with thought. On the new United Nations Charter, Broome reflected, "If it does not succeed, there is no power that can save the world from another holocaust of war." Of winter winds he wrote, "They stir our lives and then they are off beyond the ridges."[36]

THREE

Pacific Shores

From Mountains to the Sea

The expedition to the foothills south of Mount Lassen, among the canyons and gorges of Deer Creek and Mill Creek, was a homecoming of sorts—but not for the anthropologists from the San Francisco Bay Area, nor for the ranchers who joined them in the small town of Vina, in the Sacramento River valley. The ranchers knew the hill country as grazing land. Only Ishi, who had come by train with the men from the Bay Area, knew those hills as a human habitat. There he had lived for half a century, concealing his tracks, barely surviving in an increasingly hostile environment of white settlers, sharing what he had with the members of his dwindling tribe, and caring for their remains when they died. Ishi's people were Yahi, of the Yana tribe, and that country was once their land. Now he was their sole survivor, the last to tell of a way of life that stretched back some three or four thousand years in California.

Theodora Kroeber writes of this expedition to Yahi country in *Ishi in Two Worlds: A Biography of the Last Wild Indian in North America* (1961). The "two worlds" are, in one sense, abstractions: the Stone Age and the Steel Age, or modern times. They are also real places: a portion of the southern Cascade Range that comprised the known world of Ishi and his people; and the Bay Area, particularly the University of California's Museum of Anthropology, once housed in a nineteenth-century building on Parnassus Heights, near Golden Gate Park, in San Francisco.[1]

These two worlds are margins of a single watershed, traceable from the southern slopes of Mount Lassen, down Mill Creek and Deer Creek into the Sacramento River, then southward and westward into Suisun Bay, through the Carquinez Strait, to San Pablo Bay, San Francisco Bay, the Golden Gate, and the Pacific Ocean. But as Ishi moved from one world to the other in early September 1911, he did not experience a continuous flow (along with the give-and-take of tides). Rather, a "demon" on steel rails—a train—took him from the fringes of Yahi country to Oakland. Then a ferry across the bay and a trolley down city streets completed the transition. Other transitions were abrupt or slow, often awkward if not painful: from emaciation to well-being; from solitude to crowds; from silence to shared language; from hunting and fishing with handmade implements in Yahi country to buying tea, sugar, produce, meat, fish, canned goods, and ice cream on Seventh Avenue in San Francisco.

Theodora Kroeber described these transitions objectively, with a reliance on facts, yet also with sympathy and keen intuition. No anthropologist herself, she assembled from many sources, including frontier histories and writings by her husband, Alfred, and his colleagues in anthropology, bits of evidence that might form a coherent story—just as an incomplete collection of shards can be assembled so as to suggest a vessel's original form, she noted. The end product was rare: a best-seller from a university press and a fair-minded, moving story that can be read as biography, anthropology, ethnography, or human geography—people and land viewed as a whole.[2]

By the time Alfred Kroeber and his colleagues embarked on their expedition with Ishi, in May 1914, Ishi had been living for nearly three years in San Francisco, at the Museum of Anthropology, where he earned his living as an assistant janitor. He had learned to ride trolleys on his own and to know his urban environment by its signs, numbers, and landmarks. The quail in Golden Gate Park had delighted him, and urban crowds no longer terrified him. For visitors to the museum he would demonstrate his methods of making arrowheads, shafts, and bows, and of igniting sparks from his handmade fire drill. Meanwhile three white men had welcomed him to their homes and offices—Alfred Kroeber, T. T. Waterman, and the physician Saxton Pope—and each in his way had become an intimate friend. Now, in the spring of 1914, they wanted to see how Ishi would respond to his homeland—even if that return would stir painful memories. From early childhood, Ishi had been a fugitive in his own land, a survivor while others of his tribe were massacred, a reluctant raider of the occasional sack of flour or stray grazing animal, a hunter who was himself hunted. Perhaps the horror and fear had by then retreated to the past. In any event, Ishi's outward bearing was reserved, cautious, conscientious, yet often witty and at ease among friends and friendly crowds.

Piecing together a vivid account of the month-long expedition, Theodora told of stories shared over a campfire, the ample meals, the rattlesnake that Ishi would never have killed, the long-forgotten places and abandoned village sites that Ishi recognized. Theodora could only imagine the emotional impact on Ishi during that expedition—a mental journey akin to psychoanalysis, she mused. Apparently he overcame his early reluctance to return to Yahi country, then shared in the enjoyment of his fellows. In the end the white men were reluctant to return to civilization. Ishi, however, was eager to go back to the museum—the place he now called home.

Written with remarkable tact and sensitivity, *Ishi in Two Worlds* lies open to a range of interpretations regarding one man's experience, the experience of "westering" across the continent, and the nature of *Homo sapiens,* by degrees adaptable and malleable. Education, ancestry, experience, geographical place, all come into play. A few isolated observations—like shards of an ancient vessel—may also suggest a larger whole. A tall building in San Francisco, for instance, left Ishi unmoved; he knew too well the sheer walls of Deer Creek canyon, and he had seen Mount Shasta from afar. When a plane was taking off, Ishi was intrigued by the propeller blades and the great roar; but when the plane was in the air, he thought a hawk or an eagle more impressive.

Ishi impressed people with his ancient skills, his adaptability to modern life, his dignity, honesty, humor. And as he came to know something of the Bay Area—the streets and parks of San Francisco, Strawberry Creek running through the Berkeley campus, wild plants on nearby hills—he enjoyed good health for a few years, then succumbed to a series of illnesses. He died in March 1916. Afterward Dr. Pope, a close friend who had learned from Ishi how to hunt with a bow and arrow and had attended to him during his final months and days, wrote a tribute to Ishi. "He looked upon us as sophisticated children—smart, but not wise," Pope wrote. "We knew many things, and much that is false. He knew nature, which is always true."[3]

❖ ❖ ❖

In the cloth edition of *Ishi in Two Worlds,* a signature of thirty-two pages contains many black-and-white photographs that vary in size and aesthetic quality. As placed on the page, these photographs form patterns that are pleasing but not striking. And so, when we come across this signature, our attention is drawn not so much to book design as to content—photographs as documents of places and actions discussed in the text. Reading the paperback edition, too, we tend to focus on text and content rather than book design. Our experience is similar, although the paperback's signature has been reduced to sixteen pages, a few photographs have been dropped or substituted, and the back cover carries high praise for the book from scholarly journals, mainstream magazines, and newspapers.[4]

These observations emphasize some aspects of traditional bookmaking (and of the experience of reading) that are still familiar today. The design elements are not unusual for a book of the 1960s—a bit staid, perhaps, yet appropriate for a serious work of nonfiction. At the end of this chapter, we will consider a different, more daring approach to book design (also from the 1960s) that represents a conscious effort to alter the total experience of reading for both aesthetic and political purposes. Meanwhile, we will step back to Ishi's time and consider two examples of fine bookmaking that dwell on the natural and cultural resources of the Golden State. One was written by a native, a noted painter and illustrator; the other, by a writer who came to live in California at an impressionable age and later wrote from memory about places known and loved.

Romantic California (1910) opens with a few common assumptions. Yes, California has been blessed with beauty, fertility, a fine climate, and grand associations. Spanish explorers once confused this place with an imaginary island "very near the Terrestrial Paradise." But Ernest Peixotto, the author and artist, is more intrigued by similarities between California and the Old World—in its romantic past, its rich cultural life in the present, and the many out-of-the-way places that would appeal to a landscape painter. Then, too, he wants to get beyond visual similarities, beyond the picturesque vision of writers such as Charles Dudley Warner, who identified the Golden State as "Our Italy" in 1891. For Peixotto, *real* bits of Italy can be found in California where Italians carry on their traditional way of life—especially north of his native San Francisco, in the wine country of Napa and Sonoma.[5]

Heading west from a vintage festival on the slopes of Mount Saint Helena to the Italian colony in Asti, along the Russian River, Peixotto moves closer to a land and people that seem familiar. In the vineyards he finds whole families picking grapes while babies sleep in empty crates. At the winery, the grapes are crushed by modern machinery—not by bare feet—but the wine barrels are still made by hand. In the local church, the faithful sing Gregorian chants. Some afternoons, the men play bocci or go fishing down by the river, using small square nets, as in Italy. Evenings, under the trees, men play homemade reeds and pipes. Peixotto has seen it all before—or something akin to it—and sketched it, painted it, written about it, in his book *By Italian Seas* (1906). In California, however, his vision is sometimes less conventionally picturesque, more penetrating. The elderly grape-picker, for instance, done in tones of gray wash, is kneeling, perhaps for comfort, but as if in reverence. He may be weary, or he may be lost in deep contemplation or reverie. Here Peixotto has captured not a moment in time but an indeterminate period, duration. There is no image quite like it, nothing so tender, in *By Italian Seas*.[6]

Traveling in his home state after many years abroad, Peixotto was perhaps reaching for some deeper expression of a place or a person. Born in San Francisco in 1869, the son of a merchant and grandson of a physician who had emigrated from Spain to New York City, Peixotto grew up in a milieu of many cultures. His mother's surname was Davis. At the base of Telegraph Hill was the Italian quarter, where he used to enjoy marionette shows and the Italian Theatre. Out beyond the Golden Gate, Greek immigrants (among others) used to scramble up the steep, wet cliffs of the Farallon Islands to gather murre eggs for San Francisco restaurants and bakeries. And there were many others, from countries far away. Young Peixotto studied art in San Francisco (California School of Design) and in Paris (Academie Julian). His work appeared in Paris salons, at the World's Columbian Exposition, in *Scribner's* magazine, and elsewhere. He was married in New Orleans, then lived for many years in France, near Fontainebleau. By 1910 he had brought out works of travel writing set mainly in Italy and France. More books, more honors, medals, and many documentary drawings for the American military during the First World War were to follow.[7] With the ascendancy of the modern movement, however, Peixotto's representational works of art were marginalized. Now it may be time to reconsider his travel writings and drawings.

Peixotto's *Romantic California* has a certain light touch that is appealing. His perceptions are acute, confident, expressed in both word and image. And there is a fine coherence *between* words and images. He offers glimpses of people and places, often at close range, but without too much detail. The sketches of old Anglo-Spanish houses in Monterey, their fountains, gardens, galleries, fences, and varying relations to the street, all would interest an urban designer today. Literary historians would appreciate the glimpses of towns and ranches in the Salinas Valley at a time when John Steinbeck was a boy. And social historians could read between the lines of Peixotto's account of missions along the Camino Real. The pealing bells evoke a romantic past, Peixotto's own Spanish heritage; yet he knows what the coming of Padre Junipero Serra and his mission bells had meant to Native Americans. "The music of their clappers called the Indian neophyte to prayer, to decadence, and to his final annihilation," Peixotto observes. Some Indians had resisted giving up their freedom and their way of life for one that seemed "monotonously easy." In time the padres had won. Then came the gringo—the Yankee—and a way of life once sustained by missions and Spanish land grants gave way to mining, timbering, and large-scale agriculture. Main-traveled roads turned inland, upriver. El Camino Real and its traces of Spanish life along the Coast Range were left behind.[8]

In touching on these waves of conflict and shifting centers of activity and power, Peixotto blames no one. He simply selects details of his travels and lingers over some, like the old hacienda sheltered by giant oaks and nestled among the Santa Ynez Mountains, west of Santa Barbara. He tells of shady arbors, wide verandas, rooms communicating without hallways (as in the Old World), the daughter of the house (all in white), her father (tall, handsome, courtly, Castilian), their stories, their hospitality. Then he moves on. In Bret Harte's country, land of gold mines and places with names like You Bet and Jackass Hill, Peixotto is not entirely in his element, yet he remains open to whatever beauty of landscape or colorful characters he finds.

Romantic California is not a picture book but a book to be read at leisure. A few full-page plates appear among many smaller pen-and-ink drawings, but the words are equally important. Peixotto reflects on places he knew in childhood, before trains made communication easier between General Vallejo's homestead, in Sonoma County, and the outside world; and before the railroad up Mount Tamalpais, in Marin County, took away some of the adventure that he and his friends knew as boys, climbing up through dense thickets and reaching the summit hungry and tired. Then, too, Peixotto's opinions are only implied; he doesn't preach or exhort.

Beauty, mystery, ambition, greed, frivolity—all are somehow part of the romance of California that Pexiotto sets out to explore. One image, the "Cremation of Care," depicts the burning of all human troubles on a great funeral pyre while rockets burst in the air. This event was staged at one of the annual Midsummer Jinks at Bohemian Grove, some eighty miles north of San Francisco, where artists, architects, and writers such as William Keith, Bernard Maybeck, Jack London, and John Muir mingled with lawyers, bankers, and civic leaders among the redwoods by the Russian River.[9] Farther south, Peixotto caught with pen and brush the tragic quality of the contorted cypresses at Point Lobos. The tide pools below seemed like water gardens as he lay on a flat rock to study them; those he captured only in words. And one drawing recalls that of the elderly Italian grape-picker. It depicts a lone fisherman casting for trout in a mountain stream at The Bend, near Mount Shasta. A small figure in a leafy, sheltering place, the fisherman seems at home, at peace, completely absorbed in his environment.

That image and others by Peixotto—dreamlike yet believable and accessible—could have enticed many readers to visit the Golden State. And they would find the same mood of serenity in Sutton Palmer's illustrations for *California: The Land of the Sun* (1914). But the text of this book is often at odds with the images. Mary Austin, the writer, begins with a story of creation handed down from some Native American tribe of the Southwest—perhaps Shoshone, Paiute, or Mojave. Austin herself could not be certain, for the Shoshone medicine man who told her the story had never clarified its origins. What *was* clear was the spirit of conflict, a struggle of cosmic forces for control of what is now California at a time long before its mountains, deserts, rivers, and bays were formed.[10]

In the beginning, as the story goes, there was water and sky. Seeking a place to rest, Padahoon, the Sparrow Hawk, told Little Duck that there ought to be mountains, too. Little Duck then dove into the water and came up with primordial mud, which Sparrow Hawk formed into a circle of mountains that enclosed a calm sea. When Little Duck chose the western side, Sparrow Hawk built the eastern side higher. That made Little Duck envious, so Sparrow Hawk bit out chunks of the Sierra Nevada, on the east. Unsatisfied, Little Duck began to pull on the northern part of the circle, around Mount Shasta. Sparrow Hawk pulled on the southern part. The circle became an oval. It broke in the west, form-

ing San Francisco Bay. The bites out of the Sierra fell southward, forming lesser ranges (San Bernardino, San Jacinto). By then the lay of the
land was settled, yet conflicts remained, as sun, wind, rain, and fog all
challenged the mountains and shores with a continual give-and-take.
Skirmish lines were never fixed. At the margins of water and land, mountain and desert, there was always some destruction, some creation.

Mary Austin knew life on those margins. As a young woman not yet
twenty, born and reared in central Illinois, she first came to California
with her widowed mother and her younger brother in 1888. Along with
her elder brother, the family tried homesteading on the arid hills south
of Bakersfield—in Sparrow Hawk's land. Later, married, Austin moved
to the Owens Valley, another part of Sparrow Hawk's dry land. By the
time she wrote *California: The Land of the Sun,* Austin was an esteemed
writer with a foothold in Little Duck's land—in Carmel, south of Monterey. Some of her literary friends, including Jack London and George
Sterling, came together in Carmel for a while before moving on. She herself had lived for nearly three years in Europe, met the writers H. G. Wells
and Joseph Conrad in England, gained their respect, then lived in New
York City for a while. There she spent part of the year 1914, writing of
California as if some part of her had never left the state.[11]

In *California: The Land of the Sun* the colors and sounds of the coast
near San Diego and La Jolla are vivid. She hears a mockingbird scattering music "like light and laughter," singing at night, dreaming, waking
to sing, and dozing. "The lands of the sun expand the soul." So goes the
proverb that Austin quotes. Under the sun, some southern California
shores are like a dancer's scarf of many colors—aquamarine and chryso-
prase in the sea, pale green in the foliage of lupins, blue along the Coast
Range, and scarlet among the mesembryanthemums—ice plants—that
cover the slopes above sandy shores.

Many miles inland, among dry mesas and the arroyos that come alive
with water in spring, Austin had learned a few secrets from the Native
Americans. She had learned to sit still, and to see the world through their
eyes. "For the Indian has gone through all that green woof with the thread
of kinship and found it an ordered world," she writes.[12] And yet her writ-

ing in *California* is not consistently imbued with a Native American worldview. Recognizing the widely shared affection of Californians for old Spanish missions, she traces the roots of this feeling to their admiration for the spirit of enterprise, for holding out against great odds and winning. She links the padres' efforts with those of the early settlers and town builders, all struggling to rebuild their old homes in a strange, new land. "The struggle of men with men is at best a sick and squalid affair for one of the parties; but men contriving against the gods for possession of the earth is your true epic," she muses. It is a struggle of homesteaders against Pan—wild nature—with its droughts, bindweed, and sandstorms, and its rabbits gnawing the bark of tender young trees in a new orchard. If winds and weather prove unfriendly, the homesteader fails and wild growth overruns the plowed ground.[13]

Now and again Austin raises some issue of conservation in a piercing phrase or two. The logging of redwoods has been violent, wasteful, like the mining of gold. Trees have been butchered. But government forestry has begun to protect its reserves against the "Ahabs of a grasping time." Just west of San Francisco, some thirty miles out to sea, is a city of refuge for seabirds, the Farallon Islands. Austin knows of the many thousands of murre eggs that men used to take freely from the nests and sell for human consumption. She is also aware of more recent governmental restrictions against egg-picking.[14] But for the most part, rather than scold, she focuses on the beauty of certain places, their legends, and their emotional power.

Better known, then and now, for her fiction set in the arid lands of Sparrow Hawk, Austin could also write with sympathy about the watery lands of Little Duck, which she came to know later in life. San Francisco she knew through the earthquake and fires of 1906; she had seen its land shaken "as a terrier shakes a rat." Still, it was a city with a soul, a civilized place clinging to a windswept bit of earth "like a great, grey sea-bird with palpitating wings." About a hundred miles to the south, the Coast Range was broken by the wide sweep of Monterey Bay, where waters from the Pajaro and the Salinas rivers poured in and competed with the tides. The mission of Our Lady of Solitude lay in ruins in the Salinas Valley—

which remained farming country, "a place set apart, where any morning you might wake to find the sea has entered between the little, brooding hills to rest."[15]

South of Monterey Bay lay the more intimate Carmel Bay, a magnet for painters, poets, and others in search of beauty. Austin mentions raccoons, bobcats, coyotes, quail, and migrating birds in the vicinity of her own cottage in Carmel. Farther south, past Point Lobos, the narrow coast road slipped over bare hills and into dark canyons, among ancient redwoods, on its way to Big Sur and beyond. In those days, it was a road rarely taken and yet enticing—a "dramatic and unlimned possibility."[16]

Years later Austin referred to *California: The Land of the Sun* as a personal account of the place before it succumbed to tourism. One of her biographers, Augusta Fink, added that the California book was written under pressure and under contract to a British publisher; and Austin needed the income.[17] These pieces of information, though interesting, do not lessen the impression that Austin wrote the book for her own pleasure. The writing seems unhurried, reaching back into eons of prehistory.

The first American edition of *California: The Land of the Sun* and Peixotto's *Romantic California* would have appealed to similar audiences of thoughtful, perhaps well-traveled people, many of them drawn to lesser-known and wilder natural landscapes for leisurely travel or retreat. As artifacts, both books are elegant. Their cloth covers are stamped, printed, and enriched with gilt on front, spine, and top edges. But the cover of *Romantic California* is classical in spirit, suggesting a framed painting or wall panel from the Renaissance. The inset image is of an old Spanish mission, and the gilt frame is festooned with oranges and pears, backed by dark green cloth. Altogether different in mood, the cover of *California: The Land of the Sun* suggests the view from a large window in an Arts and Crafts house, looking through branches of an orange tree to a snow-capped peak. The color scheme, mainly olive, with orange, blue, and glimmers of gold, is more subdued. The name of the artist, Sutton Palmer, precedes that of the writer, Mary Austin. Today only the writer is well known.

***

Of course we don't *need* handsomely bound and illustrated books to take in the meaning of the printed word. In school some of the most memorable books we ever read were thick paperbacks. What mattered were the words, the language. Our copies of *The Grapes of Wrath* (1939) had what seemed to be a 1930s-era illustration on the cover, showing Pa and Ma Joad, a few other family members, the old truck, the open road, maybe distant mountains. Apart from that, with ample help from John Steinbeck, we formed our own mental images.

Back then no one told us about Steinbeck's *The Pastures of Heaven* (1932), a much slimmer, earlier book, with a narrower geographical range. Not a novel but a collection of interrelated stories, this work allowed the young, unknown author to write about his native Salinas Valley and draw freely from California history and his own family history while taking a few liberties with facts and literary forms. It is set in the Corral de Tierra, a small, secluded valley near Salinas that Spanish explorers had first named "Las Pasturas del Cielo."[18]

The Pastures of Heaven opens with a Spanish soldier's view from a high ridge to the valley below: a long, green valley, with browsing deer, beautiful live oaks, and hills that protect it from fog and wind. The book closes with another view of the valley, again from a high ridge. Tourists from a bus out of Monterey look down on a human-ordered scene, a vision of orchards, fields, gardens, waving grain, and snug little farmhouses. A few tourists imagine living there somehow, but their prospects for happiness seem flawed.

While each story between these bracketing scenes can be read on its own, all the stories are linked by someone's contact with the Monroes. Newcomers from town, the Monroes purchase a weedy, abandoned farm, bring it back to life, make it productive—and yet they seem to have inherited the curse that has driven previous owners away. Neighbors joke about the proliferation of curses. The very idea of a curse becomes a link between the stories in *The Pastures of Heaven*—but it may not be the most significant one.

As long as we read Steinbeck mainly for the human drama in his stories, another drama may lie unnoticed: the complex interactions among humans and the land, including nonhuman creatures, plants, trees, air, water, and sky. This drama, the ecology of a place, includes some violent conflict—earthquakes, thunderstorms, volcanic eruptions, predatory killing. In *The Pastures of Heaven* there is some killing, for food, revenge, or relief of some kind. But even the pulling up of weeds, brambles, and vines to make a farm neat and productive is a form of killing; some organic life is extinguished so that other life may take hold.

Making no overt judgment, Steinbeck shows us how others judge people and places. The neighbors think highly of Raymond Banks's large, neat farm, with its whitewashed chicken houses, its five thousand white chickens, its one thousand white ducks, and its large round pond supplied with water from a two-inch pipe. But the neighbors do not approve of the way Junius Maltby has let his wife's farm languish after she died, nor do they like to see Junius's son, Robbie, in rags. Like a Greek chorus, the neighbors uphold the values of the community, but opposed to some of those values are Steinbeck's more appealing characters.

Junius Maltby is an educated man with a hankering for thoughts that sprout and grow wild, undirected and untrimmed. He likes to spend afternoons sitting on a great horizontal limb of a sycamore, hanging his feet in the stream below, talking with his hired man about Carthaginian generals, the colors of flowers, the horses on the frieze of the Parthenon, and other fascinating things. Sitting beside them, Robbie can barely touch the stream with his toes. At school he is slow in learning to write, yet he reads easily and speaks with the vocabulary of his bearded mentors, his father and the hired man. His teacher, young Molly Morgan, considers the little boy a kind of genius. Hiking out to the Maltby place one Saturday morning, she finds blackberry vines in the apple trees and a quiet farmhouse that could have been abandoned for a century. "How run-down and slovenly," she muses. "How utterly lovely and slipshod!"[19] She is welcomed; and for a day she is happy to take part in the Maltbys' world. What unites them all is imagination.

That day Junius offers an unusual view of the eviction from the Garden of Eden. Before long, he and Robbie must leave the valley. Molly

Morgan must also leave. Even the preeminent family in the valley, the Whitesides, must leave. Perhaps they all leave because of something one of the Monroes has done unwittingly. Is the valley cursed? In any event, people make choices that shape their own fates. Molly, for instance, prefers solitude to the company of John Whiteside's pragmatic, unimaginative son, Bill. A boarder at the Whitesides' house, she is not at ease among the prim flower beds and clipped boxwood hedges along the path to their front veranda. From her walks in the hills, she brings back wildflowers and ferns to plant by the house, and these bits of wildness apparently survive—for a while.

As biographers have noted, Steinbeck was a keen gardener, who liked to dig in the earth and make things grow. In hard times during the early 1930s, he and his wife, Carol, actually depended on some of the food they grew. Not surprisingly, the gardens in some of his stories are mirrors of their owners. Helen Van Deventer, a wealthy widow from San Francisco, buys land in a canyon of the Pastures of Heaven and wants her new house and gardens to look old. Trucks haul in logs and lumber, the workmen age the logs with acid, and gardeners bring in mature plants and trees. Some old bays and oaks are left in the lawn, but beneath the oaks Helen grows showy annuals—cinerarias, in white, purple, and blue—while more annuals, brilliant blue lobelias, line the walks.[20]

Helen is no less chilling than Mary Teller, in "The White Quail," from Steinbeck's story cycle *The Long Valley* (1938). Mary, who identifies with her garden, has scarlet and ultramarine cinerarias placed in a circle of sunken pots beneath a large oak. A line of fuchsias, like little Christmas trees, keeps out some enemies—wild grasses, shrubs, and poison oak on the hillside beyond. But crawling and stalking enemies still threaten her sanctuary. Like Helen, Mary is a proud gardener but not a sympathetic one. Their gardens are not labors of love.[21]

In *The Pastures of Heaven* and *The Long Valley,* some characters identify not with the garden but with something more elusive, all-encompassing—that is, home, belonging to a place. Some never seem to belong, or their hold on a place is tenuous. Some have to assert their *right* to belong. "I was born here, the same as you," cries young Takashi Kato, and

Robbie Maltby has to figure out a way to include him in the schoolboys' little band of spies against the Japanese. He does find a way.[22]

In "The Great Mountains," however—a section of "The Red Pony," from *The Long Valley*—the elderly Gitano is not welcomed at all. "I have come back," says Gitano. "I was born here, and my father, too." Carl Tiflin and his wife do not understand; their ranch is not old. But Gitano is looking beyond their property lines. His roots are with the larger ranch, before it was broken up into smaller parcels and his family's adobe house began to wash away for lack of lime. Now Gitano wants to stay in the land where he was born, until he dies. He can do odd jobs, but Carl Tiflin has no more use for Gitano than he has for a thirty-year-old horse named Easter, once a champion racer. As far as Carl is concerned, old useless animals should be shot.[23]

Young Jody Tiflin has already seen his red pony die in its prime. He has learned something of suffering and death, but when bored or frustrated, he can be as callous as his father, indifferent toward any living creature in his path. What sets the boy apart is his youthful imagination. He can look down over the long valley and see his home ranch in the foothills, "sunny and safe." There are more ranches in the Gabilan Mountains, to the east, and Jody knows that people live there, that battles against the Mexicans were once fought there. But he wonders what lies beyond the dark, mysterious mountains to the west—the Santa Lucias. An ocean, yes, but what else? Gitano, when pressed, remembers that his father once took him into those mountains, that it was quiet there. Soon Gitano is gone.

In "The Leader of the People," also from *The Long Valley*, the elderly father of Mrs. Tifflin once led a wagon train across the plains to the Pacific. That was the one great experience of his life, and he cannot stop telling the same old stories. Carl Tiflin is not interested. But Jody listens as Grandfather tries to explain his great collective experience, getting people who had interests of their own to move as one, to carry life across the continent and set it down. Now Grandfather has come to believe that there's no place to go; that the *spirit* of westering, movement, adventure,

Crater at the summit of Mount Haleakala, Maui, Hawaiian Islands. (Photograph by Brian Muchow; courtesy of Brian Muchow)

and risk taking has died out of the people. Something has stopped them—an ocean.[24]

✳ ✳ ✳

Far out in that ocean, west by southwest, lie more mountains with a history of battles fought and vast ranches broken up. Those mountains, some rising thirty thousand feet above the ocean floor, are the Hawaiian Islands, where strangers would be greeted with "Aloha"—"My love to you," as Armine von Tempski explained in her memoir *Born in Paradise* (1940). Her paradise, located on a sixty-thousand-acre cattle ranch on the island of Maui, was a land of great beauty, a blend of gardens, corrals, pastures, hills, ravines, and trails rising up ten thousand feet above the sea to the summit of Haleakala—House of the Sun, an extinct volcano sometimes obscured by clouds. That was her little childhood kingdom, a place not owned by anyone she knew, but used, explored, lived in, and made more beautiful by people who spoke English, Hawaiian,

Japanese, Chinese, or some other tongue. For them "Aloha" was not merely a courtesy but a common bond.[25]

It was an era in Hawaii's history, so Armine's father pointed out one day. That era would pass, just as the monarchy had passed. She ought to write about it and preserve it for others, he suggested. Armine did just that, in several novels and two memoirs, the first of which, *Born in Paradise*, was picked up by the Literary Guild and reached a wide audience. A reviewer in 1940 appreciated von Tempski's dramatic stories, but thought the book oversupplied with adjectives and "very feminine."[26]

Today other qualities stand out: the intermingling of cultures, the racial tolerance, the feeling for landscape character, the emphasis on *doing* rather than owning things, the sense of permeable boundaries, and spiritual connections among people, animals, and objects in nature. Not that everyone in Armine's world felt as she did. Her mother, a daughter of the British ambassador to the late monarchy, preferred an indoor world with reliable boundaries and protocols. But her daughters, especially Armine and her younger sister Lorna, were more at home out-of-doors, in a world of cowboys, horses, cattle drives, and risks of all kinds.

Born in 1899, a year after the Hawaiian Islands became a territory of the United States, Armine grew up in a land where patterns of an older way of life lived on; where one dressed for dinner, and where raising cattle was still a going concern, even as the more lucrative sugar plantations were expanding.[27] In her family's lore, bravery, courage, charm, adventurousness, and gracious acceptance of winning or losing—with a smile, regardless—were things that really mattered. Her paternal grandfather, a military man and a political exile from Poland, had traveled and worked in Central America, Mexico, California, Australia, and New Zealand. Her paternal grandmother, a Scottish woman, had once been a governess on the island of Maui. Armine's father, Louis, had planned to travel the world when he left New Zealand at age eighteen. But he fell in love with Maui, worked at various jobs to stay there, and eventually came to manage the Haleakala Ranch. There, on some sixty thousand acres, he reigned like a wise and benevolent king, treating his people fairly, planting grasses and trees for posterity. Yet he owned no land, nor

THE REGION

even the house where he, his family, the nannies, and the servants lived. The big house was there for his use, for as long as he was able to do his work, which he loved.

An expert horseman, Louis worked alongside his men as one of them as he led them, at times driving the domesticated cattle down the mountainside to the sea, at times charging up into the hills to rope longhorn cattle that had gone wild. There were dangers to avoid, including deep lava pits hidden by brush, where bull, horse, and rider might be maimed or killed. But Louis would not be put off by lava pits and sharks. "First Born, if you want a rich full life you've got to gamble sometimes," he would say. To initiate Armine, his First Born, into his world of work and play, Louis had her fetched from the nursery one hot afternoon while the ladies were sleeping. Placing her on a pillow in the crook of his right arm, he rode off on his wildest horse, Buccaneer. Armine was a month old.[28]

Born in Paradise reads like a novel, where stories handed down in the family mingle with Armine's own memories. Every day when she was young, Makalii, an elderly Hawaiian cowboy, made a place for her on his saddle. He made leis for her, then a saddle. He taught her to ride, and to hear the land's many voices. Riding slowly, he would listen to earth spirits in the grass, the wind, the trees, and the rocks. He explained how Cloud Warriors gathered along the southern and northern flanks of Haleakala; how they fought to possess the summit or called a truce, leaving a clear sky between them—the Highway to Heaven. Makalii was with Armine when she first saw a colt being born, when she felt her first earthquake, and when she first saw the red glare of lava erupting a hundred and fifty miles away—from Mauna Loa, on the island of Hawaii. Outside her own family, Makalii was her closest confidant; no presence but Haleakala itself was so powerful early on.

In this memoir, descriptions of landscape, lyrical and fleeting like cloud shadows, mingle with recollections of people and adventures. Often it is difficult to separate places from people. On Christmas Eve at the ranch, Hawaiian *paniolos,* or cowboys, rode up to serenade the large household of many cultures and religions; they sang of their love for

Haleakala and the island of Maui, "on which we all lived and which blended our lives into a whole," Armine wrote. At election time, at a luau in the garden, the beating of hidden drums grew louder and more insistent as human voices began to chant. From a bamboo grove came ten young women to dance a ceremonial hula, their hair unbound and their skirts swishing like the sound of water flowing to the sea. As drumbeats lessened, dancers vanished one by one, like spirits. Armine recalled feeling carried on by a great tide, where past, present, and future came together as one. "Aloha, aloha," people cried before moving on to another luau.

That paradise was not without suffering and death. Even the vast crater of Haleakala held death in one of its gray cones of ash, for deep inside were ancient stone burial places that scientists later judged to be the Passing Place of Chiefs. But life was more prominent, and a mere jaunt could be an adventure, as when Armine, Louis (Dad), Grandmother ("Gan"), and Makalii rode one day to West Maui, across the isthmus planted in sugar cane. In the town of Wailuku were smokestacks, a noisy sugar mill, and powerful odors of molasses mingling with spicy odors from Chinese grocery stores, where owners sat outside and grandsons crawled on the ground. Streams were fragrant with ginger blossoms. Cottages were engulfed in shrubs and *kamani* trees. The cemetery up the hillside held Japanese graves. Battles had been fought in the Iao Valley. Some of Dad's old Hawaiian friends lived in a darker valley, among Norfolk Island pines, purple mango trees, Italian cypresses, and terraces covered with flowers. And as curtains swayed in the trade wind through open windows, the house seemed to be breathing.[29]

Von Tempski described few interiors in this memoir, for she had lived most intensely out-of-doors. But after her father's accident, which ultimately meant the loss of his position and the big house, the family settled in a small house built for them on the ranch. Armine's bedroom contained a row of french doors, many windows, a bed, a piano, a couch, and a writing desk. There she wrote drafts of books, hoping to interest a publisher. Her father would nurse his bad leg. Her brother and sister would come in with friends. Hawaiian and Japanese people came in asking for advice. The head jockey came to talk about horses. Old friends came to tea. The room was a campground for the family, Armine recalled. On sunny days it was like an indoor garden—doors wide open, no doubt. Perhaps it expressed that sense of permeable boundaries she had known all her life.

The narrative of *Born in Paradise* leaves off sometime in the early 1920s. *Aloha* (1946), von Tempski's second memoir, covers only a decade or so, ending with her marriage in southern California, in 1932. During those years, she noticed changes in the landscape of Maui—not only expanding fields of sugar cane and pineapple but also a return to wilderness of once-inhabited valleys. On the northern slopes of Haleakala, peering down into the wild ravines of the Honomanu Valley, she recalled a famous Hawaiian dancer who had lived there in retirement. That jogged her memory; Dad had once said that "the earth may be used, but it can never be owned." Now Armine felt that was true of the uninhabited Honomanu Valley; it had been there before humans and would remain after they departed. Those who had lived there had been "lovers, not masters, of the land."[30]

✻ ✻ ✻

As wilderness became increasingly rare in the United States, organizations such as the Sierra Club and the Wilderness Society tried to reach all those lovers of wild places who might actively *defend* wild places. In their publications they enlisted the forces of the printed word—including writings by Thoreau, Muir, and Aldo Leopold—as well as photographs by Ansel Adams, Eliot Porter, Edward Weston, Philip Hyde, and many others. Then in 1955 an exhibition of photographs, "This Is the American Earth," at LeConte Lodge in Yosemite Valley, gave David Brower, the Sierra Club's executive director, a novel idea. Why not extend the influence of such exhibitions in a book, something unusually large, with stunning images and freedom to wander, as in a gallery? So began the Sierra Club's prizewinning Exhibit Format books, measuring some 10½ inches by 14 inches, which drew more lovers of wilderness to their cause.[31]

In one of those books is the idea that "the greatest beauty is / Organic

Big Sur coast and State Highway 1, near Bixby Creek, in California

wholeness, the wholeness of life and things." The words are from the poet Robinson Jeffers. The book is *Not Man Apart* (1965), and the subject, the Big Sur coast of California. A diligent reader could bypass the opening pages of haunting black-and-white photographs, paired with words by Jeffers, and begin at the title page (photographs by Ansel Adams, Morley Baer, Eliot Porter, Edward Weston, Cole Weston, and others; editor, David Brower). Loren Eiseley wrote the foreword. The introduction is by Margaret Wentworth Owings, who with her husband, the architect Nathaniel Owings, had helped to keep Highway 1 from being transformed into a multi-lane state freeway through the Santa Lucia Mountains along the Big Sur coast.[32] These texts are brief, compelling, yet images beckon. And who could resist the force of certain words set against a certain image of rock, tide pool, mountain, breaker, fern, grazing horses, or spiral nebula? Who would not wander, as in a gallery, and be moved?

The Exhibit Format books were expensive, but when reduced and reprinted in paperback, they sold very well.[33] And so reasons for protecting the Big Sur coast and other places of great natural beauty reached a wide audience. Now it remains to be seen how long the "masters" of the land will tolerate Highway 1 as a narrow two-lane road. Periodically washed out by winter rains, it has usually been reconstructed on the same footprint—a slim ribbon of pavement over spectacular natural land masses and an occasional bridge.

And what of those vast areas of "unlimned possibility" along the Big Sur coast, places that Austin, Steinbeck, and many others have known and loved only from a distance? In *Not Man Apart*, large black-and-white photographs of a city engulfed in smog, a dead pelican, and metropolitan Los Angeles from the air may state the case for conservation as eloquently as the writings of Margaret Owings, Loren Eiseley, and David Brower.

FOUR

The Arid West

History, Memory,
Signs of Vitality

In some dry, seemingly barren lands of the West, widely spaced piñon pine and juniper survive the heat of the midday sun while other life persists in shadows and crevices. Some creatures are more active at night or down in the canyons. Here and there a little drama may play out unseen by all but the most patient watchers. Mary Austin was one. "Go as far as you dare in the heart of a lonely land, you cannot go so far that life and death are not before you," she wrote in *The Land of Little Rain* (1903).[1] That conviction runs through a later work of Austin, to be considered here along with works by J. B. Jackson, Wallace Stegner, and others who wrote about human habitation in the arid West. And because these writers often looked back in time, to their own past or to ruins of a vanished people, a word about history, memory, and nostalgia seems to be in order.

Hints of nostalgia—a longing for some kind of lost home—have already appeared in these pages, in writings by Louise Dickinson Rich, Robert P. Tristram Coffin, and Harvey Broome. Some would argue that Sarah Orne Jewett had a tendency toward nostalgia; if so, what of certain passages by Loren Eiseley and John Steinbeck? Since the word "nostalgia" has acquired mainly negative connotations, we could use some clarification.

In *The True and Only Heaven* (1991) the historian Christopher Lasch noted that nostalgia involves a yearning for something lost in time—childhood innocence, perhaps, or a static, unchanging society, a Disneyland. Through nostalgia, something lost can be frozen in time; and it can be preserved, idealized, so long as it remains remote, inaccessible. But memory and history are activities of an alert, inquiring mind that recognizes the past as something *continuous* with present and future. In this way the past is not dead or frozen in time but alive, an inheritance to be carried forward. What is more, the past cannot be avoided if, as Lasch pointed out, its formative influence "lives on in our patterns of speech, our gestures, our standards of honor, our expectations, our basic disposition toward the world around us."[2] In any event, it is memory and history that concern us here—not nostalgia as commonly understood and dismissed.

***

J. B. Jackson's *Landscapes* (1970), a collection of previously published essays, came as a revelation to those of us who had never heard of the man or his magazine, *Landscape*. Here were essays on neon signs and strip development written long before Robert Venturi's *Learning from Las Vegas* (1972), along with some disturbing remarks about the Sierra Club, wilderness recreation, ecology, and landscape beauty. Here, too, were bus stations, pawn shops, farm trucks, Thomas Jefferson, Henry David Thoreau, and thoughts on "Optimo City," a hypothetical town in the United States located somewhere west of the Alleghenies. These unpretentious essays were invitations to look at the American landscape in radically new ways, to question a few comfortable old assumptions and ponder how some ordinary landscapes came to be. It was a new kind of landscape history, one that might begin with a highway or a shopping center and work backward in time—or with a farm in colonial Massachusetts and move forward in time, westward in space.[3]

Looking intently at common landscapes, public and private, Jackson wrote little about himself. Even essays that gave hints of his whereabouts were not personally revealing. Years later, profiles of this provocative thinker would reveal where he had finally settled down—near Santa Fe—and something of his unusual background, in Europe and on the East Coast, through times of affluence, depression, and world war.[4] But Jackson himself was more interested in the typical qualities of a place. It might be uninhabited—a ruin, perhaps—but it would be humanized, because some human being or group had left the stamp of their way of life on it. And vestiges of that life would remain, as clues for the sharp-eyed and curious.

That is the way Jackson's own views could be detected—in small clues. He believed in what later came to be known as "environmental justice." To him it was simply social justice, noticeable—or absent—in the places where ordinary people lived, worked, played, and traveled. And, as he thought the "beautificationists" and landscape preservationists of his time seemed to have forgotten those people, Jackson set out to restructure the terms of environmental debate. Rather than focus on pollution, the extinction of species, beauty, or spiritual regeneration, Jackson asked about ordinary people's prospects for congregation, personal expression, and civic responsibility. "Would a landscape or a city conceived of in these terms be beautiful?" he asked in 1966. In time, perhaps, we would learn to recognize beauty in these qualities.[5]

To select a few of Jackson's writings on places in the Southwest, moving back in time from 1960, is to move from trailer camps to ancient Pueblo dwellings. Such a modest effort cannot really respond to the challenge posed by Jackson's former student John Stilgoe—to search in Jackson's writings for "the germ of what might grow again as the core of a wholly different landscape architecture education and profession."[6] But it does offer glimpses of a kind of landscape history that is very much alive, potent, and thus controversial.

Traveling as a tourist through the Colorado Plateau, in Utah, Colorado, New Mexico, and Arizona, Jackson was struck by two related characteristics: transiency and mobility. In "The Four Corners Country" (1960) he noted some reasons for this lack of permanent settlement—the extreme dryness, the rough ground, the high altitude, the traditional

Navaho livelihood of herding, and the white man's sporadic mining, ranching, and dam- and pipeline-building. This region without visible boundaries, better known for Mesa Verde, Chaco Canyon, and the long-disputed Glen Canyon Dam, had a great many trailers, or mobile homes, often occupied by construction workers. Jackson considered the trailer yet another step in the evolution of the American single-family home, which was being progressively stripped of traditional functions down to a temporary shell. And it occurred to him that, in a lonely, beautiful land where the Navaho, in pickup trucks, were bypassing trading posts for distant supermarkets—and where everyone else was on the move as well—these transient House Trailer People arriving out of nowhere, without roots, seemed to belong.[7]

In "First Comes the House" (1959–60), Jackson considered the Spanish colonial house in the Southwest. Owner-built, largely handmade, this house reflected the rural, conservative, family-centered culture from which it arose. It was not a good model for imitation in other parts of the country, Jackson admitted. It could not be mass-produced or replicated in a dense city, yet it could show American architects and planners just how complex and expressive a single house could be. A thick-walled shelter insulated from the natural elements and the rest of society, it was also an interior world. Based on a single room, it could grow as the extended family grew, with added rooms forming a protected little community based on kinship. At that time, mainstream American designers were dissolving boundaries between indoors and outdoors, work and play, public and private life. Noting this trend, Jackson simply recommended that designers study a house type that expressed a different cultural point of view—Spanish or Latin—and learn from it.[8]

These essays revealed a mind that was flexible, curious, open to many points of view, yet wary. In "Two Street Scenes" (1954) Jackson did not share the traffic engineer's enthusiasm for broad one-way streets through the centers of American towns. He much preferred Santa Fe, where the two-way traffic on Main Street might be clogged because of a wedding or a rodeo parade. Without pulling over, a driver might stop to chat with a passerby. Generally, the haphazard, colorful outdoor life of the city would take precedence over efficiency. Wherever traffic was efficiently dispersed, he noted, the life of a town died after working hours. In Santa Fe, that life continued, for motorists were not the sole owners of the street.[9]

At his most engaging, Jackson seems to be thinking aloud and speculating. In "Pueblo Dwellings and Our Own" (winter 1953–54) he pondered some curious findings of scholars—that the vast landscape of the prehistoric Pueblo culture had little variation in building types; and that the basic unit of Pueblo architecture was a room, multiplied in clusters—even though the Hopi language contains no word for "room." Jackson wondered if we were all victims of language, unable to see something for which we have no word. And why was the prehistoric Pueblo dwelling slow to develop as a "counterenvironment," or a complex organism of interior space, such as Europeans had developed toward the end of the Dark Ages? Was time a factor? Time could be conceived of as cyclical, based on observation of the sky—the enduring order of the heavens that regulated the days, the seasons, and the four directions. Or time could be historical, based on observation of changes on earth. These environmental changes—weathering, erosion, flood, drought—could be resisted by dwellings built to last, with durable shells, specialized, complex interiors, and rooms worthy of a name.[10]

Whether we accept the particular route and reasoning of Jackson's thought, his writing remains provocative. In fact, it's sometimes difficult *not* to pause at an inference or reframe a question. The Hopis' ancestors had no word for "room"; but Jackson knew they did have words for places where people do certain things. Well, what if those vanished people lived much more intensely out-of-doors than we do in modern times? What if they considered an *action* more important than the space where it occurred? Another point: Typically, foundations were unexcavated—merely rock and stone on the surface of the site. Jackson read this as a "lack of concern for establishing any bond with the immediate environment." But what of other bonds, spiritual connections to the land, to the place, or to the whole universe of things seen and unseen? As more ques-

Characteristic Pueblo Houses. *(Image from John L. Stoddard, Lectures, vol. 10:*
Grand Cañon of the Colorado River [1905]; photographer unknown)

tions arise, the landscape Jackson has brought to our attention draws us
in deeper. We are engaged, and he has worked his magic.[11]

It happened that Jackson left the East Coast to take up ranching near
Santa Fe in the late 1930s, the decade of Mary Austin's final years in that
town.[12] Her Casa Querida, or "beloved house," was built there in 1925,
along the lines of a Spanish colonial dwelling. She died in 1934; perhaps
she and Jackson never met, but their interests did overlap. In *The Land*
of Journeys' Ending (1924) Austin explored parts of the Southwest and
conceived of the land and people, past and present, as intimately bound
together. "Man is not himself only. . . . He is all that he sees; all that flows
to him from a thousand sources," she wrote. "He is the land, the lift of
its mountain lines, the reach of its valleys."[13]

Austin was then trying to fuse a rational, Anglo-American understanding of that land in its historical context with Native American creation stories, her own informed intuitions, and some intimations of a great cultural flowering that would arise there someday. She detected signs of a bright future in indigenous forms of architecture and art, including dance, festivals, shop signs, and baptismal fonts. One observer, Larry Evers, has noted that this late work was drawn from Austin's purposeful journeys over a few years, but not from long familiarity with a place and the acute attention to small detail that marked her earlier *Land of Little Rain*.[14] With less intimacy, then, but more ambition and grandeur, Austin tried to understand the vast sweep of land in the region of the Rio Grande and the Rio Colorado—including the prehistoric Pueblo dwellings high on the mesas and deep in the cliffs that formed canyon walls.

Writing of those cliff dwellings, Austin drew upon the findings of unnamed ethnologists to enrich her own descriptions of a way of life still faintly detectable in the ruins. But she gave no citations, dates, plans, or maps, and assumed that facts were less compelling than truths. Thus alerted, we would do well to consider *The Land of Journeys' Ending* not as history or geography, but as a work of imaginative literature.

"Corn is a town-builder, a maker of policies, mother of inventions," Austin wrote. "Out of its necessities were drawn architecture, philosophical systems, and the material of drama." Thus she compressed centuries of social evolution from hunting and gathering to dry-land agriculture, irrigation, cooperation, congregation, and religious and cultural expression in ritual, dance, architecture, and decorative pottery. She could also move swiftly from descriptions of physical nature to something metaphysical, writing of sun and silence, wind in the corn, and plants coming a long way with man through the ages, reaching up from the earth and aspiring as men aspire. If Austin's intuitions were correct, the small-house people who built round and angular towers of stone on ledges and on the terraced heights of mesas had no fear of other humans until nearly the end of their era. For most of their existence on that land, Austin imagined, they watched for the movements of wild herds, tended their corn, repaired their ditches, decorated their pottery, observed their rituals, and placated their gods. And so they lived in "the absence of those strains and resistances that stiffen us against the wind forever blowing from some quarter of the universe across our souls."[15]

Studying the ruins of Pueblo dwellings and considering their forms and materials, Austin drew conclusions for which there may be no archaeological evidence. The dwellings that are round in plan, for instance, she traced to an instinct to build around the axis of the body "as all wild things build." In time, she reasoned, men aligned their dwellings to their cedar beams and built angular watchtowers. Women, too, were involved in building, Austin noted—for excavators were continually finding "fine, feminine finger-marks, and the modulation of small, shallow palms" in the adobe clay surfaces of dwellings. The stone cliff dwellings, nestled deep within canyon walls and beneath the shelter of overhanging rock, would have been ideal places for shelter, storage, security, and visibility. Even after people had moved on to larger towns on the plains, perhaps they returned to those cliff dwellings and aerial caves for ceremonies. Enticing from a distance, those dwellings would be snug and warm inside, as people gathered around corner fireplaces and rain fell beyond the overhanging rock "like a silver curtain between them and the world."[16]

Austin had a rough idea of how those ancient dwellings had evolved, in stages. The earliest would have been the pit houses, simple cavities dug into the mesas of southern Utah and Colorado some three to five thousand years ago. Much more recent would have been the cities on the river plains farther south, each built up around an irrigation canal, or *acequia madre*. And sometime between the appearance of those two types there would have been an indeterminate period of time, when little towered villages and towns arose in places like the Mesa Verde country of southwestern Colorado. There some member of the tribe would have gazed out from a watchtower, conscious of responsibility for his tribe. And some combination of hunting and small-scale agriculture—growing corn, beans, squash, melons—would have kept the tribe nourished.

Those villages and small towns would have hovered about a certain wavering line—the line between civilization and all that had gone before.

"It is the line at which peoples cease merely to accommodate themselves to their environment, and attempt its mastery," Austin wrote. With higher degrees of mastery and control, large-scale irrigation, central organization, and more articulated buildings came higher levels of civilization. But along the way something was lost, a certain hard, sharp, decisive quality of mind and spirit. Austin alluded to it when she thought of conflicts among the vanished tribes and reflected that people deeply engaged in community had not been able to resist an enemy who fought from a different impulse, "each man for his own hand." So wrote Austin, who would soon leave New York City for good and try to reestablish herself yet again in a dry-land environment of small towns and wide-open spaces.[17]

One of Austin's friends in New York, the slightly younger Willa Cather, was also drawn to the Southwest, where she set some memorable passages of certain stories and novels. In Cather's *Death Comes for the Archbishop* (1927) nearly all the action takes place in the same arid lands that Austin presented in *Land of Journeys' Ending*. But Cather, who had lived in New York since her early thirties and would maintain a residence there, always came to the Southwest as a visitor—sensitive, curious, prepared to appreciate the land's austere beauty, yet removed from any long-term, day-to-day familiarity. And that spatial distance could be an asset, setting off one place in sharp contrast with another. Distance in time, too, could allow quick, fresh impressions to ripen and deepen.

In *The Professor's House* (1925) some memories of places and people have receded so far into the past, however, that they seem nearly inaccessible. Cather's main character, Professor Godfrey St. Peter, has reached that point in life, just past fifty, when much of what had once fed his imagination and his passions lies behind him. His scholarly volumes on the Spanish conquerors (or "adventurers," as he called them) have finally been recognized by his peers. The years and seasons devoted to his research on those volumes, in the Southwest and in Europe, will probably have no sequel. His wife and married daughters have interests he doesn't share—new houses, old Spanish furniture, jewelry, travel for pleasure. His finest student, Tom Outland, full of youthful energy and promise, was killed in Flanders during the First World War, fighting with the Foreign Legion. But Outland's story, embedded in the novel like a jewel, gives life and spirit to an otherwise melancholy tale.[18]

While herding cattle on a winter range in southwestern Colorado, the teenaged orphan Tom Outland comes across an old irrigation ditch, a few shards of pottery, arrowheads, a pick-ax. These traces of human effort and care in that seemingly empty land lead Outland and Blake, his older friend and fellow cowboy, to wonder about the ancient people who had once lived there. Later Outland pursues some stray cattle into a canyon of Blue Mesa (Mesa Verde). What follows is one of the high points of his story—one bright moment in which the whole novel, set mainly under gray midwestern skies and burdened with thoughts of death and loss, comes alive.

Outland's tale of how he came upon the cliff dwellings is marked by vivid sensations: the colors of lavender, blue, purple, gray, and gold; the "taste" of pure, cool air; the sense of enclosure in a box canyon; the warm sweat from scrambling among boulders on the canyon floor; the chance sight, through a veil of falling snow, of a stone city high up in a canyon wall. Gazing at those remains of a past civilization, Outland thinks of keeping them a secret even from his close friend Blake.

But he does tell his friend. The story of their efforts to reach the cliff dwellings, unearth, interpret, and catalogue the artifacts, then interest experts at the Smithsonian, in Washington, unfolds in a series of misunderstandings. The artifacts are carted away. Blake disappears and Outland remains at Blue Mesa, conscious of loss but also of intense happiness. For the first time he can see the place as a whole. That summer he cleans up the disturbed cliff dwellings, studies his Spanish and Latin, memorizes long passages from the *Aeneid*, and eventually ceases to worry about Blake. What began as adventure comes to seem like a religious experience. The Latin poets, writing of "filial piety," express what Outland feels for the mesa. He loves that land.

Literary critics have disagreed on aspects of the human drama—whether Outland's story is integral to the novel; whether Outland and Professor St. Peter are likable characters; and the degree to which Outland, the cataloguer of artifacts, is an artist, representing Cather's concept of a "kingdom of art." But Cather also depicts the drama of the *land*, both wild and civilized, as she draws connections between Outland's Blue Mesa and the tale of Aeneas and the founding of Rome.[19]

That epic poem would always remind Outland of two images—one on a certain page of the *Aeneid*, and one of the mesa, a once-inhabited land. As he reads on, Virgil's tale of the founding of one civilization, Roman, becomes overlaid on the remains of another civilization, prehistoric Native American. It is a tale of human love, desertion, death, war, and the roots of imperialism. But it is also about love of one's country, and it touches on two golden ages, one past, one future.

In the past golden age, which Virgil describes in more detail, there was a sturdy race of men who had come from the trunks of oak trees and had known nothing of settled life, art, and agriculture before Saturn gathered them together and gave them laws, peace, and the beginnings of civilization.[20] People may now take civilization for granted, but Cather, reared from adolescence on the Nebraska frontier in the 1880s, remembered the rawness. In her memory—and that of Outland and St. Peter—Virgil's poetry and the Spanish adventurers live on even among New World ruins and under overcast midwestern skies.

The Song of the Lark (1915), an earlier novel by Cather, contains another interlude among cliff dwellings. In this story of a great opera singer's rise from obscurity on the eastern plains of Colorado, a turning point occurs on vacation in northern Arizona. The young singer, Thea Kronborg, is shaking off the strains of her work in Chicago while she makes daily journeys into Panther Canyon (Walnut Canyon, near Flagstaff). There, the cliff dwellings are already familiar to the owner of the ranch where she is staying. Panther Canyon is not special, we are told; there are thousands like it in the Southwest. Thea first sees the "dead city" as a row of houses, like barracks, beneath an overhanging cliff. She thinks of the ancient people who lived there as timid, building homes in the cliff like swallows, who rarely fly above the canyon's rim. But after she has climbed up to the dwellings and claimed one by spreading out blankets, she begins to inhabit that dwelling in daylight hours. Touching its stone roof and scraping off carbon—from cooking smoke—she senses the presence of those people. Handling shards of pottery that women's hands have shaped, following a trail toward water that women's feet have worn, Thea comes closer to those ancient women.[21]

Moments of deeper understanding follow, not from books but from Thea's gradual surrender of her will to the power of the elements—especially the sun—and her own heightened senses. One morning while bathing in the stream down by the willows, Thea connects the precious water she stands in with the pottery vessels that women have shaped to hold it. Their art, any art, is "an effort to make a sheath, a mould in which to imprison for a moment the shining, elusive element which is life itself." And the singer's art is comparable: to make a vessel of her own throat and nostrils. It is a high point of the summer—and of the novel. In this land of bright sunlight and dark shadows, the singer finds her ideas clarified and her ambitions strengthened. But she loses something in moving on to the world of concert halls and curtain calls, a world in which she will have to assert her will and never surrender to the power of elemental forces and splendid places. When she and Fred—who arrives later that summer—leave the Southwest together in September, they leave a country that has come to seem empty, dead. In later years, when the successful singer tries to recall her stone dwelling in Arizona, the memories are too painful; she would rather not remember.[22]

Open to many interpretations, these novels can be read as primarily human dramas. But Cather's lyrical passages about landscapes vividly present or affectionately remembered suggest that the drama of the land—a humanized land—is at least equally important to the story. And how a character perceives a certain place—whether it seems dead or alive, empty or full, absolutely raw or overlaid with human associations—is a clue.

When Thea leaves the Southwest with renewed ambition, for instance, her sense of living memory is already dimmed; she leaves a land of "dead races." But Outland never quite leaves the Blue Mesa, for his reading of the *Aeneid* there has given him a new appreciation of civilization, a perception of wholeness that sustains him. He was profoundly happy there.

"It was possession," he says. And that kind of possession is about all that St. Peter has to look forward to. He holds on to the memory of the boy he once was, in Kansas, when all he cared about was "earth and woods and water." He also occupies, but does not own, a garden he is reluctant to leave. It holds memories of his earlier years in France and also of time spent happily within the garden walls, tending his shrubs, flowers, and salad herbs, working and dining there, beneath the lindens, and talking with Outland long into the evening. None of these characters is a model of perfection, as an artist, friend, husband, or father. Nor was Aeneas always exemplary. And flaws in his legacy, imperial Roman civilization, persisted in Western civilization of the early 1920s, a postwar era that left Cather profoundly troubled. Repelled by a world in which everything was for sale, Cather let a few characters turn to what they could possess only in spirit—the land.[23]

❋ ❋ ❋

"Land, land, more land! It is the cry of the ages," wrote Emerson Hough in *The Passing of the Frontier* (1918). The last stretches of that frontier he located just over the United States border, in western Canada, where a land boom occurred between 1900 and about 1913. Both the Canadian government and the Canadian railroads advertised land for growing wheat on the open plains, and homesteaders from Europe and the United States responded. Millions of acres were settled then, "as by magic." It was a familiar story: first came the most adventurous people to the far frontier, then came the civilizing ones, who wanted more than "a blanket for a bed and the sky for a roof." But north of their own border, Americans found a different climate, Hough observed. It was much more severe.[24]

An understatement. In *Wolf Willow* (1962) Wallace Stegner writes of one winter, 1906–7, on the border of Montana and Saskatchewan, when the continuing blizzards were so brutal that cowboys were literally freezing to death and survived only by extraordinary endurance and mutual support. The old ranching empires they served did not survive, however, and Stegner's family was part of the next wave, homesteaders from the United States who plowed up those plains for wheat.

The Stegners came late to that land rush in the spring of 1914, when Wallace was five years old. By then the little town he called Whitemud (Eastend) had begun to coalesce around a single main street, which was wide and dusty, without shade trees or sidewalks. Down by the White-mud River (the Frenchman) were sandbars overrun with wild roses and secret paths tramped out through the willows. There, and in the little town where the family lived for part of the year, Wallace found friends and adventure. Partly sheltered by the Cypress Hills to the west, the town in turn protected him; and in its "feminine" world of books and learning he developed a bit of self-confidence. Some fifty miles to the southwest, however, was the Stegner homestead, a man's world staked out by a tar-paper shack on exposed ground, where a slight little boy prone to illness could be marginally useful, shooting gophers before they could nibble on the wheat. Yet he could never quite win the respect of his rough, frontier-calloused father—who compared him with his robust older brother. Out there on the homestead in summers, young Stegner learned about mystery, loneliness, the power of natural forces, and self-awareness in merely being upright, casting long shadows on a flat land.

Returning to that land in the 1950s, Stegner uncovered a past that had nearly escaped him as a child. From 1914 to 1920, from age five to eleven, he had known a half-savage, half-civilized existence in a place that seemed to have no history. In school the past always had to do with England, Canada, and places far to the east. To make the local history and geography of his own early years come to life in *Wolf Willow*, Stegner wrote in several genres—fiction, history, memoir, and what is now known as literary nonfiction. Today this book can be read for the stories and the sheer beauty of the language, as well as for cautions about dry-land agriculture and reflections on the way civilized people come to terms with wildlands. In probing the meaning of his own childhood on the frontier, Stegner also raised questions that planners and designers might ask: What does this town have to offer as a human habitat? Anything? If it was a fine place to be a boy in, but always hard on women; if it has become an exporter of manpower, but not a place to hold talented, ambitious men and women, is it doomed to failure?

Not necessarily. "Give it a thousand years," Stegner wrote in 1962. By then, having adopted Salt Lake City as another hometown, he could see some positive aspects of the Canadian frontier town. Viewed from a lonely homestead on the plains, the town and its river flowing between the cutbanks had offered him sanctuary. At a time when radio and television were unknown, people found entertainment in their local organized sports, their own orchestras, their hometown newspaper, their school recitals, the lectures of an occasional Chautauqua. Among the founders, one man made violins, collected dinosaur bones, and discovered that a series of ruined chimneys nearby marked a nineteenth-century village of *métis,* the local half-French, half-Indian people. Another man had made his own telescope and invited neighbors to visit his little observatory. There was no library, but the local dump was a repository of material culture that included relics from his own family, even books they had once loaned to a neighbor. That place of childhood, divided between homestead and frontier town, had seemed unconnected, without history or geography. And yet it had nourished Stegner's imagination; "it had a wild freedom, a closeness to earth and weather, a familiarity with both tame and wild animals," he recalled. "It had the physical sweetness of a golden age."[25]

Salt Lake City was more civilized, disciplined, imbued with the values of a single religious group, the Mormons, and overlaid with monuments and institutions that reinforced the cooperative spirit of its founders. Laid out on a grid, it was a place where you couldn't get lost, Stegner recalled. It was the New Jerusalem, shining in a clear light, and accommodating even to non-Mormons like the Stegners. In 1950, reflecting on that city, where he had lived from 1921 until 1930, he felt some nostalgia, "the recognition of old familiarity."[26]

Ironically, what he relished about that city were qualities he had also appreciated in the dusty little town of Whitemud: sanctuary, security, and a feeling of closeness to wilder nature at the edge of town. Salt Lake City was conceived on a larger scale, yet it was comprehensible in a single glance from the nearby Wasatch Mountains. There was a clear line between city and mountains, and from the city's eastern edge, several canyons opened directly onto another climate—a different world—of fields, orchards, places for fishing, hunting, hiking, skiing. Writing in 1950, Stegner suppressed some of the details that his biographer Jackson Benson would later explain—the bootlegging activities of Stegner's father, the loneliness, frustrations, and yearnings of Wallace's teenage years.[27] In 1979 Stegner himself would note some disheartening changes in Salt Lake City; yet his assessment in 1950 remains a tribute to that city and its people. There he had experienced something solid and satisfying. He had no desire to recapture his lost adolescence; he wanted only to retain the memory. "Home is what you can take away with you," he concluded.[28]

❊ ❊ ❊

Writing in the early 1960s, Ann Woodin briefly alluded to the history of her adopted town, Tucson, Arizona. Two centuries earlier, it had been a walled presidio connected with other Spanish colonial towns by the Camino Real—now Main Street. From a small town of thirty thousand people at the end of World War II, Tucson had become a sophisticated city of three hundred thousand, with a university, an air terminal, and the usual attractions for wintering visitors. The suburbs were still spreading on former cattle ranches, but they had not yet reached the Woodins' forty-acre parcel of rising ground, with its mountain views and a dry wash that became a stream during summer and winter rains. Some of Woodin's friends wondered whether all that isolation in the desert was a good thing for her four boys. How would they learn what life was "all about"? Woodin's answer lies on every page of *Home Is the Desert* (1964), part narrative, part philosophical reflection about life with many half-wild, half-domesticated creatures, including bobcats, snakes, a wolf, a coyote, an owl, a tarantula, a coatimundi, a badger, and a javelina. They all came with the territory, for Ann Woodin's husband, Bill, was a herpetologist, desert ecologist, and director of the Arizona–Sonora Desert Museum in Tucson for nearly twenty years.[29]

Generously illustrated, *Home Is the Desert* conveys the impression of some "peaceable kingdom," where a human toddler and a wolf cub named Beowulf begin to explore life together, and where a lounging German shepherd calmly makes eye contact with a bobcat kitten. Family snapshots, interspersed with professional photographs of desert fauna and flora, tell a good part of the story, but not all. Woodin also wrote about the city of Tucson, which was spreading across the dry washes and bottomlands despite floods that would rise sooner or later. She noted the dust blowing from the scraped and leveled sites of future tract houses, the smog from smokestacks and cars, and lost opportunities to create parks and preserves of wildland within the city and along the watersheds—those precious threads of water where developers and engineers would prefer to rip out all the native trees and lay down concrete ditches. A New England native, Woodin was not anti-urban or averse to technological improvements. She accepted air-conditioning yet appreciated, too, the older desert ways still carried on south of the border—the rhythms and rituals of a slower-paced life, adapted to the climate and the environment.

Woodin let her sons find their own ways of adapting, living with rather than triumphing over natural forces. If the boys were as free to wander among her bookshelves as in the desert, they would also have learned from writers that informed Woodin's book—Thoreau, Aldo Leopold, Henry Beston, and her Tucson neighbor Joseph Wood Krutch, who wrote the introduction to *Home Is the Desert*. Like any mother, Woodin had high hopes for her sons, whatever they chose to do with their lives. "I hope the desert has taught our sons that they do not *own* the earth," she wrote; "that it is lent to them for as long as they treat it properly and respect the creatures with whom they share it."[30]

Those boys appear throughout the book, but they were absent on one occasion. With her husband and a group of scientists, Ann Woodin made a journey down the Colorado River through Glen Canyon in the fall of 1957, while the dam upstream from Lee's Ferry was under construction. Everyone on board knew that before long many of the living things they saw, along with artifacts and natural formations, would be driven out or inundated when the waters of the Colorado rose above the dam. The journey was sobering, yet idyllic, as they floated downstream from Hite, Utah, to Lee's Ferry, Arizona. It can be appreciated on its own, but if we retrace it along with Stegner's accounts of similar journeys in

1947 and 1965, the composite story is even more layered with conflicting emotions and irony.

In the *Atlantic Monthly* for January 1948, Stegner told of the trip he had taken in June, starting out from Mexican Hat, Utah, bound for the Colorado via the San Juan River, in a few square-ended semi-cataract boats. A writer among tourists, he was gathering material for his book on the geologist and explorer John Wesley Powell.[31] But Stegner and his wife, Mary, were also out to have a good time. While a cinematographer's camera was running, Stegner horsed around with the others. And he studied the strata of Wingate and Navajo sandstones along canyon walls. They were all latter-day explorers, he mused, in an unknown land where Pueblo Indians once tended garden crops—before other tribes came with herds and overgrazing led to soil erosion and flooding. In time, as the swift San Juan joined the slower Colorado, running wide and deep through Glen Canyon, Stegner and his fellow voyagers became drifters. Exploring Music Temple, Mystery Canyon, Hidden Passage, Labyrinth Canyon, and other canyons, he thought about returning someday to write a book while the river flowed on. But prospects for survival and escape from Cold War tensions were dimmed as a dead animal floated by, four hoofs above the water. If real sanctuary could no longer be found, at least the fishing was good. "This is the way things were when the world was young," Stegner reflected; "we had better enjoy them while we can."[32]

Time was running out. In 1948, as Stephen J. Pyne later explained, the completion of the Upper Colorado River Basin Compact began a redefinition of the river.[33] No longer wild and unpredictable, its volume of water fluctuating from day to day and season to season, the river would be controlled by dams, harnessed for power, and advertised for recreation. That scenario was also proposed for the Green and the Yampa rivers, farther north at Echo Park, where Dinosaur National Monument straddles the Utah-Colorado border. In the mid-1950s, pressure from the Sierra Club and friends, including Wallace Stegner, halted the dam project at Echo Park, in Colorado, and kept Dinosaur from being flooded; but they did not make the same efforts on behalf of Glen Canyon. Stegner, one of the few who knew the canyon, told David Brower, then Sierra Club president, that Glen Canyon was greater than Echo Park, but he did not insist upon it. In hindsight both men were wiser.[34] Meanwhile the Upper Colorado River Storage Project Act was passed in 1956.

In the fall of 1957, knowing that much of what she saw in Glen Canyon would soon be underwater, Ann Woodin looked on with wonder and sadness. The anthropologist in her party spoke of Anasazi Indians arriving some two thousand years earlier and remaining there until about 1300 AD, leaving traces of their lives in stone cliff dwellings and petroglyphs. While Bill Woodin caught tree frogs, lizards, and snakes, the ornithologist, the geologist, and the botanist pursued their own interests. Ann Woodin noticed a blue heron, a snowy egret, a hawk, a pelican. Hearing the song of a canyon wren, she imagined herself floating in sound as well as in water, slipping outside of time, belonging to the earth. It was not a pristine place. The name of Powell was chiseled in one cliff. In another were the survey stakes of Stanton, the railroad engineer, who had wanted to run tracks all along the Colorado River—even through the Grand Canyon. Some rusted dredging machinery remained. But nothing so jarred the senses as the blasts of dynamite at the dam site.

Those blasts sounded the end of a journey and the imminent drowning of superb places—Music Temple, Rainbow Bridge, Forbidden Creek, Twilight Canyon, Quaking Bog, Cathedral in the Desert. Around a campfire, everyone thrashed out arguments for and against the dam. "That the Glen Canyon Dam is unnecessary is a well-documented case," Woodin wrote. Three other dams along the Colorado already controlled the river's flow and supplied power. The stored water could not be used for irrigation. Meanwhile trucks would move up and down a road carved out of a canyon wall and restless men would keep "picking away at eternity." Woodin reflected on the 150-mile journey the group had shared, floating past traces of millions of years, thinking of dying dinosaurs and a golden age of amphibians. A line from Krutch's book on the Grand Canyon came to her—"The wilderness and the idea of wilderness is one of the permanent homes of the human spirit." And what if men went ahead with their plans, built yet another dam, and flooded part of Grand Canyon as well? Would our children ever forgive us?[35]

When Glen Canyon Dam was closed in 1963, Lake Powell began to rise. By the time Stegner returned to explore the new lake, apparently in March 1965, his power boat floated about three hundred feet above the old river. As that was some two hundred feet below the dam's capacity, Stegner knew in advance that much of what he had seen before would be drowned, and more submersion was yet to come. And so in 1965 he wrote with some misgivings about scenic improvements and losses, present and future.[36]

Stegner's "Glen Canyon Submersus" is a statement of one man's preference for wildlands and unmechanized movement through them, balanced against preferences presumed to be shared by many more people. Visiting the new Lake Powell in March, not in summer, Stegner avoids most of the motorboats and water skiers, yet he can no longer go very far without some motorized vessel himself. The river's current is gone, along with the magic of a wilderness he once knew. Judged purely as scenery, some places in Glen Canyon seem improved. The views are wider. The contrast between blue water and sun-drenched stone is sharper. You don't have to climb up rough banks to see the buttes and pinnacles at Crossing of the Fathers. The fish "sown" by airplane include rainbow trout and black bass. But some wildlife have been driven out, their habitats submerged. And Lake Powell, although beautiful, is less interesting than a flowing river. Go to the side canyons, Stegner suggests. Turn off the boat's engines. Get out and walk. Maybe the side canyon up the Escalante River could be set apart as wilderness, with a boom thrown across its mouth to keep it from being flooded. Then you could rent a houseboat, anchor it near the river's mouth, and use it as a base camp for exploring on foot.[37]

Years later Stegner noted that the Escalante Canyon had not been set apart by a boom but rather included in Glen Canyon National Recreation Area.[38] An experience of wilder country would have to be sought elsewhere. Then, too, as he pointed out in a now famous letter of 1960, wilderness need not be spectacular to renew one's spirit and inspire awe. A prairie like the one he had known in Saskatchewan, with its vast sky, small burrowing creatures, and land as grand as an ocean, would do. We need wilderness, he wrote, even the *idea* of it, as a timeless, uncontrolled portion of the earth, "part of the geography of hope."[39]

FIVE

The Heart of
the Country

Views from
a Family Farm

We have seen him so often, we tend not to notice him—the sower, reaching into a sack slung over his shoulder to cast seeds upon the ground. He is the figure in Simon and Schuster's colophon, or publisher's emblem. Leaning forward, confident, unhurried, he seems to belong to the ages, an anonymous link in a long chain of generations, passing on knowledge of the earth and its bounty as surely as he scatters seeds of wisdom on the printed page. But this emblematic figure has evolved and changed in the past century. In Josephine Johnson's *Now in November* (1934), the sower appears heroic as he strides before rays of the rising sun—a hemisphere still low on the horizon. In *Farmer in a Business Suit* (1957), by John H. Davis and Kenneth Hinshaw, the sower casts a short shadow on the title page. No longer visible, the sun is evidently higher in the sky.[1] Still later, in some works published by Simon and Schuster in the 1960s and '70s, the sower casts no shadow. The very ground he once walked on—and the horizon—have vanished.

It's eerie that slight alterations in a publisher's emblem should reflect the increasing abstraction and disengagement from natural elements that most of us now experience in everyday life, whether indoors, on the road, or in a vast, geometrically ordered farm field. In the 1930s that emblematic sun rising from the earth was a reminder of the power, the drama, the authority, and the great gift of natural forces. Later, when sun and earth were removed from the publisher's emblem, the sower himself—or the human mind and all its productions—became dominant, detached from any physical ground.

Perhaps oblivious to these emblems but conscious of economic hardships on the family farm, the authors Davis and Hinshaw remained optimistic. Rising costs, declining crop prices, and uncertain markets were problems to be overcome during the transition from the Earthbound Era to the Agribusiness Era. "We are still on a frontier," they wrote in 1957, "and many of us will be pioneering in the agribusiness area for a long time to come."[2]

In hindsight we recognize yet another frontier. In the early 1970s, molecular biologists began to map the genes on human chromosomes and to develop a whole new field of science and technology—genetic engineering. The applications of genetic engineering in agriculture, from genetically modified and patented seeds to gene-splicing and cloning in farm animals, may seem to be an extension of the agribusiness frontier that Davis and Hinshaw found alluring. Yet in many ways genetic engineering represents a different terrain. By the late 1960s agricultural experts and most farmers would have been familiar with chemical fertilizers, pesticides, herbicides, antibiotics in the feed, and high-yield hybrid seeds, which had become increasingly available since the Second World War. Then, too, grafting, crossing, and selecting for superior plants and animals had been developed over centuries. But manipulating parts of the DNA molecules in various forms of life was something new, a frontier of science not yet widely recognized.[3]

By the early 1980s, advances made in this new field since the early 1970s impressed both admirers and critics. "The redesign of existing organisms and the engineering of wholly new ones mark a qualitative break with humanity's entire past relationship to the living world," wrote Jeremy Rifkin in *Algeny* (1983). And he wondered about our journey from a world "teeming with life," spontaneous, unpredictable, often companionable, to a world of gadgets, biologically engineered, operating without flaw or feeling.[4] As if in response, Robert West Howard wrote *The Vanishing Land* (1985). This history of the uses and abuses of agricultural land in America ended with a statement of faith in biotechnology—that "genetic engineering promises to be our most effective pathfinder to a green future."[5]

Heated debates about the future of genetic engineering in agriculture—whether viewed as a green revolution or as a key factor in a "fatal harvest"—continue to this day.[6] Meanwhile, we turn to some literature that appeared between 1890 and 1970, when frontiers were generally thought to be out west, up in space, or perhaps in the boardroom—but not yet inside the strands of DNA molecules that determine all forms of life.

At that time most farmers were still earthbound, subject to many natural forces beyond their control—whatever their access to new economic tools, better machinery, or chemical spin-offs from war and aerospace programs. Some efforts to control weeds, pests, costs, and soil depletion may have seemed promising. But the finest passages in this literature are not about control or anything that can be measured or charted on a graph; they have to do with perceptions, feelings, and thoughts about cultivation, wildness, home, belonging. The authors may touch on big questions about the meaning of life and never grasp more than parts of the whole, like those admittedly incomplete answers of Rachel Peden, in *Rural Free* (1961); but at least her answers "came from the whole farm" and let her sleep at night.[7] Later in that decade, in "A Native Hill" (1969), Wendell Berry asked, "What *is* this place? What is in it? . . . How should men live in it?" And he felt he had not found the answers; rather, they had, in fragments, begun to come to him.[8]

❊ ❊ ❊

That is the way Hamlin Garland's *Boy Life on the Prairie* (1899) came to be written—in fragments, while he lived in rented rooms in and around Boston and struggled to become a writer. In the late 1880s, on visits back to his boyhood home in Iowa, he had seen many changes. The unbroken prairie had vanished, along with prairie chickens, cranes, and wolves. Sinkholes had been filled in and plowed over, and groves of native poplars had been felled. Houses on the prairie were less exposed since Lombardy poplars had grown up to shelter them. There were more dairy cows, fewer wheat fields. Some people had moved farther west. Others remained and prospered. Some would turn up in Garland's *Main-Travelled Roads* (1891), a collection of short stories in which arduous labor, debts, and futile longings outweigh the joys and freedoms of rural life. But in *Boy Life on the Prairie* Garland offsets the tedium of farm life with more adventures, even haying on the wild meadows while everyone raced the thunderheads, some laughing and shouting. The whole place—that land beneath a big sky in northeastern Iowa—comes alive, as seen through the eyes of the author and his youthful self.[9]

Born in West Salem, Wisconsin, in 1860, Garland had lived in a small coulee, or valley, in that fairly settled part of southwestern Wisconsin before moving on, with his family, to Dry Run Prairie, near Osage, Iowa, in 1871.[10] There he had labored as a boy and as a man, breaking the sod, plowing the fields, cultivating, seeding, threshing, killing gophers, herding cattle. Ten years later the Garland family took up a new homestead in South Dakota, where Hamlin would live for a while on his own claim. But the East Coast, where he had worked at odd jobs for two years, still beckoned. In 1884 he moved to Boston, where he taught, lectured, wrote articles and stories, and managed to send some money back to the family in South Dakota. He also reflected on the Garlands' westward movement, from the state of Maine, where his father, Richard, was born; to Boston, where Richard had been a clerk in a dry goods firm; to Wisconsin, Iowa, and South Dakota. By 1885 Hamlin Garland was trying to overcome his loneliness in Boston by recalling the lands of his youth. As he explained, "I had begun to hope that I might be, in some small way, the historian of homely Middle Border family life."[11]

To portray that place and its people as typical of the region, Garland invented a few names. He, as Lincoln Stewart, and his younger brother Frank, as Owen, would walk a mile to the one-room school on Sun Prairie. They would ride a horse or a pony to Rock River (Osage) for the

Fourth of July, the circus, the county fair. Their friends and neighbors, their parents and relatives, and the hired men appeared under new names but more or less as Garland remembered them. And so *Boy Life on the Prairie* evolved as a blend of memoir and fiction, along with Garland's own poems and E. W. Deming's illustrations.

In this memoir, religion is barely mentioned. Garland recalls an evangelist who had proclaimed the "wickedness of natural man," but that preacher's hold on the minds of the neighbors did not last. Women, too, are not much in evidence. Behind the scenes they prepare meals, keep house, bear children, teach school, do chores. But young Lincoln Stewart spends most of his waking hours away from women and out-of-doors. His years of more-intensive schooling in a nearby county town, beginning at age sixteen, are not covered here. Some of his farm labor is solitary and lonely—especially plowing. Other operations are cooperative, even festive in their way, engaging not only family members and the hired man but also itinerant day-laborers and neighboring farmers who come to "change work," or help out for a day or two, knowing that Lincoln's father will return the favor.

It seems that there was no place for the legendary, lone sower on the Stewart farm, where horses, men, boys, and implements had to work efficiently to complete the seeding and planting. One morning in early spring, Mr. Stewart would drive a team of horses into the wheat field, depositing sacks of grain at intervals. Lincoln would then hitch his team to the fifty-tooth harrow and walk behind it, followed by the hired man with a team and the broadcast seeder—a large box with a cover that shut with a bang as "sharp as a morning gun." Hearing the cries of wildlife on the wing, Lincoln would drag along in the mud, mechanically, feeling like a shackled convict.

Planting corn was an even more mechanical operation, based on a grid. In spring Mr. Stewart would drive a team of horses across the freshly cultivated field, dragging a marker that left several furrows in parallel rows about four feet apart. Then, driving across those furrows at right angles, he would leave a grid of furrows. On this second drive across the field, Lincoln would walk barefoot behind his father. Reaching into a pouch at his waist, he would drop three or four kernels of corn at each intersection of two furrows. Walking behind Lincoln would be a neighboring farmer and the hired man, each with a hoe to cover the kernels with earth. At that time of year, when the whole earth was teeming with new warmth and the sounds of birds and frogs, Lincoln would feel the urge to relax and take in the sensuous beauty around him. But close behind, at his bare heels, were sharp hoes. Ahead was the dragging marker, his father, and the team of horses. And so he held a steady rhythm, enduring an aching neck and back. No doubt his elders said nothing of "repetitive motion" back then, but Lincoln knew the pain and welcomed the end of each furrow.

Between the lines of these stories and beyond the colorful expressions like "Hello! the house!" (a universal greeting), there emerges a pattern of work and leisure, intense focus and freedom to wander, unity of purpose and diversity of tasks and environments to work in. The pattern might not be so clear if Garland had written from an adult's point of view. Mr. Stewart routinely roused his sons from sleep by shouting, "Roll out, boys, roll out! Business on hand!" But young Lincoln's attitude was not businesslike. He liked some work. He loved to go hunt the cattle, mounted on his favorite horse, Ivanhoe, alone or with his best friend, Rance. While a man was scything brush, Lincoln enjoyed piling and burning it in the field. But he did not enjoy any task for hours on end. He disliked tedium, sore muscles, blisters, a dull mind; he liked variety, stimulation, and unexpected pleasures along the way, in a bird's song or a slough's dark mystery. "Every change of work brought joy," Garland recalled, "like a release from prison."[12]

As on the plains of Saskatchewan, in Wallace Stegner's memory, so on the prairie in Iowa, a farm boy's tasks included killing little burrowing, crop-menacing creatures like gophers and ground squirrels. With gun and snares, Lincoln and Owen were sent out to get rid of the little creatures, with the promise of a few pennies for each tail they produced. But Lincoln soon learned that, as in fishing, the real reward was simply being out on the prairie or by a stream, looking, listening, or lying peacefully in "the downpour of spring sunshine."

Stories of school days on the prairie and Saturday evening debates at the lyceum in the Grove School do not absorb many pages of *Boy Life on the Prairie*, yet they show how Garland could develop the ambition to study in the nearby county town and make his own way in the larger world. Books, debates, recitations, even competitive games that degenerated into fistfights formed part of his education. Another part of his education came from the land. In the flight of wild geese he found poetry. Fifty miles from home, the woods by Clear Lake seemed mysterious, like wilderness. But now that Sun Prairie had been tamed and civilized, now that dairy farms had replaced wheat fields and meadows of wild grass, a bit of real prairie sod by the railroad tracks was at least proof that the wildness had not been merely a dream.

One detail did remain dreamlike, however—a mental image that Lincoln carried with him from southwestern Wisconsin to Iowa. It was of a house nestled in a hillside. That image grew dim as the boy became absorbed in his new life on the prairie, but now and then he would recall the house, the hill, the snow, and a red sled coasting down to the meadow bog.[13]

Less than ninety miles to the southeast—as the crow flies—stood another house nestled in a hillside in Wisconsin. Built after the Civil War, it was the farmhouse of Richard Lloyd-Jones, his wife, Mary, and their ten children, many of whom would settle in the valley, cut down trees, clear fields and meadows, rear their children, worship their God, and shore up their clan. One grandchild, Maginel Wright Barney, told their story in *The Valley of the God-Almighty Joneses* (1965), which remains a source for architectural historians interested in the author's brother, Frank Lloyd Wright, and in the buildings he designed in his ancestral valley.[14] Here our main interest is in the valley itself, site of many small family farms and one, in particular, that remained a home while becoming a school.

The Lloyd-Jones family came to their "Valley of the Clan" after twenty years of pioneering in Wisconsin. In 1844 Richard Lloyd-Jones, Mary (known as Mallie), and their seven children had left their ten-acre farm in Llandyssil (or Llandysul) in the south of Wales to join Richard's brother, Jenkin, in America. In the spring of 1845, Richard and his older sons were clearing stands of oak, elm, and basswood from their land in Ixonia, near Milwaukee. By the spring of 1856, Richard was ready to move on to another, less crowded frontier, and their new farm on rich bottomlands near the Wisconsin River was soon thriving. Within another ten years, however, Richard's son Jenkin had returned from Civil War battlefields, and another move was imminent—for their land was less fertile after constant cropping, the soil was sandy, and there was not enough land in the area for the next generation of Lloyd-Joneses. And so the family moved across the Wisconsin River, to a hillside above a broad valley. There they stayed.

Barney's memoir is more affectionate and richer in detail than this bare outline suggests. She dwells on spiritual satisfactions of living and working in intimacy with the land, both cultivated and wild. She shows her family's love of music and poetry, their respect for learning, their informal gatherings for prayer and song in their own little chapel, their ample feasts at threshing time and on holidays, their characteristically Welsh devotion to the clan. And her sketches of family members show each as an individual. Her grandmother Mallie had brought flower seeds from her garden in Wales to the frontier in America. Her grandfather Richard had been a farmer, a Unitarian preacher, and a hatter in Wales. Uncle Jenkin, his middle son, became a well-known Unitarian minister in Chicago. Uncle Enos, the youngest son, was more easily driven to tears of joy or sorrow than the others. On his living room wall hung a copy of Jean-François Millet's *The Sower,* a figure that always reminded him of his father.[15]

In these glimpses of pioneer experience, the virtues of discipline, thrift, and industry are prominent while between the lines is at least one disturbing tendency—a lack of long-term commitment to certain tracts of land.[16] That tendency, traceable to a pioneer's optimism and longing for the ideal place, perhaps, or simply to a lack of stewardship, would persist as long as "unimproved" land remained cheap and seemed to be unlimited. Then, too, at a time when improved, or cleared, farmland might sell for ten times its price as virgin woodland (a fact Richard Lloyd-

The Sower, Jean-François Millet, ca. 1865–66. (Pastel on paper, 1982.8; courtesy of Sterling and Francine Clark Art Institute, Williamstown, Massachusetts; gift of Mr. and Mrs. Norman Hirschl)

Jones discovered in Wisconsin), there would be strong incentives to cut down forests and cultivate the land intensively while the soil remained fertile, then move on.

Commenting on one of those moves, Barney insisted, "A rift in the Clan could never be considered." And yet tensions did arise. Most of Barney's aunts and uncles were content with a modest sufficiency on a single family farm, but after the death of the patriarch, Richard, in 1886, Barney's uncle James invited his siblings to join him in a venture while government land could still be bought cheaply. "If one field can make a man a living," he argued, "twenty can make him a fortune!"[17]

The Lloyd-Jones siblings declined to enter a partnership with their

*Landscape of Taliesin, Spring Green, Wisconsin—now a National Historic
Landmark, encompassing the residence, studio, farm, and school of Frank Lloyd
Wright*

brother James, but some, including Nell and Jennie, cosigned documents
and mortgages.[18] A few good years followed. Then came the depression
of the early 1890s. After some frantic purchases of more machinery and
strenuous efforts to increase yields while crop prices fell, James's ventures
ended in tragedy. He died, leaving economic hardships for the clan.

Meanwhile Nell and Jennie had been pursuing another enterprise—
a school—on the original family farm that they had inherited from their
father. Some might view the Hillside Home School, established in 1886–
87, as a bold experiment, a coeducational boarding school in which rules
were few, narrow disciplines were unknown, and the neighboring farms,
gardens, woodlands, and streams were all extensions of the classroom.[19]
A few women remembered it as a place unlike any other, less a school
than a way of life.

Nell and Jennie—known in the valley as "the Aunts"—were already experienced teachers when they opened their own school. Nell had headed the history department at the River Falls State Normal School in Wisconsin, and Jennie had directed the kindergarten training schools in Saint Paul, Minnesota. Barney remembered the Aunts as tall, slender, somewhat worldly in their satins and silks, when their school first opened and she was a student there. Years later Mary Ellen Chase had a similar impression of those graceful women, white-haired, dressed in silk, when they interviewed her for a teaching position in early September 1909. Already aware of Chase's qualifications, they did not question her knowledge of history and English. They asked if she liked animals, rode horses, knew about birds and wildflowers, and loved music. Did she like the country? And, coming from the coast of Maine, would she miss the sea?[20]

Chase's answers were satisfactory; she got the job and remained at the school for three years before going on to graduate school. If she had any inkling that the Hillside Home School was then going bankrupt (as Meryle Secrest, one of Frank Lloyd Wright's biographers, explains), Chase did not mention it in her memoirs of academic life, *A Goodly Fellowship* (1939). There she dwelled on the school's environment of homelike dormitories, barns, fields, pastures, gardens, the river, the hickory and black walnut groves, and the valley as a whole, along with a mysterious outbreak of rashes and some traditional remedies. Classes might be canceled for a sleigh ride in winter or the gathering of violets in May. Food on the table might come from the students' carefully tended gardens. Students could also care for ponies and horses—their own, or those of the farm. They could learn to milk cows or help in the fields, going out with teams of horses on Saturdays. Sunday service in the chapel would be led by an aunt, an uncle, a teacher, or an older boy or girl. On weekday mornings, the service in the school's common room was simpler. Above its great fireplace were a few Welsh words carved in stone: "The Truth against the world." In winter, logs would be burning. And as a clock struck nine, all seated in the room, young and old, would fall silent for five minutes. That memory of silence and stillness was especially gratifying to Chase at a time of widening unrest, in 1939.[21]

By then a well-known author of novels and nonfiction works, some translated into several languages, Chase would have reached a fairly wide audience with *A Goodly Fellowship*. There she acknowledged a debt to two women from a Wisconsin farm, particularly for their vision and imagination, qualities that she in turn hoped to encourage among her students at Smith College. By then, too, the first few printings of Frank Lloyd Wright's *Autobiography* (1932) would have conveyed his impressions of the valley, the original Lloyd-Jones homestead, and the buildings he had designed for his aunts' school. By the late 1930s he was re-using those buildings for his own unique architectural school at Taliesin, where aspiring young architects worked in the fields as well as in the studio. He loved that place, that land. "After a while the Valley taught me everything," he once told his sister Maginel.[22]

It taught many others as well, including one Florence Fifer Bohrer, class of 1895 at Hillside. One year Bohrer roomed with a very bright, talented African American from Chicago, and learned of the young woman's longing to be white—or treated as such. One evening at the school Florence heard a "Mohammedan" speak—about religion, apparently. Another time, she heard Robert La Follette give a talk when he was running for office. And more memories of Hillside came back to her: getting to know the birds and wildflowers, riding horseback the year round, walking to Sunday chapel along a country road with people from the valley, and getting into mischief now and again. A spoiled young woman when she arrived—so she recalled—Bohrer left with standards subtly shaped by two patient and understanding women, the Aunts from the Valley of the Clan.[23]

✳ ✳ ✳

When the New York writer and editor Carl Van Doren looked back on his hometown—Hope, Illinois, a crossroads in a cornfield some twenty miles east of Urbana—he read the story of America's westward movement. In 1860 the site of Hope had been open prairie, where his ancestors came to break up sod with grass roots as thick as a man's arm. By 1885, when Van Doren was born, Hope was a settled community with a resident physician, his father, who would soon buy a farm and maintain his practice while tilling the soil. By 1890 the early pioneer farmers' lands were worth forty times the purchase price. In 1900 the Van Dorens moved to Urbana, in part for the education of their five boys. And there were other reasons. As Van Doren explained in his memoir, *Three Worlds* (1936), his family was "in the drift of an impulse which in 1900 was common in Illinois and throughout the Middle West. Farming had become old-fashioned."[24]

That is, by 1900 successful farmers in the region were no longer working their own land. Van Doren recalled that they were leasing it to less successful farmers or hiring laborers. Living in a village or town, those older farmers—patriarchs, like Van Doren's grandfather Butz—"looked upon the future as a perpetual adventure" and assumed that any patient, industrious fellow could prosper just as they had done. They doubted, however, that the inheritors of lands already cultivated and ordered could ever quite measure up to their pioneering forebears.[25]

Reflecting on those patriarchs during hard times in the 1930s, Van Doren was appreciative and mildly ironic. He recalled his own happy childhood as one of books, chores, good family relations, and Fourth of July celebrations. He recalled, too, the family farm, where he had lived and worked from age five to fifteen. At sunrise on the morning of his family's uprooting from the farm, he had felt—briefly—at one with day and night, earth and sky, but soon he was eager to move on. Years later, in 1933, he returned to Hope, his nearly vanished hometown, and read the "essential story of an older America . . . compressed into three generations," from unbroken prairie to crossroads village to a few remaining houses, a church, not much more.[26]

Some frayed threads of that story of an older America appear in Josephine Johnson's *Now in November,* published in one of the bleakest years of the Great Depression, 1934. The situation of her main characters was also bleak, strained, and nearly overwhelming with bad luck and thwarted desires. And yet the book itself is luminous in its vision of something whole and enduring in the land and the people. Arnold Haldmarne is first seen as a farm-reared man in his late fifties, thrown out of work at the lumber mill, now struggling to provide for his family on a long-uninhabited, mortgaged farm. His wife, Willa, is patient, trusting, with her braided raisin roll and her faded church dress. They have three un-married daughters, one hired man who leaves, and one who would like to stay. There are also neighboring farmers, some of whom would rather dump their milk in a ditch or a hog trough than sell it below their costs.

Not all these characters are depicted in depth. No one is saintly (Willa comes close). No one is evil (not the bald-headed tax assessor, not even the preacher who evicts Willa and her daughters from church). The Haldmarne family and Grant, the second hired man, are central to the story, but so is the land itself—the barnyard, the stony place in the woods, a valley of pear trees in bloom, and the pond on a windy night in spring when the frogs' chorus is "thrust up like spears of sound." While the ground is still hard, Mr. Haldmarne plows up acres of wild phlox and cuts down old oaks and sycamores to plant corn. Focused on his family's material needs, he neglects other needs. His wife is generous and for-giving, living through others' lives. Kerrin, the eldest daughter, is willful, passionate, a night wanderer, and an intimidating teacher in the school-house. Merle, the youngest daughter, who walks in a clear, straight line down a hillside, is solid, strong, purposeful. Her father appreciates her. The hired man loves her.

Marget, the middle daughter and narrator, wishes that she too could "march steadily in one road" and be loved. But Marget is plain-looking, introspective, troubled by fears and doubts. Sensing things she cannot make sense of or share, she takes comfort in the healing qualities of the earth and stumbles along toward a vision of wholeness—which has nothing to do with success or failure. It is about what can be learned from the cycles of the days and the seasons, the rootedness of two scrub-oak trees in the north pasture, the healing of the night sky, and small, eter-nal things, "the whip-poor-wills' long liquid howling near the cave[,] . . . the chorus of cicadas, and the ponds stained red in evenings."[27]

We can imagine this story unfolding somewhere near Kirkwood, Missouri, where Johnson wrote *Now in November*. Born in 1910, she came to know several houses and landscapes in and around Kirkwood, southwest of Saint Louis; and near Columbia, Missouri, where an uncle had a dairy farm and two aunts lived in a cottage. Images of these places appear in Johnson's memoir *Seven Houses* (1973). And yet a search for the actual pastures or barns or kitchens lighted by kerosene lamps that appear in the novel seems unnecessary. *Now in November* embodies the family farm of the American heartland just as, say, James Still's *River of Earth* embodies the farms and mining camps of the Kentucky hill country and Robert Frost's "The Death of the Hired Man" embodies a family farm somewhere north of Boston.[28]

Time in *Now in November* is elusive. The narrative shifts from a distant past to recent months, during a span of ten years, from about 1924 to 1934. Most of the action occurs during the thirties. The Haldmarnes, the conscientious hired man, and a few neighbors keep on working, often grimly, in the face of debts that are never paid off or accidents that leave someone crippled. Bankers and landlords hold the balance of power. Farmers, organizing to hold back their milk until the price rises, are no match for them, or for the economic system they uphold. One generous and trusting man, the African American tenant farmer Christian Ramsey, is callously pushed off the land he farms with his wife and their many children. Death comes to two women. Nature seems cruel, benign, indifferent. The drought is tenacious, and Marget searches for reasons to go on year after year, weighed down by debt. Her solution, as always, is to return to the land, some high ground like the hill above the orchard. From there, in November, bare branches blowing in the wind seem beautiful "in the clean sharp way of winter things."[29]

Is this novel really a meditation on land, earth, water, sky, light, and darkness? Or is it mainly about social and economic justice and thwarted, wasted lives? Or an autobiographical account of coming-of-age? In the view of one critic, Nancy Hoffman, Johnson's vision fuses these three literary traditions with "an economy, clarity, and intensity that are nothing short of a miracle."[30] The novel is a poem in prose. Whether it remains a distillation of its own place and time may best be judged by a dwindling few—those who lived on a small midwestern family farm during the Great Depression.

✳︎✳︎✳︎

Rachel Peden's *The Land, the People* (1966) reveals a sensibility akin to Johnson's, nourished in upland pastures and the wilder margins of orchards and fields. But Peden's voice is that of an older woman who has made her peace with whatever may have been perplexing and painful in her youth. Since 1946 Peden, a "farm wife," had been writing a column for two Indiana newspapers, the *Indianapolis Star* and the *Muncie Press*. By 1961, with the publication of *Rural Free,* drawn from those columns, Peden had gained a national audience. Then came *The Land, the People,* Peden's effort to combine histories of her own family and that of her husband with tales of neighboring farmers as they adjusted to changing economic conditions and adapted to (or resisted) new machinery and methods. Here and there a lyrical passage appears as an aside, a conclusion, a grace note, or merely an acceptance of things as they are. One day, watching a robin and envying its ability to fly, Peden feels earthbound. Another time, she reflects on two sharply different views of the soil that covers strata of fine Indiana limestone. To a geologist or a stoneman, that soil is simply "overburden." To the farmer it is the "precious flesh of earth itself."[31]

Rather than attempt to fuse all these elements of human and natural history, anecdote, and reflection into a coherent story—a novel—Peden wrote *The Land, the People* in four parts, including three overlapping histories of farm families and one brief sketch that reads like a short story. The land is in central Indiana, mainly in Monroe, Owen, and Johnson counties; the people are members of Peden's extended family and their neighbors. One main theme, a shared love of the land, underlies several recurring issues: possession, ownership, boundaries, waves of invasion, and degrees of a farmer's independence.

Peden's questions are compelling: As old patterns of life and work continue to change, will the family farm survive? Or rather, how long will it survive without "off-the-farm" income? At what point does all the powerful new machinery cease to serve the farmer and make him a captive? And what about the presumed separation between the human world and the natural world? Peden leaves most of these questions wide open while revealing her own feelings of kinship and cooperation with the earth, not dominance or control. "The earth does not belong to man," she writes, "but rather he belongs to the earth."[32]

In the opening pages of *The Land, the People,* one generation is passing. Peden's widowed mother, Laura Mason, is dying. "High Gap," the place where Mrs. Mason and her husband reared their seven children for nearly two decades, was once a Monroe County orchard; now it forms part of the Morgan-Monroe State Forest. The Masons' old farmhouse, once an inn built by a pioneer, had been burned by an arsonist, and a collection of old Indian arrowheads and hammers found in the soil had disappeared in that fire. Now picnic tables, shelters, a CCC camp, a supervisor's house, and an artificial lake occupy land where Peden's father, B. F. Mason, had once perfected his prizewinning peach, the Shipper's Late Red. Now all traces of the orchards and the old dirt roads are gone. "The land, never completely possessed by any holder, soon forgets its temporary owners," Peden remarks. And yet she and her sister Nina still feel a kinship with that land, a source of wisdom and strength at a time of sorrow.[33]

Peden's family histories give glimpses of American agricultural history as well. Peden's father-in-law, Walter Beem Peden, born in 1867, was part-owner, along with his brother and his father, of four farms in Owen County, Indiana; and he helped to manage them while living in town. Walter Peden was also part-owner of a family-owned bank that failed, apparently around the time of World War I. The family's livestock and three of their farms were sold to pay the bank's depositors. The last farm was nearly lost in the Great Depression, yet Walter remained optimistic, an "insatiable" farmer who loved the land. He found comfort in that farm, which Peden describes as both his mistress and his business.

After their own children were grown, Peden and her husband, Richard, continued to live and work on a farm in Johnson County, Indiana, which they expanded to 239 acres. Their main crop was feeder cattle, fed by the corn, hay, and silage they raised. With some misgivings Peden describes some operations on her farm, on neighboring farms, and along the public roads—the use of pesticides and herbicides, fields plowed at night by tractors' lights, and automatically controlled "farm safety lights" that diminish the light and magic of the moon. Peden also mentions the planting of hybrid seed corn; the staggering costs of new machinery; the increasing size of farms in the region, worked by fewer people; the burdens of debt; and farmers' loss of whatever independence they once enjoyed.

Raising these issues, Peden points to no villains, but she does mull over land ownership and possession—which she sees as a history of invasion. Pioneering settlers in her region invaded the land of Native Americans—who were mainly hunters, Peden assumes. More recently, industry has been "invading agriculture," and the real victim is the small farmer. Offering no solutions, Peden looks about her at the new spring grass and the wildflowers. The woods are magical. She and her guests pick mushrooms on a hillside—land that she and her husband have recently bought from departing neighbors. That land is not yet truly owned, she feels. But over time, with greater familiarity and layers of memories, she and her husband will own it, possess it, at least for a while.

The Land, the People might seem complete without "The Starling's Voice." But this brief sketch of Dakin, a middle-aged farmer, provides a contrast to the enterprising, improving, progressive farmers in Peden's extended family. A bachelor, Dakin carries on the old ways, living in the kitchen wing of the two-story farmhouse built by his grandfather. Against the advice of more prosperous neighbors, he keeps a few cows, sheep, and chickens, mainly for his own use and pleasure. He repairs his own harnesses by hand, with a tool his father had discarded. And he looks forward to breaking sod in a stone-fenced field that had been used as pasture for many years. Driving his team of horses and walking behind the plow, he takes time to admire the appearance and savor the smell of his newly turned soil. When an accident disables him for a while, a kindly neighbor sets out to plow the field for him—with a tractor. But Dakin will not allow that. "Kindred of the earth," Dakin will take time to heal and wait for another spring.

If Dakin's opposition to the tractor, an indicator of modernization and mechanization, is extreme, Peden's father-in-law takes the middle road. Born in the era of implements driven by horses and mules, Walter Peden eventually drives a car. In his eighties, around 1950, he acquires a tractor but has someone else operate it. Meanwhile Rachel Peden remains a "farm wife," observing, writing columns, reminding readers of the old ways and questioning the wisdom of certain new ones. Before highway maintenance men sprayed herbicides along the public road, she had intended to dig up and transplant some wayside yellow raspberries. After the spraying, she is grateful for what has been left unsprayed along a private fence row. Odd patches of weeds and brambles are part of the land's charm, and Peden likes to see a bit of land left unproductive. A touch of luxury, she admits—but it is also a kindness to the wild creatures, part-owners of the land, who will find food and shelter there.

Clearly Peden regrets that small family farms like hers and Richard's are on their way to extinction. And yet the mood of *The Land, the People* is not gloomy. The sane, measured pace of rural life in Indiana in the mid-1960s is evident in the stories she tells and the phrases she repeats. "Come over," one neighbor will say to another after a chat by a roadside mailbox, even as time for leisurely visits is slipping away. Farm neighbors may have part-time jobs and other commitments, yet the friendliness, the shared values, the willingness to pitch in and help, in celebration or in sorrow, seem to be part of a rural culture that will not disappear overnight or within one lifetime. Some of it may disappear as the economic base of this way of life erodes. Peden makes few predictions. She implies, however, that her native culture runs deeper than economics and may survive in some form, so long as farmers can still maintain a degree of independence in their work and feel some kinship with the earth.

※ ※ ※

By the end of the 1960s, Wendell Berry and Josephine Johnson were writing of farmland that had been bought and sold a few times or passed on in the family and converted to new uses, new patterns of living. Johnson and her husband, Grant Cannon, were then living in southern Ohio, east of Cincinnati, on a thirty-seven-acre parcel of farmland where they and their children had lived for over twenty years. Now they were letting the land revert to the wild as suburban development encroached on all sides. Berry had brought his wife, Tanya, and his young children to live in Henry County, Kentucky, where his family roots went back several generations. For both Berry and Johnson, making a living from the farm was not an issue; they had other sources of income, in writing, editing, and, in Berry's case, teaching. But the land was part of their way of being in the world. For Johnson, those thirty-seven acres of hills, ravines, woodlands, and open fields were essential, her "lifeblood." And some of the land in Henry County was, literally, a part of Berry's inheritance.[34]

A generation younger than Peden and Johnson, Wendell Berry was not yet widely known for his rural values and critiques of industrial agriculture when a few of his autobiographical essays were published in 1969. In "The Long-Legged House," he writes about a swath of woodland along the banks of the Kentucky River, where his great-uncle Curran Mathews had built a two-room cabin in the 1920s. The lumber for that cabin had come from a log house of one of Berry's ancestors; and over time the cabin became a "wilderness place" for Berry's extended family—some farmers, a lawyer (his father), and others, who had settled within about four miles of Port Royal, Kentucky. Some incidents of their lives flow around and through this essay, just as the rising river in spring flows around and through the old cabin. Berry rebuilds the cabin higher up the bank (and inadvertently disturbs a phoebe's nest). Later another rise, and yet another, engulf the rebuilt cabin. But after the floor is washed clean of silt, Berry continues to work there on his novel *A Place on Earth* (1967). Over the years the heronlike cabin-on-stilts draws Berry back home from writing and teaching—in California, New York, Europe. He purchases adjacent land, rebuilds its old farmhouse, and turns to farming part-time.[35]

Having returned from far away, Berry realizes that his life at the cabin is not provincial after all. Lights arrive from distant stars. Migrating geese fly past, to the tropics, to the Arctic. The place is unique. Berry aspires to belong to it as herons and thrushes and muskrats belong—yet he realizes that he'll have to work at it. He thinks of Thoreau, Gilbert

THE REGION

White, Andrew Marvell. Perhaps he has come across something of Rachel Peden's as well. She had prefaced *The Land, the People* with thoughts of a farmer's blend of hope and humility, kindness and gaiety—all qualities the farmer would need in order to fulfill "his personal obligation to the land." And in her words is more than a hint of Wendell Berry's now well-known stance.

"A Native Hill," another of Berry's essays from 1969, is composed of short sketches brought together as if from notebooks and journals. His moods vary from incident to incident, remotely past and present. And a sense of urgency builds as he moves from vivid details of his native place to something more universal. "We must abandon arrogance and stand in awe. We must recover the sense of the majesty of creation," he writes; "it is only on the condition of humility and reverence before the world that our species will be able to remain in it."[36]

That year, 1969, Josephine Johnson's *The Inland Island* appeared. And in its month-by-month reflections on the beauty and mystery of an old farm slipping back into a half-wild state is also a sense of urgency, which builds slowly, deliberately, from traces of aggression among the small wild creatures to signs of human aggression and harsh words about Mars, the god of war (in March). On a warm day in May, Johnson feels nostalgic for the summers of childhood that will not return, for her aunts and their roses, for the "unreturning dead." In September she hears the sounds of guns and propane explosions, meant to drive the redwing blackbirds from the cornfields. One day in autumn she senses a cold front coming, a storm coming. "Now, in November, I do not see our lives as a whole. I see a great breaking up and out. . . . It is as though the very stability of the physical earth, founded on gravity, were changed."[37] Some readers will recall Johnson's novel *Now in November* and its fine passage about wholeness—which is distorted here, in 1969. "Stop the killing," she writes in November. "Stop the killing!" she echoes in December.

The links between the war in Vietnam and the war against nature are intertwined in *The Inland Island,* such that we cannot always separate one from the other. Nor does Johnson, who sees a "world of war and waste" in the soapsuds flowing down the stream, in the smell of sewers, the air pollution from factories, the target practice nearby, and planes overhead. Writing of old men with no roots and great power, of dead roots and poisoned land, Johnson finds sanity in 1969 just as her character Marget found sanity in 1934—in a portion of land known and loved. Despite Johnson's bitterness, she cannot help noticing white snow on the "lovely darkening land." And although "there is nothing in all of nature that can compare to this enormous dying of the nation's soul," Johnson ends not on the dying year, with the temperature falling to zero, but on the first day of the new year, dawning "with awesome clarity."[38]

The January-to-December progression is understandable, but had Johnson begun in May, she would have ended in April, the time of vernal pools that she watches year after year, always rising in the same place. To experience these "seasonal miracles" we don't have to seek out wildland or great wilderness, Johnson reminds us. We need only to live for a while in one place and watch for the pools to rise, flower briefly, then disappear.

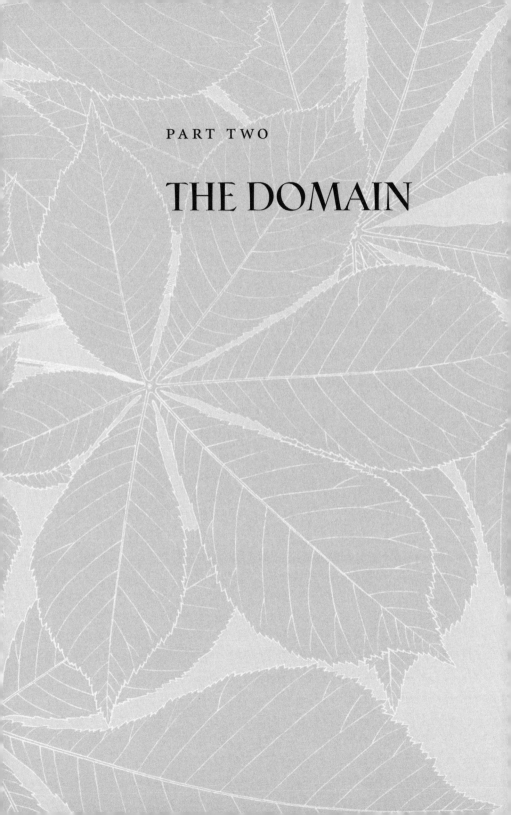

PART TWO

THE DOMAIN

The Small Place
and the Little Garden

"The word 'home' appears in but few languages." And yet "the love of home has always been one of our deepest human feelings." So wrote the Boston landscape architect Fletcher Steele in *Design in the Little Garden* (1924), a work written primarily for Americans of modest means. Reflecting on the meaning of hearth, roof, and walls for people who must endure long, cold winters, he thought of other amenities for people of more benign climates—the vine, the rose, the fountain. If natives of southern lands had no word for "home," perhaps they did not need it, he mused. They had the word "garden" instead. They also tended to live more out-of-doors than northern peoples. Around the world, little gardens were as different as nations. Yet among them were common traits, based on common needs, which Steele mulled over as he distinguished the typical little gardens of England from those of Italy and France.[1]

Steele's slim volume was one of a series of books on the little garden, edited by Mrs. Francis King. With their drawings, plans of gardens and houses, and many appealing photographs, these books provided practical hints and also inspiration for improving a small urban or suburban backyard in the United States. But one photograph in this series stands out for its somber mood and mystery. Entitled "The Little Garden at Vauvillers—March 1919," it shows four men and two women, all dressed for cold weather, standing by a ruined brick wall. A distant tree lifts bare branches to the sky, and a few people hold mugs or bowls. This grim scene had been the site of a garden before the war. There the lady in the dark hat and coat (who was touring battlefronts with the men in trench coats) noticed two small peony plants pushing up out of the blasted earth. They moved her to tears. Then the French peasant woman, who had lost nearly everything, offered her one of the plants—for she could see that the lady loved peonies.[2]

That lady, Mrs. Edward Harding, wrote the volume on peonies in Mrs. King's little garden series. There, and in other volumes of the 1920s featuring the iris, the rose, the kitchen garden, the season of spring, economy, variety, and design, we recognize a wider phenomenon—a certain phase of suburbanization—and what it meant for people who had grown up in cities or on farms, who had never before owned cars or never had to make something of a lot measuring, say, fifty by one hundred feet. Americans were more mobile after the First World War. Land was changing hands and being converted to new uses—from farmers' fields and woodlots to suburban acres, from old country properties to new subdivisions, from lonely mountains and rocky coasts to summer colonies and rows of cottages facing the sea. People without roots in a new place needed some guidance, and it was mainly for them that the "little garden" books were written.

These books sometimes rise above the level of genial advice to stimulate another part of the mind and touch the heart. The authors might mention their own garden—or a garden they once knew and loved and labored in, then left, perhaps because of a death in the family. At times they, too, had had to make adjustments and begin again on unfamiliar soils and contours.

It is for personal reflections, then, as well as for a broad understanding of gardening in the 1920s, from the Northeast and Middle Atlantic states to the Midwest, that we turn to the "little garden" series. There, and in a few works written in the 1930s, we will notice changing views on horticultural matters—hybridized plants, wildflowers, weeds, pests—as well as on design problems, such as where to place the garage on a small lot. But for a closer look at a single garden, much loved and cared for, we might turn back to a time "before the war," that is, to the 1890s and early 1900s, when the life of some American homes flowed quite naturally into the garden.

* * *

One iconic image of that era is Childe Hassam's 1892 painting *Celia Thaxter in Her Garden*, a study of forms, colors, and textures bathed in the intense yet somewhat diffused light of the summer sun just past midday. The white-haired Celia, then an exceptionally popular poet, stands by a wooden gatepost, her white-clothed figure backed by the low wooden fence and a calm, pale blue sea. Looking down, she seems absorbed in her own thoughts while white sails hover about the horizon and, in the foreground, red and pink poppies and yellow-orange coreopsis all but obliterate any sense of path or boundary. In fact the garden gate is wide open, allowing the mass of cultivated flowers inside the garden to merge, visually, with the wilder flowers and seed pods beyond the gate.[3]

This image of abundance and serenity, familiar in reproductions, resists a single, definitive interpretation.[4] It may suggest financial security, long vacations, or a life of leisure and freedom—although we know from writings by Thaxter and others that she was never wealthy, that her creative life and domestic relations were both blessed and heavily burdened. Then, too, the image may suggest a middle-class woman's passive or limited role in late-nineteenth-century America. But compared with another painting of a woman in a garden, this depiction of Celia Thaxter seems remarkably self-contained, as if she were some sort of earthbound goddess, willful and determined.

In one catalogue of an exhibition, Hassam's *Celia Thaxter in Her Garden* is juxtaposed with an earlier painting, his *Gathering Flowers in a French Garden* (1888). There, a fragile-looking young woman, in white, stands on the gravel walk of a small garden. Framed by tall hedges and horse chestnuts in bloom, she holds a bouquet of flowers. In the middle distance a balding gentleman, in black, sits on a bench near the house, reading a book. This is the sort of traditional French garden that Fletcher Steele would later characterize as a small, intensely private place surrounded by high walls and hedges, where the man of the house reads the newspaper, his wife sews or shells peas, and his children play discreetly, never upsetting the prized begonias. "Everywhere is personified the immemorial order of French family life," Steele wrote, just as Hassam had painted.[5] And the contrast is dramatic: in the Old World, an enclosed, ordered, and protected space in subdued, dappled light; in the New World, a sunny, open, seemingly wild tangle of flowering plants spilling down to the sea. Both women, ingenue and matron, are dressed in white, but only the matron seems relatively free and conscious of an inner peace, whatever the weight of her unknown thoughts.

In *An Island Garden* (1894) Celia Thaxter tells how she maintained her precious fifty-by-fifteen-foot garden on a windswept island in the North Atlantic—Appledore Island, among the Isles of Shoals, some nine miles off the coast of Maine and New Hampshire. Prompted by her friend Sarah Orne Jewett, Thaxter also included a plan of the garden—which became invaluable when, in the late 1970s, the garden was restored.[6]

The plan is simple. All beds and borders are rectilinear. Every path is straight. Steps, gates, and main paths are all aligned with some feature or other. Numbers indicate plants from the accompanying list. If not for the airy, impressionist treatment of color and form in Childe Hassam's illustrations for the book, the plan alone would suggest geometries that Thaxter does not mention; in any case, those forms are obscured all summer long. In one dreamlike meditation on a day in June, Thaxter has just left her work in the garden for the hammock on the piazza. Below the vine-draped posts is the garden, to the south and west. Beyond the garden, rocky land slopes down to the sea. The hot sun brings out the fragrance of Jacqueminot roses as a few crimson petals fall. Other sensations follow—colors that flare up, the stir of a cool breeze, the hum of a bee, the song of a martin, "melodiously content."[7]

Thaxter was better known as a poet then, and also as a painter on porcelain who sometimes illustrated her own books.[8] Born in Ports-

Celia Thaxter's garden on Appledore Island, Maine, as re-created on the original site, beginning in the late 1970s

mouth, New Hampshire, in 1835, Celia Laighton Thaxter was reared from age four on a series of islands, beginning with tiny White Island, among the Isles of Shoals, where her father was keeper of the lighthouse before his interests in commercial fishing and hotel management drew him away to the larger islands nearby. How, at age sixteen, Celia married her tutor, Levi Thaxter; brought up her three children; became estranged from her husband; helped her mother and brothers run a resort hotel on Appledore Island; and attracted a coterie of writers, poets, painters, and musicians to her own cottage near the hotel is a romantic story known to historians of a widening range of American arts and letters.

Celia Thaxter's granddaughter Rosamond has traced a wide web of literary connections (Thaxter's husband was a college friend of James Russell Lowell, the *Atlantic Monthly* editor who first published one of her poems). Rosamond Thaxter's biography also includes excerpts from some of Thaxter's letters to Sarah Orne Jewett, Annie Adams Fields, John Greenleaf Whittier, Bradford Torrey, and others.[9] Caleb Mason tells more about the musicians that Thaxter welcomed to her music room and salon in summer, among them, Edward MacDowell, William Mason, and John Knowles Paine.[10] Alan Emmet has set Thaxter's little wooden-fenced garden in its rich social, cultural, and horticultural context of the late nineteenth century.[11] And Vera Norwood has broadened that context, comparing Thaxter with environmentalists and ecofeminists of our own time.[12]

In her thirties, Thaxter described one context while it was still vivid—her childhood home, where she first developed an uncommon bond with wild creatures, especially birds, and learned to cherish living things that struggled in the face of ocean winds and storms. In *Among the Isles of Shoals* (1873) she moved swiftly from the islands' bleak, lonely appearance to their enchanting, magical qualities. The sound of the sea—the rote—reduced the sharpness of things, perceptions, and feelings to softer, more blurred impressions. The place was wild, and strangely beautiful, with its storms of rain and snow and the minutely varied effects of fog, light, clouds, wind, and stars. Living things were precious in their seasons—anemones, violets, shadbush, jewelweed, sundew, clover, ferns. "For these things make our world," she wrote; "there are no lectures, operas, concerts, theatres, no music of any kind, except what the waves may whisper." And she had no regrets. Although her first garden was a mere patch of African marigolds, Thaxter recalled the devotion that she, a "half-savage" child, felt for the little golden flowers.[13]

In *An Island Garden* the much older Celia Thaxter wrote of flowers as lifelong friends. By then, however, she was a civilized woman with an admittedly civilized garden, from which she had to pull up some wildflowers she had loved as a child—clover, mallow, sorrel, and goldthread (or "dodder"). In her later years, Thaxter could be delighted by a "wilderness of bloom" seen from a train window as well as in her own garden.[14] But to achieve the *appearance* of wilderness in her cultivated island garden, she had to banish some of the wildness. As Chris Robarge and John M. Kingsbury later observed, her garden contained more annuals than perennials, and many of the plants had been crossbred or hybridized.[15] And, as the newer plants were also highly susceptible to pests and diseases, Thaxter could no longer cherish all manner of living things.

Among the pests that threatened Thaxter's happiness as a lover of flowers were cutworms, wireworms, pansy-worms, thrips, rose-beetles, aphids, and slugs. To combat them she used powdered hellebore, powdered sulphur, yellow snuff, air-slaked lime, salt, Paris green, cayenne pepper, kerosene emulsion, and whale-oil soap. She also had help from many birds and the toads that a friend had sent from the mainland. Some garden writers have described their wars against pests and weeds with mock-seriousness, but Thaxter remained earnest and intense; to find peace she felt she had to exterminate the enemies. Only the songsparrows, who ate her planted seeds, were forgiven.

It is a familiar gardener's story. Behind it lies ambivalence—an appreciation of wild things and natural forces, and a yearning to control them in the name of art and civilization. In two works of fiction that appeared around that time, however, some gardens flourished without excessive care or anxiety. Inviting, unpretentious, they may have been especially appealing to people long accustomed to certain conventions and constraints, between four walls as well as out-of-doors.

❊❊❊

Sarah Orne Jewett read Thaxter's manuscript of *An Island Garden* in rough drafts and offered suggestions that Thaxter appreciated and heeded. In turn, Thaxter and her garden may be dimly reflected in *The Country of the Pointed Firs* (1896), which appeared two years after Thaxter's death.[16] Jewett's *Pointed Firs* stories are set along a part of the Maine coast and among islands that Thaxter would have found familiar. In any event, Mrs. Todd and her tangled garden of wild and cultivated herbs are central to Jewett's narrative, which itself seems to grow freely, without plan. Stories unfold, some more colorful than others, like flowers that blossom for a time, then fade. But bright colors and dramatic tales of shipwreck and strange creatures in arctic fog are only incidental in a story where muted tones prevail. In Mrs. Todd's garden, as well, shades of green and fragrance are more prominent than the few colorful flowers, for that garden is devoted to plants with medicinal properties—pennyroyal, horehound, balm, sage, wormwood, southernwood, mint, thyme, and others.

Steeped and blended with molasses, vinegar, or spirits, these plants have powers to soothe and heal. They are the means by which Mrs. Todd earns her living and greets the local doctor on terms of equality. A middle-aged widow, she works calmly—not exhaustively but knowingly, dutifully—especially in early summer, when she must seek out certain herbs in the wilds. The growing season on the coast of Maine is not long. Neighbors with ailments may knock at her door at any time, and some remedies require precise instructions. It is all serious business; improper use of her herbal remedies might cause harm.

There is no mention of insects or diseases that harm Mrs. Todd's plants, however. No weeds seem to menace the garden, nor does she appear to order plants from a catalog (as Celia Thaxter did). The tame and the wild simply grow together in profusion. The narrator, who boards with Mrs. Todd one summer, may not know which plants are rare. But by the fragrances that drift in through an open window, she comes to recognize just where Mrs. Todd may be walking or standing in the garden. And that little detail of recognition, emblematic of the sympathy that develops between boarder and landlady, speaks for the garden as well. All summer long it is predominantly green, fragrant, useful, and moderately profitable—a natural place for natives and strangers to come together.

Mabel Osgood Wright alluded to a similar ideal of mingling when she wrote of native and exotic plants in her novel *The Garden, You, and I* (1906). At a time when old farms in southern New England were giving way to cottages and more summer homes were rising on the bluffs overlooking Long Island Sound, Wright wanted to offer newcomers from the city some basic knowledge of gardening. Born and reared in New York City, she had acquired that knowledge in the gardens of her family's summer home in Fairfield, Connecticut. She had also attracted a wide following with her *Garden of a Commuter's Wife* and *Flowers and Ferns in Their Haunts,* both published in 1901. In all these novels, practical advice on gardening flowed from the dialogue. In *The Garden, You, And I,* Wright used yet another literary device, letting her characters communicate by letters. The result, a hybrid of fiction and gardening manual, is not quite comparable to Jewett's *Country of the Pointed Firs. The Garden, You, and I* is better appreciated on its own terms—as an engaging, mildly satirical tale of suburban and ex-urban life, showing in words, plant lists, and photographs what might be done with a bit of land in the village, by a woodland edge, in a new subdivision, and down by the rocky shore.[17]

Although a century old, *The Garden, You, and I* reflects a world that seems familiar today. Real estate prices are rising, there is a market for old stone walls, and the Opie Farm will be renamed "Opal Farm" once Amos Opie agrees to sell. When an overworked lawyer needs a change of scene for his health, his friend, a civil engineer, suggests a vacation in the garden. "What greater change can an American have than leisure in which to enjoy his own home?" he asks.[18] Meanwhile a reservoir project is under way—to dam a stream and drown a valley of woodlands and wildflowers. In a suburb of Bridgeton (Bridgeport, Connecticut), a dozen "Colonial" houses will be built as rental units on one-acre lots to attract urban dwellers with limited means, long summer vacations, and a love of gardening. This might be a dubious venture today, but the pattern of development and the traditional style of the houses are familiar.

One woman's tale seems vaguely medieval yet also modern. Mrs. Marchant, a genteel widow, is mentally disturbed and may never fully regain her sanity. Dwelling in a one-acre portion of the lovely old Herb Farm, however, she can wander among its borders, dressed all in white, drifting as in a dream, breathing in fragrances that calm the nerves and relieve a tormented soul. Apparently the powerful scents carry Mrs.

Marchant back to an earlier, happier time, to a place of the mind, where her late husband and son are still alive.

The woman in white may be a faint allusion to Celia Thaxter. In another scene a character recalls that Thaxter used to arrange flowers on a mantel or shelf so that a looking glass would double their beauty, "making the frail things seem alive."[19] But this is merely a passing remark. Many more pages are devoted to planting schemes and mundane problems in the garden, such as insect pests, fungus, mildew, rust, and black spot. The rose chafer, a beetle, should be picked off and dropped into a jar of kerosene. Other aids for the vigilant gardener include powdered hellebore, phosphates, whale-oil soap, and Bordeaux mixture. Wright's persona, Barbara, admits some qualms about using insecticides and fertilizers. She also warns against too much weeding and neatness in the hardy, or perennial, garden. In her own garden she has her perennial beds dug up every three or four years to set aside the plants, rework the soil, and add manure. Replacing only as many plants as will fit without crowding, she would give away the rest. Her gardens represent a great deal of labor behind the scenes, then, but the result is meant to appear casual, nearly effortless.

Plants for these hardy gardens can be started from seed or gathered—with caution—in nearby woodlands and fields. On one trip to Hemlock Hills (the Berkshire Hills, perhaps), Barbara and her husband gather ferns in a deep ravine. Not far from Gray Rocks, a little cottage on Long Island Sound, their friends find some native New England cactus (*Opuntia opuntia*) and transplant one in their seaside garden, among rockroses, beach heathers, sea lavender, rabbit-foot clover, beach pea, and other plants. This little garden is unlike its neighbors, where brilliant geraniums (pelargoniums), nasturtiums, and petunias fill window boxes overhung by red-and-white striped awnings. Clearly Wright leans toward quieter colors and simpler native plants, while she lightly mocks whatever seems brash and boldly artificial, in people and in plants. And yet her persona, Barbara, cannot resist the pleasure of a labor-intensive rose garden or certain splendid, short-lived, disease-prone lilies. Interestingly,

THE DOMAIN

Barbara does not mention insecticides or herbicides while discussing ferns and wildflowers.

And what of the place—Wright's little world of southwestern Connecticut, alongshore and up-country? Despite the passing of a century, the world of *The Garden, You, and I* is still recognizable. Some characters are vividly reflected in their gardens. And the gardens they create—as well as the gardens they long for—tell us a great deal about who they are.

✳ ✳ ✳

In *Gardening in California* (1923) Sydney B. Mitchell addressed another generation of gardeners, many of them transplanted easterners like himself. (Mitchell was born in Montreal, educated there and in Albany, New York, before moving to California in 1908.)[20] From the outset he clarified for nonnatives any lingering confusion about the two seasons (rainy and dry), the limited rainfall, and seasonal temperatures as modified by ocean, desert, prevailing winds, and circling storms. Noting a few similarities among the climates of California's regions and other parts of the world, he suggested the wide range of trees and small plants that would grow well in the state—including one large genus introduced from Australia, the eucalyptus, "one of the most characteristic features of the California landscape."[21]

Mitchell, who would later serve as president of the California Horticultural Society and editor of its journal, was addressing the concerns of beginning gardeners and amateurs for the most part. And yet a professional might glean something from his chapter on planning the small garden. Consult an expert, Mitchell advised; for any good architect and landscape architect would always want to visit the site, study its contours and environs, and consider the client's interests and needs, so that the final product might reflect the client's personality.[22]

The hypothetical clients Mitchell described were all men of various temperaments, each apparently about to build a custom house with a unique garden. Today that client group could be broadened to include renters and remodelers, women as well as men, with or without children. And what if a planner of new towns and subdivisions had to consider *all* the wishes of these clients? One man wants mainly to present a good impression toward the street, with a lawn and fine trees in front, and very little behind the house. Another man wants an outdoor room to live in. Along the street he wants either screening for privacy or very little land. To him, trees, shrubs, and garden furniture are more important than flowers. A third man has such a keen interest in flowers that he would omit a lawn, trees, and anything else that would steal nourishment and sunlight from his flowers.

The frontispiece of *Gardening in California* depicts the author's own garden in Berkeley, with masses of irises on a steep slope and a path to one side, bordered by *Nepeta mussini* and little gray-leaved, white-flowering annuals, *Omphalodes linifolia.* An avowed iris enthusiast, Mitchell tells a great deal about their species and varieties, but he writes very little about the place—his garden, his neighborhood in Berkeley, or the Bay Area. Years later, we learn that Mitchell had lived high up in the Berkeley Hills, on Woodmont Avenue, between Grizzly Peak Boulevard and Wildcat Canyon Road.[23] Evidently he represented that third type of client—a flower lover—who understood the limitations of his climate and soils and knew what to expect of his favorite plants from year to year.

Fletcher Steele was more intrigued by the qualities of an outdoor room. "Too many flower-gardens become slave drivers," he remarked in *Design in the Little Garden.* "Their owners never dare sit down in them." But in a green garden, the boundaries of hedges and trees could be studies in texture, light, shade, and silhouette, while the color of flowering plants would be incidental and seasonal. There serenity, repose, and the chance to mull over some particular refinement of detail would be more important than colorful display or rare varieties. And only in a small garden could one strive for perfection in minute detail; one could study its forms and textures as a sculptor studies a work that is always in progress, never completed.[24]

Steele is perhaps best known for the design of large country places such as Naumkeag, the Choates' summer place in Stockbridge, Massachusetts; the Backus residence, in Grosse Pointe Shores, Michigan; and other properties discussed in Robin Karson's critical biography of Steele.[25]

Modern gardens of the 1920s in France intrigued Steele, but so did small, ordinary gardens in America.[26] It was all a matter of spatial design that did not stop at the front steps or the kitchen door.

Within the confines of a single lot, Steele could address faults such as unimaginative foundation planting, lack of seclusion, and lack of connection among structures and garden elements. Other shortcomings called for more imaginative town planning, with flexibility on building setbacks as well as in floor plans. As George Tobey noted, Steele was a few years ahead of the planners Clarence Stein and Henry Wright in orienting the living and dining rooms of a house toward an interior lawn, while kitchens and garages faced the street. A prophecy of "functionalism," Tobey called it.[27] But that was only part of Steele's agenda.

In *Design in the Little Garden*, Steele includes a hypothetical street plan of three houses, each set on a lot 75 feet by 125 feet, along Maple Cove Avenue. His fictitious characters, Mr. and Mrs. Brown, first consider the merits of a front porch as a truck roars past, spewing exhaust. Looking over the rear terraces and tiny gardens, some screened by shrubs and trees, others left exposed to any neighbor or passerby, the Browns imagine how they might live on one lot, then on another. One garage, placed close to the street, seems at first to be an eyesore, but the Browns notice that such an arrangement eliminates the need for a long driveway and frees up land for growing vegetables and roses—and even for drying laundry. In this street plan, there are no back alleys to accommodate garages and delivery trucks. Steele mentions one means of public transportation—the trolleys. Other details suggest a way of life that may be less common today than in the 1920s.

Each garage, for instance, holds only one car. Each lot contains a vegetable garden, a drying yard, a lawn, some flowers, a few trees. And so, regardless of the property they choose, the Browns could expect to spend a fair amount of time at home and out-of-doors. On any of these lots, "home" would be more than a house. On the lot that Mrs. Brown gradually comes to prefer, the house is merely one element in a well-considered series of gardens. "Henry! we could *eat* out there Sunday nights, looking on that delicious little wild corner," she cries.[28] And in that wildness may be traces of the past, for Steele suggests that plants from the original site may have been preserved—old pears, birches, shadbush (*Amelanchier*), dogwoods. The vegetable garden could be hedged by blackberries. Foxgloves, lilies, cimicifuga, and hostas could grow among the shrubs. And these are merely suggestions. Some gardeners might devote most of their leisure hours to perennial borders, a vegetable garden, a cutting garden, a rock garden, or a "wild" garden.

But why? The reasons for creating and tending these gardens are best known to the individual. Steele's own affection for a small place surfaces now and again, as in some secluded little garden in a great city, a suburb, a village, or wherever—some "cool quiet green place, rarely drawing attention to itself, but content to be, like a dim, old room full of books— a place to live and think, and perhaps at times to dream."[29]

Some reasons for gardening were self-evident—beauty, nourishment, mild exercise, contact with the earth, or perhaps a memory of happiness in childhood. "The little garden will save the children," wrote Mrs. Francis King in 1921, reflecting on the formative influence of home, flowers, gardens that express affection and care, and a pervasive loveliness of the land. "If our children grow to manhood and womanhood without the love of beauty, we are a nation lost," she added.[30] Writing from Orchard House, her home in Michigan, Mrs. King also encouraged people to enclose their gardens, despite local prejudice against walls and fences. "Build your wall, hang your gate, and then invite everyone to enter!" she wrote, without fear of being inundated by visitors—for she lived in the small town of Alma, and the nearest city, Saginaw, was forty miles away.[31]

Born in rural northern New Jersey, Louisa Yeomans King was uprooted several times in her life. She lived with her husband and three children in and around Chicago before coming to Alma, Michigan, a fairly young town, settled shortly after the Civil War.[32] These facts help to explain the warmth with which she recommended another work in her series, which reflected the experience of several generations of one family living and gardening in one place.

Frances Edge McIlvaine, author of *Spring in the Little Garden* (1928), was still living on the old Glen Isle Farm, in Chester County, Pennsylvania, west of Philadelphia, where she had lived as a child. The place dated from 1780, and even earlier her forebears had been landowners in that valley of the Brandywine. Her grandfather was an avid horticulturist. Her grandmother, a lover of fragrances, would let no one depart from the place without a little nosegay of herbs or bits of a fragrant shrub. McIlvaine was herself a gardener who cherished native plants. Despite the national tendency for families to move every few years, she urged people to get to know their local plants, to experiment, propagate, create a bit of romance about those plants, and perhaps engender the sort of love that the English have for their native primroses and hawthorns.[33]

Each of these "little garden" books of the 1920s contains some practical hints from the author's experience, sometimes a glimpse of a place preserved or on the brink of change. Generally the authors wanted to see the grounds of a home enclosed—for the beauty of the gardens within and for privacy. Steele, McIlvaine, and Kate Brewster, author of *The Little Garden for Little Money* (1924), all urged that the garage be placed near the street to preserve more land for gardening. There would be objections, of course. But Brewster, then president of the Garden Club of Lake Forest, Illinois, explained that the house could still face the street politely, formally, as if meeting a "well-mannered stranger," while the garden side could be reserved for ease and intimacy among friends.[34]

Discussions of pesticides and other poisons were frank in these "little garden" books—although threats to human health disturbed some authors more than others. Gardening near New York City, Mrs. Edward Harding stressed prevention; rather than spray the peonies in her garden, she grew them in beds of their own and watched them carefully. Any diseased or attacked parts of a plant she would cut away and burn, then remove the nearby soil. A friend of hers in Connecticut would use powdered sulphate of iron to combat the rose bug, but Mrs. Harding relied on cultivation—"the regular and thorough stirring of the soil." Then, too, as peonies were known to be hardy, they were often neglected. Give them attention, she advised; let them grow apart from other plants, in good, not overfertilized, soil.[35]

With these notes, Mrs. Harding's *Peonies in the Little Garden* (1923) nearly came to a close. It ended with a childhood memory: the author as a little girl, tracing lilies, irises, poppies, and peonies in the needlework of an old chair. To have a little garden with all those flowers would be Heaven, thought the girl. Many years later the mature woman concurred. "For it is Heaven."

* * *

Leafing through these books on gardening and listening to the several voices, we may wonder if they represent more than a pool of information or a fleeting bit of harmony when three or more people happen to agree. Could they represent a conversation carried on across time and place? "Only Connect," Mrs. King wrote in *Variety in the Little Garden* (1923), quoting two words from the title page of E. M. Forster's *Howard's End* (1910) and thereby linking a whole prewar world of assumptions about land and inheritance with her own postwar concerns in the little garden. The connections she had in mind were those among the rich and the poor of whatever country or race, all united by their labor in the garden. "We work in faith that the seasons will still roll for us and for our sowings and plantings," she wrote. "There is no other such meeting ground."[36]

Meeting Ground. Living Museum. Heaven. Paradise. Private World. The garden could be all these things, and more. For Herbert Durand, a regular contributor to *House and Garden* magazine, the garden was a sanctuary for plants that were disappearing from the wild in the 1920s.

Durand lived in Bronxville, New York, only a half hour from Broadway. Three miles south of his home lay the northern boundary of Greater New York, and suburban development was spreading. Behind his house on a sixty-by-one-hundred-foot lot lay a rocky hillside, which he had made a haven for native trees and plants. One of his neighbors, who had planned to have a stone wall carted away, let Durand take rocks for retaining little pockets of soil. Another neighbor allowed him to gather wildflowers in his woodlands before the land was sold for development. For more plants, Durand visited nearby ponds and swamps and went by train to northern New Hampshire. In time his garden held plants from all over the United States.[37]

With his own garden, his magazine articles, and his books, including *Taming the Wildings* (1923) and *My Wild Flower Garden* (1927), Durand showed Americans the beauty of their common landscapes. He gave them a means to connect their own little gardens with the larger natural world. Even more, he encouraged them to garden without pesticides and poisons—mainly by allowing garter snakes, toads, ladybugs, spiders, bats, owls, and other birds to come and go freely. "And as for the innumerable fungus diseases that spoil the plants in 'civilized' gardens," he wrote, "they are as yet practically unknown to our untamed and aggressively healthy natives."[38] And so chemical spray pumps never cluttered Durand's garden.

For all these efforts—disseminating ideas about gardening with native plants, birds, and other wild creatures, doing away with pesticides and herbicides, rescuing plants from the path of the bulldozer, saving plants from near extinction—Durand should be better known. But over time readers ask for something more. They want to be enchanted, to dream a little. And Durand could not get a reader to dream through words alone.

That was an ability that his Bronxville neighbor and colleague, the garden writer Louise Beebe Wilder, had acquired somehow. She had also suffered losses. Married in 1902, she and her husband, an architect, and their two children had lived on a large country place with many gardens in Rockland County, New York. Soon after the First World War, however, Wilder took her two children to live in Bronxville on an acre of neglected pastureland, once part of an old estate. But why? What happened to her husband and the place in Rockland County? Biographical sketches do not explain.[39]

Wilder was reticent about her domestic affairs—and yet cheerful about beginning again on a bit of unpromising land. To her it was "a New Heaven and a New Earth." Having grown up among the mellow old gardens of her parents and grandparents, in Maryland and Massachusetts, Wilder knew the appeal of flowers that had been blooming for generations within their protective walls, freely giving, asking little. The new garden was demanding—a rough, blank canvas—but it offered adventure. She would have to find out which plants would grow in a given soil or exposure, alone, or in close company with mingled roots, in full sun or in shade. Even more, she would often have to discover and gather up the plants themselves.[40]

Like her neighbor Herbert Durand, Wilder was a collector who advised readers on when they might take plants from the wild—and when they should gather only seeds. Both were keen collectors of *American* plants, in particular. And Wilder had an especially sharp eye for the beauty of individual plants—the "rough-finished, homespun sort of foliage" of the juniper; the slow-growing *Ilex opaca*, a native holly; the tiny, fragrant alpine from Colorado, *Primula angustifolia*, with its flowers like stars.[41]

And yet Wilder seems to have been most deeply moved not by a single plant or a collection, but by working with the earth, enhancing it. Her idea of happiness was "to be at work, to help the earth give the best report of itself, to call into being beauty where were neglect and unloveliness. . . . In very truth are the roots of delight buried in the heart of the earth."[42]

Reading Wilder's books of the 1920s and '30s, we notice suburban growth enveloping her small place in Bronxville, yet something rural remained—a bit of old woodland, a lane with wild flowers, scampering wildlife, the song of a thrush. Her house was small and relatively easy to maintain—an ideal situation for someone who loved to be in the garden. She knew the flaws of her garden, but it was not for show. It was for work, experiment, peace of mind, joy.

It was also a foothold in a changing world. In 1931 Wilder wrote of nearby country roads that were being cleaned up as city dwellers bought old properties for weekend retreats. Before those roads were shorn of their tangled weeds, vines, ferns, and plants escaped from old gardens, Wilder thought of collecting a few "escapes" into a garden of their own— old friends like clematis, Bouncing Bet, Joe Pye Weed, watercress, daylilies, campanulas, dianthus. Herbs, too, crept along old roads, up the banks, and into the fields: marjoram, thyme, nepeta, hyssop, horehound, rocket, tansy. An escaped plant might be traced to an abandoned garden, an old recipe, or a childhood memory, to Marie Antoinette, or to Shakespeare. Each plant had a life history, she mused; "they are so human, so natural, and they seem to have a common past with us and common traditions."[43]

In a brief chapter Wilder could only begin to suggest those traditions. In *Herbs and the Earth* (1935) Henry Beston devoted a volume to them. Like Wilder, he was intrigued by the plants' life histories—which were cultural and social histories as well. He also imagined a small garden that would have resembled Wilder's proposed garden of escaped plants. Beston's would be a patch of "simples," or medicinal plants, many of them too weedy for his herb garden. They were wanderers—tansy, catnip (nepeta), goldthread (*Coptis trifolia*), wild basil, wild mint, wild ginger, and others. Collected in some out-of-the-way place, these plants would represent a middle ground between the cultivated and the wild. And still some might escape. Half-domesticated by many years of human use, they seemed to need a "freer existence" than any well-maintained herb garden could accommodate.[44]

Beston's main concern was the herb garden proper, a garden small enough to receive affectionate, patient care. In it might be forty or fifty kinds of herbs, not more—so that the gardener could know each one intimately. The garden would be predominantly green. Apart from their use in the kitchen, the herbs would be enjoyed mainly for their form, texture, habit, and fragrance. The color of flowers would be incidental—as it had been for gardeners of ancient times, Beston noted. And the presence of herbs would always recall something of the past, a "human past."[45]

What distinguishes *Herbs and the Earth* from many other herbals is the intricate weaving of that human past with a human present and prospects for the future. Among passages from Shakespeare, memories of street cries in London, notes on the loss of Dittany and the magic of Rue, and allusions to Pliny, Charlemagne, and trade routes to the Far East are glimpses of the place where Beston and his family lived: the farmhouse, the fields, the shale and granite in old foundation walls, the cry of a loon, the snow in winter. For many pages it is not clear where, exactly, the Bestons lived. Nor is it critical. What matters is the recurring sense that all is grounded in *some* place and time. Early on, the mowing of the fields has begun, and something of the motions and rhythms of the earth are stirring in a human being. The winds are strong, but walls shelter the herbs, and peace with the earth is possible.

Beston describes his little herb garden—enclosed on three sides by house and shed, and open to the morning sun—with just enough detail so that it has a real presence. From the garden, beyond and below an old apple tree, he can see a bit of the lake and fields of hay. It is his garden, but it might be anyone's. Gradually, among stories of sweet marjoram, balm, sage, and other herbs, the place becomes more specific; it is in New England, where three dry weeks of August are followed by a blessed rain. One evening in midsummer, coolness rises from the earth and fragrances are intense. Later clues, such as dew in the morning, and a bird migrating from inland to the sea, are followed by the casual, long-withheld words "here in Maine." By that time, readers may be curious about the place (in Nobleboro, Maine), about the lady of the house, and the "Two Young Persons Who Never Pull up or Step on Father's Herbs," to whom the book is dedicated. But again and again, Beston moves from human dramas to other dramas, those unfolding beneath and above the earth. "We are not conscious enough in our human world of this other shaping of life beside us," he writes, having dwelt on the endurance of plants and their will to rise above hardships and lift even a single flower from a ruin.[46]

On the fragrance of certain plants, Beston added his voice to a chorus of garden writers, ancient and modern, including Mabel Osgood Wright and Louise Beebe Wilder. Like them, he wrote of fragrant flowers and herbs for treating medical and psychological illnesses.[47]

Beston also touched on the "emotion of place" that a fragrance may arouse in us—the smell of freshly cut hay in spring, for instance, or some other odor expressive of earth and life, of joy or sorrow. We breathe it, sense it. And all at once, the physical reality of the place where we are is fused with an "emotion of ourselves as we were in time and the place remembered."[48]

The appeal is to the senses and feelings, not to the logical, rational mind. And it is personal. In Beston's own experience, the uses of basil and rosemary, the association of bergamot mint with eighteenth-century music, brocades, jewels, and politics, the movements of sun and moon, and the beauty of the earth, all are somehow connected, intertwined. "It is only when we are aware of the earth and of the earth as poetry that we truly live," Beston insists, early on.[49] And his epilogue is poetry in prose, an epic in miniature, about the parting of the earth to bring forth new life in spring.

Beneath the quiet beauty and civility of *Herbs and the Earth* lay traces of sadness, however. Quite apart from the strains of the Great Depression, the age was a troubled one; "it is without a truly human past and may be without a human future," Beston wrote. His tales of herbs in history would help to restore some of that human past. But more was needed. "Only Connect," Mrs. Francis King had written, echoing E. M. Forster. Beston, too, sought some connection, a deeply spiritual one, writing of humans "torn from the earth," wandering in space, without meaning. Working with the earth, patiently, knowing and caring for plants as individual living things of great beauty and use, perhaps people would in time reconnect with the earth, make some peace with it instead of abusing it, poisoning it. "Peace with the earth is the first peace," wrote Beston, words that may yet prove to be prophetic.[50]

SEVEN

The Abandoned Place

In *Country Neighborhood* (1944), a collection of stories and reflections on life in midcoastal Maine, Elizabeth Coatsworth told of one encounter between a fox and a mild-mannered pit-bull terrier. The large black terrier was entirely domesticated. The golden-red fox, once a pet among several others in a village household, had been returned to the woods when still young. Reappearing in the village one day, the nearly full-grown fox showed no fear of the unknown terrier; she seemed to want to play. And Coatsworth found the fox enchanting—"neither wild nor tame, but something beyond either."[1]

The same could be said of many abandoned places—where cellar holes are filled with standing water or growing trees, where pastures and fields are reverting to woodlands, where mill wheels and mine shafts have been made obsolete by newer technologies, where rutted roads and stone walls seem to run without purpose through second-growth forests. We know these things through the poetry of Robert Frost, the photographs of Wallace Nutting, essays by John Burroughs, Bradford Torrey, and Walter Prichard Eaton, stories by Sarah Orne Jewett and Mary Wilkins Freeman, and the writings of historians and critics. Or we may have come across these abandoned things in our travels.

We are also aware of the unkempt land, but often vaguely—as background. Much more vivid are the nails that are pried out by warping boards in Frost's poem "The Black Cottage" (1914).[2] We remember the widow who had lived in that cottage, dwelling on the meaning of the war that had claimed her husband's life at Gettysburg—or was it Fredericksburg? We see the windowpanes blazing as the narrator and the minister leave at sunset. But what of the tar-banded cherry trees and the rank grass? And why was the old house set far back from the road, rather than conveniently near it? In focusing on people, things, events, ideas, have we missed seeing the land, the place itself?

This chapter gives more attention to the land without losing sight of people who once dwelled there and made it a memorable place. The chapter begins on some abandoned farms in New England, reaches across a continent and half an ocean to the Hawaiian Islands, then returns to the continental United States. It considers articles, essays, poems, personal narratives, diaries, and a novel, all of them dealing with a place that has been humanized in some way but not completely dominated by human will. To some writers, the land is a presence, with a will of its own that is sometimes opposed to, or indifferent to, human will. For a while the land may be subdued by human forces. Then natural processes set in—erosion, siltation, weathering, sometimes revegetation and healing. There may be an observer, alone or with others, who wants to reclaim the abandoned place and transform it, make it more beautiful or productive. Sometimes it is enough to observe, to reflect on how a place came to be abandoned and ponder the consequences.

❖ ❖ ❖

In November 1901, Liberty Hyde Bailey launched a new magazine, *Country Life in America,* with a lead article on abandoned farms. Whether Bailey, the eminent botanist and professor of horticulture at Cornell University, actually wrote that unsigned article is not clear; perhaps he had a hand in it. In any case, as editor, he wanted to attract a wide range of people from rural and urban areas of the country. The son of a pioneer farmer in Michigan and grandson of a Vermont farmer, Bailey knew the country as a workplace, but also as a place for unstructured play, wonder, curiosity, and delight. As he explained in his first editorial, this magazine would be written in the country (Ithaca, New York) "for the country man, and for the city man who wants to know the country." Bailey would seek out the finest work of photographers and writers, but he was not aiming at a rarefied audience. "We hope that the smell of the soil will be on its pages," he added.[3]

That earthy, gritty sort of reality permeates "The Abandoned Farms." The tone of the article is upbeat, confident, with a trace of disdain for fanciful illusions. Any regrets or bittersweet feelings about the abandoned farms of New England were beside the point. With changing economic conditions and widening opportunities, as new industries developed in the East and richer lands opened up in the West, shifts in population were bound to occur. It was not a question of agriculture, the writer asserted; it was about economics.[4]

The main interests in this lead article—efficiency, modern methods of farming, profit, utility—are in keeping with the times, the Progressive Era, yet they are presented in a context of old, or timeless, values and allusions to quiet lives, rich and deep. Bailey's first editorial, too, dwells on enduring qualities—contentment, satisfaction of the soul, harmony with one's environment, love of country life—without a hint of conflict between, say, profitable farming and proliferating summer places. It was a time when nature study, gardening, hiking, camping, hunting, fishing, and other outdoor activities were widely popular. Then, too, despite the flow of migration from rural to urban areas, despite waves of immigration to the largest cities, the U.S. Census in 1900 had revealed that more than 60 percent of the population lived in places of four thousand people or less.[5] The trend was toward greater concentration in cities, of course, but as railroad and trolley lines extended the reach of cities and towns, boundaries between urban and rural lands became somewhat blurred. Many farms, once remote from neighbors and markets, were no longer so isolated. It seemed that the time was right, then, for enterprising people to take up an abandoned farm in New England and make it both attractive and profitable.

Today "The Abandoned Farms" reads like an engaging piece of public relations for the good life on the farm—except for one sobering passage. The writer mentioned bleaching branches and rotting trunks in an orchard, the wind blowing through an old roof, stone walls tumbling down, and swallows nesting in a damaged chimney. He (or she) knew that a stranger from the city would not look upon these things as the owner—perhaps the last in the family line—might see them, overlaid with memory and respect for ancestors. A prospective buyer would focus on the present and the future.

A decade later, in "The Abandoned Farm" (1911), Walter Prichard Eaton wrote about traces of neglect and decay that were colored by his own memories and desires. When he was a boy, his father, a schoolteacher, had managed to purchase an old farm south of Franconia, a village in the White Mountains of New Hampshire. That became the family's summer place; in other seasons Eaton attended a series of schools in small towns near Boston. A few miles farther from the city (in Reading, Massachusetts) was his grandparents' farm. Such are the bare outlines of what Eaton recalled as a "country boyhood"—bits of city, incipient suburb, rural fringes, and remote countryside.[6]

A generation younger than Bailey, Eaton would have shared many of Bailey's rural values, particularly his mission to get the country man to see rural land in a new light and appreciate its many forms of beauty, humanized and wild. Writing in a manner much more personal than Bailey's, however, Eaton alluded to tensions developing in the changing, modernizing world about him, tensions that he himself could not—like a magazine editor—resolve with one piece of writing set against another between two covers. Rather, he would try to reconcile conflicting values—the melancholy beauty of abandoned farmhouses, the pleasure of seeing neat, well-ordered places, the desire for stimulation and self-advancement, the longing for rootedness in a place, the wish to conserve, the need to consume. As a writer, then, Eaton avoided the format of a factual, impersonal article in favor of the familiar essay, a more flexible mode of expression that could accommodate abrupt shifts in mood and let him work through his ambivalence toward some temporary resting place if not a conclusion.

In "The Abandoned Farm," Eaton begins in a middle ground, the pasture behind his parents' farmhouse in New Hampshire. Some three or four miles to the north lie the village and resort hotels of Franconia, a social nucleus for the prosperous-looking farms owned by summer people from the city. Beginning a mile or two to the south lie several abandoned farms, strung along a few winding roads that rise from the valley floor up the flanks of the great local presence, Mount Moosilauke. Eaton is familiar with both worlds, but his affections remain with the southern one, where places have been left behind in "half-wild, beautiful, pathetic desolation." His descriptions amount to a personal tour of deteriorating farmhouses, a sawmill, a blacksmith's shop, a graveyard, with now and then a story of a few old characters he once knew. One centenarian (whom he never knew) is remarkable for the dates on her gravestone, an evocation of English poetry from Pope to Wordsworth. This might be so much "local color," except for jarring elements like the motorcars with out-of-state license plates creeping through Franconia Notch, the profitable hobby farm of a wealthy manufacturer, and virgin hardwood trees on the steep slopes of Moosilauke, seen against clear-cut patches that had been logged for pulpwood, then abandoned. These were all part of the landscape of abandoned farms, a blend of decay and prosperity.

Rather than try to account for these contrasts by some failing among the local people—or by evil cities that had drawn young people from the hinterlands—Eaton identified a wider context and a tentative solution. "Civilization opens a Pandora's box of desires and ambitions and discontents," he observed, "and it creates, too, an increased expensiveness of living which a pioneer society, without changing its methods, is unable to meet." Not that the descendants of that original pioneer society were doomed; and their family farms did not have to be bought up by millionaires. To avert a return to feudalism, Eaton would promote Progressive Era measures such as the scientific management of forests, governmental restrictions on logging, and greater attention to soils, crop rotation, and local markets. He would eliminate middlemen and encourage more social and cultural interaction among natives and summer people. The melancholy beauty of the abandoned farm buildings he found on his solitary walks would slip away, of course. But Eaton believed that a solution to rural poverty and environmental degradation could be found in a repopulation of the countryside with people able and willing to own their own bit of land, work the soil with their own hands, and put down roots. And some of those people would necessarily come from the city. "The country needs these people," he insisted, "and these people need the country."[7]

"The Abandoned Farm" was reprinted in Eaton's *Barn Doors and Byways* (1913), a collection of essays mainly about rural places, particularly in two areas of New England, the Franconia area and Berkshire County, in western Massachusetts. Two years later Robert Frost was delighted by the book. He and his family had recently returned from England, having been away for two and a half years. They had just settled in a farmhouse about a mile south of Franconia when Frost received a copy of *Barn Doors and Byways* from a friend. In July 1915, he wrote to Eaton, expressing his appreciation and hoping to meet the author. "Yours is a lovely book—full of things I wish I had thought of first," he admitted.[8] Some time later Frost inscribed a copy of his *Mountain Interval* (1916) to Eaton.[9]

Not much is generally known of Frost's exchanges with Eaton, beyond a couple of published letters.[10] Evidently Frost would have liked to have at least a few good conversations with Eaton, whose description of taking shelter in a strange barn during a thunderstorm seemed to Frost like a poem itself. Then, too, they had in common a keen interest in drama. After reviewing plays for about a decade in Boston and New York, from 1900 to 1910, Eaton would eventually write a few plays for the stage. Frost was particularly attentive to the sound and cadence of natural speech; and some of his finest early poems, including "The Death of the Hired Man" and "Home Burial," are based on dramatic encounters. "The height of poetry is in dramatic give-and-take," Frost once told an interviewer. "Drama is the capstone of poetry."[11] In any event, a long conversation between Frost and Eaton would inevitably touch on some abandoned place or thing in landscapes they both knew and loved.[12]

In "Ghost House," a poem first published in 1906, Frost shows a grave-yard to be teeming with life—in the trees of orchard and forest, in mosses, in the wild grapevines that straggle over the tumbling stone wall. Whip-poorwills, woodpeckers, bats, and toads are all active, and an old foot-path has been healed by the new growth of plants. The narrator, a ghost who dwells in a cellar hole full of wild raspberries, has a "strangely aching heart"; he should be cheerful, given all the signs of vitality around him. The ghost is not lonely; he has companions whose names are recorded on gravestones. And once the nonhuman forms of life are recognized as players in this little drama, the place is anything but abandoned.[13]

In "The Wood-Pile" (1914) the narrator is walking in a frozen swamp that has about it nothing memorable, nothing to mark its place. Then a bird flies past, seeks cover, and finds it behind a woodpile—which really does mark a place because of its mysterious setting, far from a dwelling of any kind. Why would someone make the effort to cut, split, and stack that full cord of wood, then abandon it to clematis and the elements? In the end the narrator's casual speculation leads to a thought that takes us beyond the preoccupation with human action to the infinitely patient actions of weathering and warming—the "slow smokeless burning of decay" that will to some extent "warm the frozen swamp."[14]

These and other poems by Frost that treat themes of desolation and abandonment are often read only from a human point of view—which would seem to be fair, given Frost's well-known insistence on human drama in his poetry. As he remarked to a sympathetic reviewer in 1921, "We have had nature poetry now for a hundred years. Now we must have the human foreground with it."[15] But as biographers and critics have observed over the years, Frost's life and work were full of contradictions, paradoxes, periods of depressions, and tendencies toward play, humor, puns, games, mischief, fun. Jay Parini, for one, has emphasized the masks

and games of deception in Frost's life, along with the elaborate con-
structions in Frost's poetry.[16] Could it be that some of those construc-
tions have been so well crafted by a crafty fellow that we have been
diverted from seeing the nonhuman dramas unfolding in the poems? Is
it possible that, on some level, Frost also wanted us to read some of his
poems from the point of view of the mountain, the brook, the glacier, or
the wildflowers?

Considered from these shifting perspectives, two poems in Frost's
New Hampshire (1923), "A Brook in the City" and "The Need of Being
Versed in Country Things," have much in common, for both deal with
nonhuman responses to changes on the land. When a growing city absorbs rural land, any farmhouse not torn down must "square" with the
new city street. If not buried in fill, the brook is diverted to run under-
ground, as a sewer; and so it is abandoned, "all for nothing it had ever
done." When a house in the country burns down to a lone chimney, the
phoebes don't sigh or dwell on the past; they keep on building nests
among the ruins and do not weep. In "The Birthplace," first published
in 1923, the first seven lines sketch in the strenuous work of a pioneer on
a mountain farm, who clears the land and rears a dozen children. The
remaining seven lines show the farm abandoned to wilderness—from
the point of view of the mountain, a willful presence, who will cheerfully
tolerate the pioneer family for a while, then reject and forget them, once
"her lap is full of trees."[17] Here, again, Frost dispels the gloom from an
abandoned place by shifting perspectives and inviting us to consider the
land in its own right.

In yet another poem of the 1920s, "The Last Mowing" (1928), Frost's
main concern is not abandonment but the natural processes that will
unfold in the aftermath. Far-away Meadow will no longer be mowed, or
so they say at the farmhouse. It will revert from tame to wild. Trees will
eventually reclaim the meadow, but for a short time it is "ours." That is,
the narrator shares the place with sun-loving wildflowers—plants that
will have only so much time to bloom and proliferate before trees
spring up and cast their shade. The moment is fleeting—and joyous—

especially for the narrator, who apparently holds no title to the land but possesses it just as the wildflowers do, for a little while.[18] And that narrator is no ghost; it could be Frost himself.

In 1932, writing from his farm in South Shaftsbury, Vermont, Frost sent his friend and fellow poet Louis Untermeyer some reflections and a bit of advice. He wrote about the value of land that is not tilled or otherwise considered part of a system of intensive agriculture. That was the sort of land Frost liked for himself—"unconsidered land," where he could take time to mull over ideas, like so many crops that he would turn under again and again, back into the soil, until the moment when he had something to take to market (to publish). "Don't come as a product till you have turned yourself under many times," he advised Untermeyer.[19] It was a double metaphor—the slowly evolving literary product, viewed as a crop finally taken from the soil; and the slowly evolving individual, who needs to be withdrawn and "almost wastefully alone" for a while before engaging in social life again.[20] Behind that advice lay the poem "The Last Mowing," about one normally unconsidered moment—a few seasons, maybe a decade or two—when wildflowers can "waste and go wild" in an abandoned meadow.

Whether Frost intended these poems to be read with shifting perspectives, from a human to a nonhuman point of view, or whether he wanted us to see the land and natural processes at work without us, is debatable. In any case, some of his own published conversations would lead us away from contemplating the nonhuman in nature like some reverent nineteenth-century figure, studying leaves or berries or mountain vistas. Rather than stand in awe of the land and natural processes, Frost would have us at least be interested in these things, see them more clearly—and even get lost in the process, in order to find ourselves, as he suggests in "Directive" (1946). In that poem, among traces of abandoned houses and ruts left by wagon wheels, he calls attention to evidence of glacial action on the ledges, which extends the poem's time frame from barely two centuries to eons of time.[21]

And there were other ways of stretching the mind in abandoned places, once the preoccupations of modern life were set aside. Walter

Prichard Eaton liked to walk along lost roads in second-growth forests, looking for traces of human habitation and any interesting shrubs or garden flowers that might have survived. In "Cellar Holes" (1921) he mentioned a few treasures—an iron pot, a few handwrought hinges, a clump of spirea—that he could haul back to his dusty auto, left miles behind. But more intriguing were the cellar holes themselves, which he "collected" by finding, naming, and remembering them, often making up stories about them and their pioneer inhabitants. His collection of cellar holes amounted to a sort of museum without walls, stretched out over more than two hundred miles—about the distance from his own farmhouse in Sheffield, Massachusetts, to his favorite haunts in Franconia, New Hampshire. Each site in the collection was more or less protected by its own remoteness from civilization. Together they represented the passing of an old pioneer way of life, yet the decaying remains did not seem melancholy. They were "brave, brambled records of the pioneers who bred us," tough yet highly civilized men and women whose hewn stones and corner cupboards Eaton could still admire, while a hermit thrush sang and daylilies bloomed in a place he called Sky Farm.[22]

In "Cellar Holes" and other essays by Eaton, a human foreground and its once-domesticated, now half-wild setting are often intertwined, a bit like the wild grapevine coiled about a young maple in his essay "Sweets for Squirrels" (1932).[23] There, in one of his more introspective moods, the simple pleasures of squirrels (tapping the sap of old sugar maples in early spring) and the recent visit of a young poet (walking ten miles from a shack in the woods to Eaton's farmhouse) lead to a meditation on the complexity of life in a society organized around acquisition and consumption. In a time of austerity—the Great Depression—could one really warn against the tyranny of things, alluding to motorcars, movies, telephones, tiled bathrooms, and the wisdom of Emerson and Thoreau? In any event, Eaton kept at it, just as he tugged at the coiling grapevine, to free the young maple and let it grow into a thing of beauty. He was thrilled by wildness, but he also wanted an interesting rock garden with a tall tree to shade the ferns. He drove a car, but only part of the way, in search of his cellar holes.

Cellar hole, Sutton, New Hampshire

And so the tradition of solitary wandering among abandoned places in old New England continued well into the mid-twentieth century. Less common, it seems, were tales of abandoned places discovered by little groups of people or families—as in one vignette from Elizabeth Coatsworth's *Maine Ways* (1947). Setting out one day in search of a beaver dam not far from home, Coatsworth came across some houses that seemed to be abandoned; windows were shuttered, a roof was falling in, a floor was missing, a fireplace had been bricked in. These and other objects caught her attention. But land, in varying stages of neglect and care, and views up to the skyline and down from high ground were at least equally compelling to her.[24]

Coatsworth was not traveling alone. Accompanied by her husband, Henry (Beston), and her daughters, Meg and Kate, she shared the adventure, which began by car and ended on foot, through tangles of blackberries, past traces of animal trails and a lone horse in a pasture, to one house that was evidently deserted and another that might have been, but for signs of habitation—the mown hay, the fenced-in garden, the milk

THE DOMAIN

bottles and a string of dried alewives by the back step. In the end, someone at the crossroads explained the situation of the lone bachelor, last of
his family line, who was looking after some of the old homesteads and
living in one of them, while a distant relative had remodeled another
homestead for a summer place.

Coatsworth's story is marvelously compressed—the prose work of a
poet. It could have been depressing, but it is not. Something in her tone—
calm, humane, at once engaged and gently detached—allows us to see
abandoned places as part of a larger environment in evolution, a real,
physical environment of sand roads, elm trees, mown fields, orchards,
woods and sky, bachelors and grandchildren, car doors that slam, and
candles that burn in the night. What lingers in the mind, here as in some
other writings about abandoned places, is a feeling for both the people
associated with an abandoned place and the half-tame, half-wild land
itself, its beauty and its promise.

❊ ❊ ❊

In *Hawaii* (1970), one of those sumptuously illustrated National Geographic monographs, the island of Kahoolawe was briefly described as
an uninhabited place used as target range by the U.S. Navy and Marine
Corps. Flown to the island one day by helicopter, along with military per-
sonnel who would be observing the gunnery practice, the author William
Graves noticed that the remains of weapons were mingled with volcanic
debris, such that it was difficult to distinguish nature's "violent handi-
work" from that of man. But no photographs in *Hawaii* document those
fragments on the pummeled ground—or anything else on the island. On
maps and in renderings, the forty-five-square-mile island of Kahoolawe
simply appears as a tiny fleck of land to the southwest of Maui. Its geological history—as part of the Hawaiian Ridge, rising up from the Pacific
Ocean's floor—was said to reach back some twenty-five million years.
But of Kahoolawe's human past Graves had nothing to report.[25]

By that time a popular novel set on Kahoolawe, Armine von Tempski's *Dust* (1928), may have slipped into obscurity. This was a fictional
account of a young man's passion to reclaim the desiccated, dying island,
based in part on a true story. Von Tempski knew personally two men

who had begun to make the island once again fit for cattle grazing; the men were family friends. She also lived there for a while, working on her novel and watching for signs of grasses and trees taking hold in the once parched, overgrazed earth. As a work of literature, *Dust* does not rise to the level of von Tempski's *Born in Paradise* (1940), but some passages, conveying intense feelings for the land and elemental forces, make it worth a fresh reading—if only to learn about a once-cherished island during one moment in time between volcanic eruptions and military bombardment.[26]

The hero of *Dust,* twenty-three-year-old Saxon Kingsley, has little to lose but his youth and perhaps something of his sanity as he sets out to reclaim the abandoned island for cattle ranching. The tall, lean, red-haired fellow with a desk job in Honolulu has no family, no friends, no financial resources, and little experience working on the land, except for a couple of years herding cattle on a ranch on Maui. Before signing a lease for the island and assuming a hefty debt (rather than work for hire), he learns of the island's recent past. Some forty years earlier, a cattle ranch on Kahoolawe had supported about twenty-five hundred head of cattle and three hundred horses. Eager for more income, however, the ranchers had imported sheep and goats, "close feeders," that devoured the grass down to the ground and effectively destroyed its roots. The soil, no longer held down, began to blow away. Water supplies dwindled and vegetation withered. After a few years, the ranchers had departed, taking their cattle and horses, eventually their sheep as well. The goats, left behind as worthless, continued to graze on the scanty grasses and multiply. Since then, other men had tried to reclaim the island—and failed.

How young Saxon begins to bring life back to the dust-blown island with the financial and moral support of some individuals in Honolulu, and with the help of hired men—Japanese, Chinese, Hawaiian, and Portuguese—is a story of adventure, romance, opium smuggling, and deaths, some tragic, some mysterious. Read along with von Tempski's second memoir, *Aloha* (1946), the novel can be understood as a fictitious human drama, based on some knowledge of local history, grazing practices, native plants, erosion, trade winds, and cycles of drought and storm.

Differences of race, religion, socioeconomic background, and age are simplified, sometimes to the point of caricature, so that the relations among a few characters—mainly two young men and a young woman— may be more finely drawn.

Saxon, the central figure, is somewhat larger than life, a mythic hero who resembles a prince or a young king disguised as a workingman. Having known poverty and loneliness all his life, he is immediately drawn to a lonely, gaunt, mistreated island that has been eaten away by the abandoned goats, and by winds that blow soil into red clouds of dust when no rain falls. On his first visit, he becomes committed to the place. People have warned him that living in such a desolate land will take its toll, but the omniscient narrator gives more clues to Saxon's motives— glimpses of his room in a scrappy boardinghouse, and evidence of his feeling for beauty in a flower, a bird's song, even in the eyes of the young goats that he must get rid of, somehow, so that the island may recover.

At first Kahoolawe is a means to an end—a business venture, a step toward a way of life that might include a garden like one Saxon has lingered in at the home of some kind, generous people in Honolulu. And, like any island, Kahoolawe is a refuge, a place for turning inward and living deeply, apart from civilization. In time the island becomes an end in itself. Saxon loves it; he is a part of it. Returning after a trying period away from it, "he felt reabsorbed by the island, as rain is absorbed by the earth." Yet he can also appreciate the place on its own terms: "The faint dry scent of the scarlet island set between sky and sea, the vast unruffled calm of ocean spaces that hinted at eternal things, air like a benediction coming off the clean, sharp edges of the world."[27]

Only the omniscient narrator and Nollie, a young painter, can see the island of Kahoolawe as Saxon sees it. Nollie falls in love there and eventually paints a portrait of the place, entitled "The Death of an Island." The narrator's perspective is more distant: "Dawn came as it comes only in the desert and in Hawaii, pure, pale, luminous as radium." In fact, some years before the novel appeared, von Tempski had traveled in the Southwest and visited the Grand Canyon and Monument Valley. She had seen the Navajo country covered in snow and also colored by blooming lupins and purple sage. She had fallen in love there—with the land, and with a geologist whose work had brought him there. The geologist later dropped out of her life, but von Tempski's appreciation for spare, dry places and the quality of desert light and air remained. "These deserts and mountains, the great mesas and raw colors, fascinated me," she wrote of the Southwest. "This, I chose to think, was Hawaii, translated into another language. It had the primal force of the Islands, the inviolate spaces, the strange, haunting magic that goes deeper than the surface of things."[28]

Behind Saxon's love for the overgrazed and abandoned island of Kahoolawe, then, lies the author's feeling for dry, lonely places. Behind it, too, is Saxon's determination to make Kahoolawe a finer, richer place. He sends for books on grasses and land reclamation. He scatters seed, sets out saplings, thinks of building beehives, maybe planting coconut and *hau* trees and making the island a real home. When the *kona* rains finally arrive after three dry winters, Saxon is thrilled to recognize native grasses that he has never seen on Kahoolawe, grasses he knows only by their Hawaiian names: *pualili, lauki, kakonokono, kukai-pua.* Riding over the island, he absorbs the fragrances and colors of blossoming *kiawe* trees and looks for other signs of recovery. Much of the island, to the south and west, is still bleak and bare, but on the northeast slopes, facing Maui, some life is returning.

Despite the red hair that blazes in sunlight, despite his youth and limited experience of life, Saxon embodies some of the finer traits of von Tempksi's father, Louis, of whom a close family friend recalled, "It wasn't for himself he planted grasses from all over the world, developed fine herds, and set out thousands of trees. He built for posterity. The island of Maui will be richer forever because old Von lived on it." Saxon was not quite so altruistic, perhaps, but he, too, envisioned an island with pastures of waving grasses, herds of cattle, a garden, a wife. Even against great odds he was "creating a world out of chaos"[29]—an ironic commentary on the island of Kahoolawe, which neither Saxon Kingsley nor Armine von Tempski could have imagined under routine bombardment, day after day.

THE DOMAIN

✲ ✲ ✲

Forty years later, in a book littered with abandoned objects and places, Edward Abbey offered a compelling reason to have faith in a world where nothing abides and everything is in motion. Near the end of his *Desert Solitaire* (1968), as he prepares to leave his seasonal job as a ranger at Arches National Monument, in Utah, Abbey reflects on nature's ability to reclaim a place. And it is not some mountain pasture in New England that he has in mind, or any other place in a temperate region with fairly abundant annual rainfall. It is Trinity, New Mexico, "where our wise men exploded the first atomic bomb and the heat of the blast fused sand into a greenish glass," he writes. "Already the grass has returned, and the cactus and the mesquite."[30]

Abbey's *Desert Solitaire* has become such a classic of nature writing that, despite its irreverence and blunt criticism of the National Park Service, it comes highly recommended in a standard guide to our national parks and monuments.[31] In 1971, when Arches was redesignated a national *park,* its boundaries were redrawn and the total area was doubled. When Abbey worked there as a ranger in the 1950s and '60s, the territory he covered extended only thirty-three thousand acres—some fifty-one square miles—but that was sufficient for what he called his "terrace." Partway through the season, when the house trailer that came with his job felt like a kiln, he abandoned it—except for storage and the kitchen. Outside he slept, ate, smoked, watched the sky, and tried to work through some of the paradoxes and mysteries of his existence there, alone for the most part, yet much less lonely than he would have felt indoors. Out on the terrace he could see for many miles, hear a great horned owl, study constellations, and reflect on the passing of a way of life for many in the region—for the Hopi, the Zuñi, and others, whose ancestors had lived in now-abandoned cliff dwellings; for cowboys, at a time of increasing mechanization and automation; and for himself, a seasonal ranger in a rough, wild land soon to be tamed by paved roads and modern conveniences. As he warns at the outset, *Desert Solitaire* is itself an expression of something that is passing, an elegy, a tombstone, heavy and dangerous.

Unlike Saxon Kingsley, Edward Abbey is not out to reclaim or otherwise improve the land he works on. He mentions no debts, lives with few belongings, and even puzzles over whether naming things—rock formations, landmarks—is tantamount to craving them, like possessions. Resisting the trappings of his culture, he remains aloof for the most part, and critical. But when he chats with a group of tourists one evening over Labor Day weekend, Abbey admits that he, too, is an exile from an America made up of concrete and iron. On other occasions his thoughts turn to loneliness, a woman he once knew, the red dust of Utah, the distant mountains that seem like islands in a sea of desert. One cool mountain peak becomes his refuge from desert heat for a day or two. Another high peak, seen from a distance of twenty miles, leads Abbey to reflect on the value of wilderness, not only for himself but for all people—whether they ever immerse themselves in it or simply know it's there, a refuge apart from civilization.

In *Desert Solitaire,* abandoned places—old cabins, camps, "ghost villages," abandoned mines—are not really destinations so much as landmarks or catalysts for thought. Turnbow Cabin stands as a ruin at the beginning of the trail to Delicate Arch. Abbey mentions the cabin's namesake, a man with a terminal illness who had fled an eastern city for the Utah desert, where he lived for many years in a cabin he built by a brackish stream (the nearest potable water was a half mile away). But more compelling is the natural object at the end of the trail—Delicate Arch, an eroded fragment of sandstone that is, by any standard, strange, weird, marvelous—and yet tangible and real. Abbey thinks of the wonders of natural processes that had shaped that arch, and the wonders of anyone's journey here on earth. Once the mind is jolted out of its habitual rut, he realizes—once one can see the wonder and mystery in the commonplace, nothing on earth can be taken for granted.[32]

When not on duty at Arches, Abbey made some journeys in desert and mesa country to the south, including a one-week excursion with a friend down the Colorado River toward the site of Glen Canyon Dam, then under construction. Traveling with a friend while the river was still running wild and free, Abbey gathered impressions somewhat as Wallace Stegner and Ann Woodin did while negotiating the wild river in small groups.[33] But Abbey and his friend often separated for a day, to fish or hike alone. Once, while hiking alone on a side trip up the Escalante, Abbey thought about the abandoned cliff dwellings he saw high up in the canyon walls. Like others before him, he wondered why those ancient cliff dwellers had left their "ghost village" of stone—but also what quality of life they had known in that place. Beyond architecture and artifacts, what atmosphere did they leave behind? Was it fear? Distrust of innovation? Were they driven out by human enemies, he wondered, or by disease or pollution of air and water? Abbey's return journey down the Escalante, mainly in darkness, left him eager for his friend's campfire—and for civilization.

A longer sojourn among abandoned dwellings left Abbey grateful not only for civilization but for life itself. Based in an abandoned mining camp along Havasu Creek, a tributary of the Colorado, just south of Grand Canyon National Park, Abbey lived for over a month, mostly alone. He could get supplies and find society at the village of the Havasupai Indians. In the abandoned silver mines, he found a few sticks of dynamite, not much more. In a side canyon he nearly lost his life. That story is harrowing and humbling; three times this fearless middle-aged man admits to crying, without restraint. But by his own wits and with uncommon agility, he evades death. The stories that follow seem anticlimactic. He has pushed solitude to the extreme. Some connection to society and civilization, along with an acceptance of flux and change, seems to be the inevitable conclusion. "I want to hear once more the crackle of clamshells on the floor of the bar in the Clam Broth House in Hoboken. I long for a view of the jolly, rosy faces on 42nd Street," he writes in the autumn, knowing that the desert will still be there (however changed) in the spring.[34]

* * *

More than one writer mentioned in these pages has noticed that wild creatures of the air and on land don't seem to care if a place is abandoned. If not barred from entering, they move in and out as they please. In time someone may appear—a hunter, a trapper, a wilderness guide, an ecologist—and stay there a while, conscious of company and perhaps even grateful for it. Edward Abbey, for one, was content to share his house trailer with some of the smaller creatures that had made it their home over the previous winter. And Aldo Leopold once wrote of an unnamed, uninhabited island in a stream that, despite the poison ivy in summer and unreliable ice in winter, held some attraction for the deer. That piqued Leopold's interest. When the title to the island reverted to the county, Leopold commented, "The county holds it in trust, as it were, for the deer and myself. The peculiarity of this arrangement is that the county knows nothing about it."[35]

Here was one way of looking at the natural world: with a blend of curiosity, affection, and the detachment of someone equally at ease in a lecture hall or a lean-to. A younger colleague of Leopold's, the wilderness guide and nature writer Sigurd Olson, wrote about wild and abandoned places with a comparable ease and affection, but with less detachment—as if he and a friend or two were swapping stories while seated around the campfire. "I have always felt that cabins belong to the animals of the woods as much as they do to us," Olson reflected in *The Singing Wilderness* (1956); "the animals should feel as much at home in them as though there were no doors or walls." And he went on, writing of trust between humans and animals, of caves and overhanging ledges as shelters, and of his own thoughts that sometimes merged with the sounds of trees creaking in the wind.[36]

As a writer, Olson took longer to develop his own distinctive voice. As it happened, *The Singing Wilderness,* one of his best works, appeared three years after Leopold's posthumous *Round River* (1953), a selection of journal entries and essays-in-progress. Today, a fresh look at what Leopold and Olson had to say about abandoned places reveals something of the kindred spirit between them as well as differences in aim and temperament.

One piece in Leopold's *Round River,* "The Deadening," reads like a prose poem. A farm has been abandoned. The uninhabited house may be brought to life again, but once an old oak is girdled, deprived of water and nutrients, it will die. A long essay on the life and health of the land

THE DOMAIN

might have followed; instead, Leopold reflected briefly on the degrees of resilience among living things—and the short-sightedness of humans, acting in their own "economic" interests, as commonly understood. In another piece, "Natural History: The Forgotten Science," Leopold questioned a prevailing view in academia, that laboratory work is more valuable than fieldwork. A trained forester and a professor of wildlife management, Leopold preferred to consider work in lab and field as complementary efforts in the quest for an ecological understanding of a place—an abandoned field in the Ozarks, for instance. In such a field he would begin by asking questions about the sparseness of the ragweed, the farm's mortgage, the whole watershed, future floods, and prospects for trout and quail. A conventionally trained biologist might find these questions absurd, Leopold admitted; but an ecologist or an amateur naturalist would begin to see the interrelations and move on from there.[37]

Sigurd Olson was an ecologist with a master's degree in that field from the University of Illinois. But as his biographer David Backes pointed out, Olson hated laboratory work. Out in the field, as he studied timber wolves and coyotes, it was the beauty of the whole place that intrigued him—not the quest for data and behavioral patterns. For these and other reasons, Olson never pursued a doctoral degree under Leopold at the University of Wisconsin. Leopold's invitation had tempted him; but Olson, married, with children, had many reasons to pursue other paths.[38] For one thing, he had a fine gift for storytelling. And, with less irony than his friend Leopold, he could show an apparently abandoned place to be endearing, full of life and the amenities that matter.

In Olson's *Singing Wilderness*, it was not only the wind in the pines or the rapids in the stream that made music. In the sounds of a deer mouse nibbling on the floor of a trapper's cabin, Olson heard an "elfin note." That cabin, like others he knew of in the Quetico-Superior lake country of northern Minnesota, was for the most part abandoned to the elements. The trapper needed no luxury, only the essentials of shelter, warmth in winter, a stove for cooking, a table, a bunk. Entering one trapper's cabin, Olson "felt as much a part of the out-of-doors as when sleeping under a ledge." There a red squirrel was not an intruder but a partner. The cabin of rough logs was itself part of the forest, someday to merge back into the moss and duff.[39]

Having quoted Thoreau on simplicity, Olson could have gone on to rail against the comfortable "mouseproof" cabins he had visited, along with the motorboats, highways, and airplanes that made those cabins easily accessible. Instead he focused on why he had come to the woods and sought shelter in a trapper's cabin: to get away from urban living, to find solitude, to do "primitive things in primitive ways." Back in Ely, Minnesota, where he lived, and in other cities where he traveled to speak on wilderness issues, he would need to state his views in more pragmatic, rational terms. And those pressures would intensify. During his term as president of the Wilderness Society, from 1968 to 1971, the increasingly complex issues of conservation would have to be framed in the terms of scientists, lawyers, economists, and government administrators.[40] But in his calm, knowing little book, *The Singing Wilderness,* he could simply tell a good story and dwell on mysterious things like sounds in the night and moss in the chinks between logs of an abandoned cabin.

THE DOMAIN

EIGHT

The Reinhabited Place

In 1965 Congress appropriated nearly eight times more money for aero-space exploration than for urban renewal. The figures, according to the *Washington Post* architecture critic Wolf Von Eckardt, were nearly $5.2 billion for landing an astronaut on the moon and $675 million to rebuild the nation's cities.[1] A strong defender of federal urban renewal programs, Von Eckardt was then urging a reversal of these priorities—for American cities had reached a crisis. That summer of 1965, tensions broke out in the Watts riot, in Los Angeles; and in other cities as well, the problems of poverty, unemployment, crime, racial injustice, inadequate public transportation, and polluted air and water could not be ignored. The frontier was not out in space but in the public realm.

So concluded a fictitious character in the epilogue of Von Eckardt's book *A Place to Live* (1967). It is a long, well-illustrated book, a blend of architectural journalism, history, and firsthand reporting on places seen and admired, mainly in the United States but also around the world, from the new town of Tapiola, outside Helsinki, to the building conversions and renovations of Ghirardelli Square, in San Francisco. Von Eckardt, who lived on a Victorian street near Dupont Circle in Washington, D.C., appreciated fine old buildings and other urban amenities within walking distance of his home. He also applauded the bulldozers then leveling slums to make way for new urban vistas and orderly, modern places for working, shopping, congregating, and relaxing. In his Utopian view of the United States in the year 2003, there is a place for historic preservation and urban renewal, along with clean industrial districts, cities of a million people, clustered communities, greenbelts, "radarmatic speedways" between cities and airports, FBI agents communicating via closed-circuit television, and more. In effect, funds formerly poured into the nation's aerospace program had, by the year 2003, been diverted to make cities the focus of technological and social change in America.[2]

Von Eckardt's *A Place to Live* did not become a classic work on the level of Kevin Lynch's *Image of the City* (1960) or Jane Jacobs's *Death and Life of Great American Cities* (1961). No doubt the timely, topical nature of journalism had something to do with it. Crises subside. Bulldozing whole neighborhoods falls out of favor, and treeless plazas above parking garages become hotter in summer as global warming continues. In any event, *A Place to Live* now reads like an item from a time capsule, revealing some of the optimism that mayors, developers, planners, and urban designers may have shared as they promoted slum clearance and wholesale urban renewal.[3]

Unlike some of these city builders, Von Eckardt underscored the need for options. He recognized that not everyone in his visionary America of the twenty-first century would choose to live in a high-rise building or work in a small greenbelt town. He welcomed Jane Jacobs's fresh perspectives on the rehabilitation of inner-city neighborhoods, but apparently he didn't read all the fine print. That is, he could commend the inclusion of a pub, a Laundromat, and a "Ma and Pa" store in a new housing complex on a formerly bulldozed urban renewal site as "the Jane Jacobs kind of thing."[4] And he was not alone. Others, too, might hear Jacobs, an editor of *Architectural Forum,* speak at a conference on the vitality of old urban neighborhoods such as her own, on Hudson Street in Greenwich Village, in New York, where long-time residents and newcomers live and work in buildings of different ages and conditions, developing friendships, community, and levels of trust. Yet Jacobs's meaning could get lost in the details; people might recall mainly a phrase or two—"eyes on the street," or "leave room for the corner grocery store!"[5]

Meanwhile, some of Jacobs's more penetrating insights had to do with what we might call "reinhabitation." New ideas and fledgling businesses need old, affordable buildings for incubation. People adapt to an old building or place and gradually make it suit their needs and desires through renovation, expansion, conversion, or restoration. Even Jacobs's own house on Hudson Street had reverted to its original single-family use. These kinds of reinhabitations depended on some financial resources—but not massive funding, even in lower-income neighborhoods, as Jacobs learned. They also required some continuity and self-determination on the part of local people. The outcome might be unpredictable, but the essential idea was sound: that as the life of a neighborhood in a great city is intertwined with many human lives, over generations, its physical fabric may be continually renewed, *piecemeal,* in response to local interests and needs, both public and private.

The Death and Life of Great American Cities contains a few intimate glimpses of urban neighborhoods Jacobs knew and appreciated, including Boston's North End and her own block in Greenwich Village. Omitting illustrations, however, she urged readers to study real cities—to forget about how a city should *look* and pay attention to how it *works,* economically and socially. She noticed the "intricate and close-grained diversity of uses" that cities need and listed its four essential conditions: a mix of primary functions, short blocks with frequent streets, a mingling of buildings of different ages and conditions, and a fairly dense population. Urbanity was her main interest, yet she also mentioned the "real countryside" that big cities needed nearby. Then, too, "countryside—from man's point of view—needs big cities," she added, "with all their diverse opportunities and productivity, so human beings can be in a position to appreciate the rest of the natural world."[6]

If the city and the countryside really are mutually sustaining, as Jacobs argued, then how has this come about, beyond the obvious exchanges of

Central Park, New York, looking west from Fifth Avenue

people, food and other raw materials, products, and services? What about those "unaverage" clues that Jacobs liked to examine, apart from statistical studies and abstract measurements? She thought some unaverage details, such as the business hours of a bookstore, might be meaningless to a statistician yet reveal something vital about a place. And so we turn to some unaverage little books that Jacobs and her colleagues might have found intriguing.

***

Before the Second World War, apartment buildings such as the one Alan Dunn depicts in *East of Fifth* (1948) may have seemed fairly impersonal—places of "reinhabitation" for a shifting, transient population. Tenants would have remained for an average of two years or so before moving on. But, as Dunn explains, the wartime housing shortage in New York left apartment dwellers less mobile, and air-raid drills brought together residents who would otherwise have gone their separate ways. Although differences of class, race, and social status remain, Dunn's omniscient narrator detects a new ethos emerging from the war years among the population of this inconspicuous fourteen-story, fifty-two-unit apartment building on a street somewhere east of Central Park. The place has become like a village, where residents and those who attend to their needs indulge in gossip from time to time, speculating on one another's comings and goings, while pursuing their own interests much as they had done before the war.[7]

This apartment building is an older masonry structure, neo-Georgian in detail, dating from the 1920s. In keeping with New York's zoning law of 1916, its upper stories have been set back to allow more sunlight to reach the adjacent buildings and the streets below.[8] As a result, the more spacious upper-floor apartments have terraces, some filled with trees and flowering plants, while smaller, more affordable units look out onto an air shaft or the street. Another consequence of the zoning law, perhaps unintended, is that this "drab" but solid apartment building can plausibly house the range of people that animate Dunn's story—the socially prominent and the obscure, bridge players, poker players, European émigrés, mothers with baby carriages, a boy on a scooter, an assistant minister, a retired general, the hostesses of cocktail parties and dinner parties, the would-be novelist who writes advertising copy at night, the elderly collector of *Life* magazines, the jilted lover, and the man who regulates the flow of steam piped in from a plant on the East River to the tenants' radiators.

Dunn's narrator, apparently a resident in the building he describes, finds humor in the tragic and the commonplace. His tone is a bit distant, bemused, yet gently sympathetic, like that of his colleague E. B. White, who surveyed the city of his own youthful aspirations in *Here Is New York* (1949). Both White and Dunn were regular contributors to the *New Yorker.* For many years White's essays appeared in the magazine's "Talk of the Town" section, while Dunn produced cartoons—on average, nearly one cartoon per issue for forty-eight years, according to another colleague, Brendan Gill.[9]

The cartoons that complement Dunn's running text are hard to resist. You read *East of Fifth* from the middle to a page at random, forward or back, and you marvel at a facial expression, a gesture, or the scene along a sidewalk at night, as shadowy figures, all wearing hats and dark coats, take their animals for a discreet walk at day's end. But to begin at the beginning and follow the story to its close is to move through a vertical village in the city with an urbane guide who sees it whole, through fragments. Some people depart in the morning for Wall Street, by cab. Some depart in the evening for Harlem, probably by bus. We don't learn where the window washers and the men with jackhammers sleep at night. We do know, because the hostess has given explicit instructions, that one African American, a noted poet, will not be directed to the service elevator.

"His drawings can be read as a history of the transformations, both physical and psychological, of much of twentieth-century New York," Gill wrote of Dunn's work.[10] And within the twenty-four hours of a single day, as Indian summer gives way to autumn, Dunn shows us the passage of time in urban nature—which resembles rural nature yet remains apart. The opening scene in *East of Fifth,* a luxuriant garden, might be anywhere; it turns out to be on a terrace thirteen floors above the street.

In the city, as in the country, summers can be debilitating with heat and humidity. But cooler autumn is *the* season, the spring of New York life, when people are inclined to congregate once again, grateful for indoor warmth and social life in "the cold metropolis of the north."[11]

Farther north, in upstate New York and New England, were villages, camps, resort hotels, cottages, and renovated farmhouses where Dunn's apartment dwellers and their neighbors might spend a weekend or more in summer. Guidebooks, postcards, memoirs, and the biographies of summer or seasonal visitors have made some of these places familiar. They have a charm that makes visitors dream of staying on indefinitely. Meanwhile natives notice changes about the place—an unaccustomed neatness, a dirt road newly paved, a new building, a house torn down or converted to a new use. Some people may regret changes that others hail as progress. A remote village may become too fashionable, its taxes too high, for natives to remain. With new prosperity, what was once the place's reason for being can disappear.

But that is not precisely what happened to Manchester, Vermont, as Margaret Hard explains in *A Memory of Vermont: Our Life in the Johnny Appleseed Bookshop* (1967). A village of taverns and inns since the eighteenth century, Manchester also attracted some industry—sawmills, gristmills, carding mills, and a tannery. For a while local farmers raised sheep. Lying in a valley, the village became a crossing for stage routes, both north-south and east-west. By 1850 the main business of the village was tourism—that of a summer resort.[12]

Writing an informal guide to Vermont in the mid-1930s, Margaret Hard and her husband, Walter, described Manchester as a visitor might see it for the first time: the tree-lined main street with elegant historic buildings, framed by mountains—the northernmost Taconics on the west, the Green Mountains to the east. "Of course it loses the lovely tranquillity of smaller villages by being a summer resort," Margaret noted, "yet much that is fine has come to it through that very fact."[13]

In *A Memory of Vermont* Margaret Hard tells two anecdotes, among others, that begin to explain why selling books in Manchester could be much more than a business venture for her and Walter and their two children, Ruth and Walter Jr. One wet day in late September 1930, Ruth was tending the bookshop in the family's orchard, off the main street of the village. Caught in the rain, a man dashed in for shelter; and before long Ruth was listening to him read aloud from a book he had found on a shelf. His name was Ray Stannard Baker; the book was his own *Adventures in Contentment,* about the joys of country life and the pleasures of reading, written under the pen name David Grayson.[14] A few years later, in October, when the bookshop was housed in a drugstore's annex, Sinclair Lewis came in from the rain. And something about the place and the well-chosen titles intrigued him. Margaret Hard, then minding the shop, read to him from her husband's volumes of poetry, including *Mountain Township* (1933). Lewis was reminded of Edgar Lee Masters—"without the sting and bite." When he wondered about the lack of bitterness in Walter Hard's poetry, Margaret alluded to the gentle influence of a whole countryside "bent on embracing one." And she gathered an impression of Sinclair Lewis—a shy, boyish person, talking of wistfulness and loneliness. When the rain let up he said a few kind words, then disappeared.[15]

The shy author of *Main Street* and *Babbitt* found the Hards' bookshop in the drugstore annex charming, an "idea-in-a-cubbyhole." And that idea developed without any elaborate plan or strategy. It was based on one family's love of books, along with an interest in people, and a willingness to risk time, energy, and life savings on a business that could grow slowly, moving from one unlikely place to another. Ruth Hard had first broached the idea in the summer of 1929, after her freshman year in college, but the germ of the idea could be traced to a shelf in her grandfather Hard's drugstore in Manchester.

In the 1890s Walter Hard's father had cleared a shelf in his drugstore for books to sell—and also to read for his own pleasure. Years later, while in college, Walter inherited the drugstore business and felt obliged to forgo a career in journalism. He made room in the store for a table of books and a bench where summer visitors gathered. But evidently Walter did not think an independent bookstore could survive in Manchester.

With the willing labor and enthusiasm of the next generation, the

Johnny Appleseed Bookshop opened on July 1, 1930, in the only purpose-built structure it ever had: a two-room wooden structure with a stone fireplace, sheltered by the largest apple tree in the Hard family's orchard. Furnished with books, tables, comfortable chairs, reading lamps, and vases of wildflowers, the place seemed more like a home than a shop. In another northern New England village, under different management, this bookshop might not have survived the Great Depression. But Manchester was an unaverage summer resort, a gathering place for the Southern Vermont Artists, the Poetry Society of Southern Vermont, the publishers Alfred Harcourt, John Farrar, the Doubledays, and others, some of them willing to send books on consignment to the little shop beneath the apple tree. Word of the place got around. In *Publishers Weekly* Ruth outlined the region's attractions and her ambitions for the bookshop—including the children's story hour and an in-house lending library.[16]

In the mid-1930s, while Ruth was working elsewhere, the Hards moved the Johnny Appleseed Bookshop closer to Walter's business—the annex to the drugstore, formerly an inn. Adapting the old structure was a challenge; lines were not true, walls bulged, windows did not match. The odd space was like a mirror of Walter Hard himself: a man who loved to write, still wearing a white coat and selling aspirin and toothbrushes, while his volumes of poetry were drawing national recognition and speaking engagements accumulated. The Hards did make some adaptations. In 1935, while Walter Jr. was still in college, they sold the drugstore business but maintained the Johnny Appleseed Bookshop in the drugstore annex—a rented space—until 1949.

The bookshop's third venue was a historic landmark. Built as a bank in 1832, the two-story brick structure was later occupied by the fledgling sporting goods company of C. F. Orvis—who rented out part of the main floor to the post office. In 1949 the Hards bought the building and rented out office space upstairs. On the main floor were walls of books, etchings, paintings, and the photographs of a New York photographer whose friendship with the Hards went back many years; she had once converted the Hards' former bookshop under the apple tree into a summer studio. And other items were familiar from the earlier venues—tables, chairs, a children's corner, a fireplace. The bookshop's hours were 9 AM to 10 PM, June to October, and Christmas holidays; 9 AM to 6 PM in winter. The place became an informal information bureau and a sort of "non-ecclesiastical parish," where people felt welcome to drop in and share some great joy, grief, or wonder.[17]

And Margaret Hard encouraged that openness. Her stories of people who turned up in and around Manchester—famous and unknown, natives and newcomers—reveal her warm interest in people, whatever their origins. Robert Frost, Carl Sandburg, Dorothy Canfield Fisher, Lewis Gannett, the *New Yorker* founder-editor, Harold Ross, and his colleague Alexander Woollcott were all from somewhere else, as she was. Although born in Manchester, while her parents were summering there, Margaret had roots in Philadelphia and New York; whereas her husband had five generations of Vermonters behind him.

That contrast is sharply drawn in Walter Hard's poem "A Newcomer." There, a woman dismisses the local doctor's opinion on fencing in the burial ground with the remark, "Land sakes, he ain't lived here more'n thirty years."[18] Such attitudes among her neighbors may have troubled Margaret, for one day she openly regretted her lack of a Vermont background. Her son, about twelve years old at the time, reassured her: "Just think of all the Vermont *foreground* you're getting."[19] That foreground could not be inherited; it was like the home Margaret referred to when, long past the age of retirement, in 1965, she and Walter sold the Johnny Appleseed Bookshop. By "home," she was referring not only to the historic house they had restored and settled in but the extended landscape for miles around, a "singing greenness" of hills and mountains, remembered in winter, in a poem of her own.[20]

❊ ❊ ❊

When Lewis Gannett bought the old Reed place in West Cornwall, Connecticut, in 1924, he was not aware of his own roots in the area. He was simply giving in to a desire that many city people feel on a visit with friends in the country—to acquire their own quiet place nearby and seek the "best of both worlds," city and country. At midcentury, Gannett and his family still loved the city, however hectic the pace. Weekends spent gardening, chopping wood, and scything a few acres were a form of recuperation. And it did not disturb Gannett, a journalist, to realize that, after twenty-five years, the old Reed place was not yet known as the Gannett place. He and his family were still newcomers—a recognition that runs as one long strand throughout his memoir, *Cream Hill* (1949).[21]

Another strand is the sense of belonging. Some time after Gannett had bought the old Reed place on Cream Hill Road, in West Cornwall, he learned that one of his forebears, the clergyman Ezra Stiles, had owned a couple of farms nearby. Reading Stiles's diary of the 1750s and '60s, Gannett came across a map that his great-great-grandfather had drawn of the area. Much had changed, of course. West Cornwall's population had risen steadily and peaked in 1850. As people left the land, trees reclaimed the fields, houses fell into cellar holes, stone walls tumbled, and some roads disappeared. Wandering among these traces of old settlements, Gannett never found evidence of a ruin Stiles had mentioned, but he did recognize plants that had escaped from old gardens. Newcomers had brought some of them from Europe—useful herbs and fruits, but also crab grass, Queen Anne's lace, mullein, chicory, yellow rocket, and Bouncing Bet (saponaria). After centuries of spreading through fields and along the roadsides, these immigrants seemed about as wild as the real natives—goldenrod and aster, white pine, oak, maple, birch. It was an ever-changing, accommodating land.

The illustrations in *Cream Hill*—lithographs by Gannett's second wife, Ruth—give the impression of a coherent, orderly world with the innocence of Norman Rockwell's small towns and the stylized charm of a landscape by Grandma Moses. Children file into the board-and-batten schoolhouse, girls through one door, boys through another, as in a dream. More realistic are the images of acorn squash and skunk cabbage—two of many plants that Gannett describes in his chapters on gardening, month by month. And yet *Cream Hill* is more than a garden book to read by the fire in winter.

A staff writer for the *Nation* when he bought the old Reed place, Gannett moved on in 1928 to the New York *Herald-Tribune*, where he wrote a daily column, mainly on books, for twenty-six years. In 1944 he was a war correspondent in Europe, traveling with the Ninth Army. He had covered the Paris Peace Conference after the First World War, and he served as director and vice president of the NAACP. It is not surprising, then, to find a wide range of topics in *Cream Hill,* from race relations and religious diversity since colonial times, to civic responsibility in a mobile society. Then, too, a counterpart to the Cream Hill garden was the Gannetts' roof garden in the city. There, before the zipper makers moved in, aromas from the cigar factory on the floor below helped to keep away insect pests.[22]

Gannett was an engaging, elegant writer. Parts of *Cream Hill* had previously appeared in the *New Yorker* and *Harper's Bazaar.* He was also self-critical. "We are developing in America a large class of folk who pay taxes in both city and country but give primary allegiance to the city," he wrote. "Many of us love the country precisely because we are not really a part of it." And he wondered if his rural retreat was a form of escapism, while ward bosses controlled the city's affairs and rural towns were run by a few well-meaning selectmen and board members from a dwindling pool of year-round residents. West Cornwall was not really a summer colony. Rising property values had not yet driven working farmers off the land, and the old town-meeting form of government still operated— effectively, if not entirely democratically, Gannett observed. He wrote the editor of a Hartford newspaper, alerting him about West Cornwall's deteriorating covered bridge—which was promptly examined for structural weaknesses and rebuilt. But Gannett's notion of civic responsibility was more demanding than that. "I no longer quite belong either in the country or the city," he confessed. "I accept no deep responsibility anywhere. And there are dangerously many like me in the United States."[23]

Later, in the 1950s and '60s, a related phenomenon would draw more attention among planners and urban designers—the departure of middle-class people from the city, or "white flight." As of 1949, however, the Gannetts were still committed to their city flat and roof garden, where tomatoes, beans, chives, parsley, petunias, and zinnias flourished in season. Some Sunday nights, returning from West Cornwall, they brought back a more varied range of produce to the elevator man. Like most gardeners, they enjoyed passing on something of their harvest. What they probably could not pass on was the family home—in the city or in the country.

It was not only that Gannett's children had jobs elsewhere and families of their own. The American pattern was to move on, or so it seemed: to tear down, build on a clean slate, rebuild, or rearrange what others had left behind. The home of Gannett's father in downtown Boston was gone; even the street, Bumstead Place, was gone, covered by a large building. A garage stood on the place where Gannett was born, in Rochester, New York. Uphill from the Gannetts in West Cornwall, friends from New York—the writers and editors Carl and Irita Van Doren—lived in the Wickwire place. In fact, it was a visit to the Van Dorens back in 1924 that had enticed the Gannetts to acquire the old Reed place. But in the long run they were all passing through, perhaps leaving something of value behind.

Pastures, tilled fields, woodlots, forests, shade trees and specimen trees, all appear in Ruth Gannett's illustrations for *Cream Hill,* along with freight trains, white picket fences, a covered bridge, a burying ground, and wooden frame houses of various sizes and ages, some with front porches, all set fairly close to the street. Her image of the town is an appealing fantasy—an American town, pre–World War I, in miniature. From diaries and town histories, Lewis Gannett reconstructs a more realistic old West Cornwall. His great-great grandfather Stiles (who once served as president of Yale) and other white settlers of northwestern Connecticut come to be known by what they planted, ate, drank, worried about, and celebrated. Some protested courtships across ethnic lines, but without success; Gannett tells about the romance and marriage of the deacon's daughter, Harriet Gold, and Elias Boudinot, a man of Cherokee origins, who later founded the first American Indian newspaper in New Echota, Georgia.[24]

With a trace of nostalgia, Gannett imagines that his own fondness for forests may be linked to an atavistic sense of "at-homeness" there. And yet his lines between past and present, city and country, are clearly drawn. He and his wife are nonnative New Yorkers who, like many of their friends, find a workable pattern in their hybrid form of urban and rural life. They need the city for a livelihood. They seek the country as a respite—a link with Mother Earth, as Gannett put it, where a modern-day Antaeus could touch down at intervals and regain his strength.

Much of what Gannett had to say in *Cream Hill* is still resonant. Today, on any weekend, people make the same sort of migration from an urban area and back again, mainly by car. But the Gannetts and the Van Dorens also took part in a more intricate process still under way in our time, a shifting of population and a mingling of land uses, such that categories like "urban," "rural," "industrialized," "developed," and "wild" become merely relative terms.

Theirs was an earlier phase of the process, beginning around the 1920s, when many people's ties to a densely built city were still strong. As those ties weakened for whatever reason—depression, war, postwar relocation of jobs, suburban sprawl, new information technologies, personal pref-erence—some people moved into once-remote rural areas, built a house, and settled there. Others found an old place to fix up and reinhabit. Down the road would be a church or two, a service club, the volunteer firemen's garage, and a liars' bench in front of the general store. Some newcomers made their way into town government and onto boards of planning, zoning, education, and conservation. Some started new busi-nesses and maybe wondered if they would ever belong. Meanwhile, peo-ple with roots in the area would try to keep the old farm going. If they sold some land, they might keep up the haying and sugaring, and mind the farm stand on weekends. Harvest festivals and craft fairs would help to keep some skills and customs alive—but for how long?

❊ ❊ ❊

Henry Beston and Elizabeth Coatsworth acquired an old farm near the coast of Maine, on East Neck in Nobleboro, and took part in a way of life that was gradually passing. It was the early 1930s, not quite two years after they were married. That part of Maine, about midway between the Kennebec River and Penobscot Bay, was still mainly agricultural. Some traditions had died out—house-raisings, husking bees—as Coatsworth noted in *Country Neighborhood* (1944). But people still came together at town meeting, the grange, the church, the county fair. Country auctions were as much a form of entertainment as a sale of usable old things and treasures. Some families were largely self-sufficient, but mowing, haying, harvesting, canning, "housing up" for winter, and reopening the summer kitchen in spring might require help from a neighbor or two.[25]

Many of those kindly, knowing neighbors appear in both Coatsworth's and Beston's writings. If husband and wife happened to describe the same event, some details would differ. Each writer's voice remained distinct—like the two layers of clouds that Coatsworth mentioned in *Maine Ways* (1947), writing of the much-prized, somewhat unreliable weathervane that came with the deed of their farm.

Made of tin, the weathervane represented a galloping horse and rider, complete with whip, reins, and jockey cap. "Johnny-Ride-the-Sky," Coatsworth named it. In that sky were often two layers of clouds, one moving inland from the sea, the other traveling in the opposite direction, from the land. As the two streams of air collided, strange and delightful cloud formations would appear. Meanwhile, Johnny-Ride-the-Sky detected only the currents at his own level.[26]

For Beston, the farm in Maine was a place where writing in solitude could be balanced with work in the barn, out in the fields, and in the garden. In *Northern Farm* (1949) he wrote about all these places without forgetting about the city, the nearest highway (U.S. Route 1), and developments in science, technology, and foreign affairs—including war and violence. Reflections on these aspects of modern life often intruded on the tranquil scene. But Beston's main focus was country life, on land, by the water, in the sky, and in some timeless realm of memory, where innovation and change occur slowly, almost imperceptibly, like ice breaking up on the pond in late winter.

Moving through the seasons and drawing from isolated incidents and reflections, Beston conveys textures and moods, rather than a single story. Readers who know and love his earlier work of natural history, *The Outermost House* (1928), may miss the drama of a storm at sea or the sustained reflections of a single day's walk. Those who have read his river study *The St. Lawrence* (1942) will find here much less history, as commonly understood. *Northern Farm* has more to do with memory—which is less dependent on fact and linear time. This memory, filtered through one writer's mind, is collective as well as personal. What matters is the memory of a place, and of people in that place, over many generations. Dates are rarely mentioned. Time is cyclical, marked by daily and seasonal changes. It is as if Beston's rural life had no beginning and no foreseeable end, as if it were one with the life of all ancient rural people, who had taken up the same plow handles and made the same furrows. "Linked with this past," Beston writes, "is all the human past of man as a part of Nature, of one living by the sun and the moon, and waiting for the clearing in the west."[27]

In *Northern Farm* the moon in winter casts shadows as if it were the phantom of a summer day. Beston studies the sky and knows the Big Dipper by its medieval name, "The Plough." In late summer, as a young couple complete the haying of Beston's field, backlighting from the afternoon sun transforms their two little blond-haired daughters into tiny maenads, dancing on the load. On a morning in spring, around March 15, the sun's path has moved far enough north to come around to the kitchen ell and flood the east-facing kitchen windows with light— light that had been denied the kitchen during the coldest months of the year. It is a joyous moment, a flooding of light that, in another age, would be met with trumpets, pipes, and timbrels.

The memory of a preindustrial way of life, dependent on the land and light from the sky, is kept alive by the entire farm, including a small cemetery. "When we bought the house we felt that we should accept the responsibility of looking after the cemetery," Beston once told a writer for *Yankee* magazine, "since we do owe something to the people who developed this land and built us an honest house."[28] That house is the physical and emotional center of *Northern Farm,* yet Beston describes it merely in passing, as a well-built cape, more than a century old, with additions. Thoreau MacDonald's illustrations show only its essential form and a few details. Often the artist depicts the house as merely a small form, in light or shadow, set in a larger landscape of low wooded hills, a pond, sloping ground, expressive skies. And that seems exactly right. Although *Northern Farm* contains no explanation of how Beston and his wife came to live there, Coatsworth recalls that it was the *landscape* that had appealed to him from the beginning. The house, somewhat dilapidated, he first saw only from a distance.[29]

In *Country Neighborhood* (1944) Coatsworth writes of *her* first acquaintance with the farm. She lingers over details of living for a while in a cove of the nearby pond. Friends had lent the Bestons their houseboat. There were frequent trips to a neighboring farm for fresh milk, eggs, and well water. There was a loon, seen long before it was heard. Tall pines and hemlocks grew by the water's edge. Bluets grew in a pasture and thrushes sang in the woods. Later, in *Maine Ways* (1947), Coatsworth dwelled on a perception of land that was not yet widely shared in America—that the deed to the farm could hardly grant them possession of the granite, wild grasses, forest trees, apple trees, songbirds, porcupines, and deer. She and her husband could own the house and barn and a few other things, but the farm, in some form or other, would outlive its owners and all humankind. Meanwhile she was grateful. In her poem "The Farm," she mentions treasures freely offered by nature as well as the cleared fields, the small, south-facing house, the lilacs, and other gifts that previous inhabitants had left behind.[30]

Beston, too, is conscious of those who have left something of themselves in the place. "An old farm is always more than the people under its roof," Beston writes in *Northern Farm*. "It is the past as well as the present, and vanished generations have built themselves into it as well as left their footsteps in the worn woodwork of the stair." Like Coatsworth, he rejects the idea of absolute ownership of the earth. Wise use of it—yes. But humans are the servants as well as the masters of their fields. The earth is not a commodity; farming is not a merely utilitarian activity. The ancients were wise, recognizing a quality of divinity in the earth, mother of life. They knew "that the shadow of any man is but for a time cast upon the grass of any field."[31]

Passages such as these, perhaps written no more swiftly than one sentence in a morning (as Coatsworth tells us), appear among notes on the humble rounds of a country year. In *Northern Farm* Beston gathers them all, along with reflections on his life in Maine and some dark thoughts about American life at midcentury, and makes of them a work of whole-ness and great beauty.

Elsewhere we learn that, in the 1930s, the Bestons spent winters back in Hingham, Massachusetts, where family members lived; and that they too felt the impact of the Great Depression, materially and spiritually.[32] In *Northern Farm* Beston dwells instead on little details and grand universals that together transcend the successes and failures of American life, circa 1949. He writes of the fine clam chowder that a neighbor made for the Grange dinner, the cowslips from Elizabeth's wild garden, the autumn changeover from the pond water system to cistern and spring water, Arcturus above the ridge in the winter sky, alewives running up-stream from bay to pond, and tracks of fox and varying hare in the snow. He ponders the increasing mechanization of modern life and worries about a people alienated from nature—and from one another. They need community. And so he urges a return to beginnings—to responsibilities of the family and the village, and to "our universal and neglected duty to the earth."[33]

Coatsworth understood the spirit behind these words. "Henry will not compromise," she once explained; "more foolish or more wise, he demands a harmony of elements." She herself had made some accom-modations in an imperfect world, where the view from the road included gas tanks and burning waste dumps as well as attractive little towns by the bay. She had accepted amusement parks along with the sunset-colored breasts of soaring seabirds. Evidently she was more accessible to her daughters, Meg and Kate—who often figure in her poetry and prose, and who might at any moment show her something marvelous. She wondered if these differences between her and Henry had to do with gender—simply being a woman. "I say that almost everywhere there is beauty enough to fill a person's life if one would only be sensitive to it," she wrote. "But Henry says No: that broken beauty is only a torment, that one must have a whole beauty with man living in relation to it to have a rich civilization and art."[34]

***

It is a long way from Wolf Von Eckardt's Washington, D.C., in 1967 to Henry Beston's Nobleboro, Maine, in 1949. The Washington-to-Boston corridor gives way to two-lane highways and back roads. We move from a Utopian vision set in the future to a poetic vision of the present, linked with the ancient past. We give up linear time for cyclical time. The journey is punctuated by real places, yet something has been missing—the land between city and country, or suburbia.

Such an indeterminate place can be difficult to see clearly, after decades of commentary and waves of efforts to make it more urban, more rural, or more sustainable as resources become scarcer and global warming continues.[35] Some writers on gardening and natural history, living in suburbia or some place in the process of *becoming* suburbia, have explored their half-wild surroundings and reported on things of beauty and wonder we might otherwise miss. And then there is that rare person, a native with deep roots in a rural area who may bring something old back to life yet also welcome change—even suburban development. As George Woodbury shows, in *John Goffe's Mill* (1948) and *John Goffe's Legacy* (1955), it may not be necessary, or even desirable, to preserve every historic detail of a place. In fact, a blend of the old and the new may be more satisfying.

Woodbury, a young anthropologist, had just completed a long, inconclusive report on ancient human remains when he found himself out of a job and in poor health. It was the mid-1930s. Since he and his wife, Connie, could not live on what she earned at Harvard's Peabody Museum, they left Cambridge for Woodbury's hometown of Bedford, New Hampshire, where they settled into a large, drafty old house that his family had been renting out until recently. When the 1938 hurricane swept through New England, the destruction created a demand for rebuilding—and lumber. To support his growing family, Woodbury then decided to restore and operate the old Goffe mill, on Bowman's Brook, which had been in his family for seven generations, since 1744. Rebuilt in 1845, the mill had kept going until 1909, when its dam finally gave way to the force of high water in spring.[36]

For many years Goffe's Mill had seemed obsolete—even in 1909, when

Woodbury was a boy. The industrial revolution had reached nearby Manchester, on the Merrimack River, about the time of the Civil War. When Goffe's milldam collapsed, industries like the Amoskeag mills in Manchester were operated on a vast scale, by power much greater than that provided for only half a year, spring and fall, from a brook's high water. Then, too, Woodbury recalled the impact of innovations like town water, electricity, gas buggies, and a rare biplane. "We were caught up in the heady excitement of the new and the sensational," he wrote. Not that he had since lost interest in the new; but his work in anthropology and archaeology had taken him far enough from home to get some perspective on mechanical improvements. Labor-saving devices did not *save* labor; they changed its character. People still worked long hours, less arduously. Instead of making what they needed, they worked for hire and bought what they needed. It was a legacy of the industrial revolution: "buy, throw it away, buy a new model." Now Woodbury would return to an earlier maxim: "Make it yourself, fix it up, make it do."[37]

To reconstruct a dam fourteen feet high across a brook seventy feet wide, using original and new materials—granite, wood, poured concrete, iron for pipes and gratings—Woodbury engaged a skilled mason, a barn framer, and a crew. The mill's wooden waterwheel had been replaced by an iron turbine in 1845, and he would need more replacements. Across the Merrimack, in old machine shops in Manchester, he found elderly skilled craftsmen who took an interest in his mechanical problems. With their help and from old books, Woodbury rebuilt and expanded the mill, where in time he produced sawn timber, stoneground flour, wooden rocking horses, wooden stools, and other items. And it occurred to him, as he studied the mill building in progress, that everything about it was obsolete—tools, methods of construction, the skilled workmen, even himself.

While his hands were occupied, Woodbury had time to reflect. The stream, powering the mill while flowing in its own time, was indifferent to him; yet he felt a responsibility toward it. He was humbled, yet exhilarated, working with this primordial force. Was he the master, he wondered, or the servant?

Working among old lathes, millstones, and a modern sawmill, Woodbury was happy to pause and give visitors a tour. The mill was not a period restoration. It was a business, and he could work at his own pace. Connie would bring the children to swim in the millpond. Or the pond would be calm, stirred only by a kingfisher or a muskrat. The place was idyllic. There were temptations to daydream and also opportunities to take on profitable, repetitive work. But Woodbury would not turn his mill into a factory. Machines were not a problem; what mattered was how one used them—with alertness, or mindlessly.

As the Depression wore on, Woodbury felt as pinched as the farmers who came to him for small jobs and repairs. They made various arrangements—cash payment, toll (a portion of the grist to be milled), barter, goodwill. Woodbury did custom work and sold things ready-made, wholesale and retail. The whole operation seemed to be a kind of "industrial counterrevolution," supported by business practices of the past, the present, and perhaps the future.[38] Then war and its aftermath brought changes. After a century of decline, Bedford's population grew. New building crowded out farming, the old way of life. And the Woodburys hired carpenters to remodel a few old tenant-farmers' cottages that young couples from the city were happy to rent.

One young carpenter bought part of the Woodburys' woodlot to build his own house there, on weekends. When winter was near and the house was not yet habitable, the rest of the crew came to help out on a holiday. In a day the house was closed in from the elements. That became a pattern: the whole crew helped one carpenter at a time, weekends and holidays. The woodlot became a cluster of houses and, in time, Bedford formed part of the suburban fringe around Manchester.

John Goffe's Legacy ends with a few verses from Ecclesiastes, about generations passing away: "but the earth abideth for ever."[39] Today Goffe's Mill, converted to offices, forms part of the Wayfarer Conference Center and Quality Inn. The brook still flows over the dam, out to the Merrimack River—through a culvert—and down to the sea.

NINE

The Lost Place

Changing, vanishing, passing, disappearing: are there any less painful words to describe a place about to be lost? And what of that place when the earth itself was young, its land and waters not yet configured as they are today? In *The Everglades: River of Grass* (1947) Marjory Stoneman Douglas brings together these two time frames—human history and vast stretches of geological time. From one ice age to another, through flood and fire, in tales of one drainage scheme after another, her history flows like a river. Some of her figures were villains and some, visionaries, now remembered for a railroad, a botanical garden, a hotel in Palm Beach, or the plan of Coral Gables.

Much less understood in those days was the delicate balance of natural processes in that region of southern Florida. For many years the Everglades were vaguely assumed to be a swamp and not, as Douglas realized, an infinitely slow-moving river. By 1947—the year a portion of that region was set aside as Everglades National Park—Douglas held out some hope. If people could learn from past errors, overcome greed, and work together, the Everglades might not be "utterly lost."[1]

It was not until the late 1960s—in her late seventies—that Douglas became an environmental activist and founder of the Friends of the Everglades. In the 1940s she was simply trying to understand the Everglades as a place, some kind of river, emerging from changes over millions of years. "The course along which for a little way one proceeds, the changing life, the varying light, must somehow be fixed in a moment clearly," Douglas wrote, "from which one may look before and after and try to comprehend wholeness."[2]

Not all the authors considered here had quite that aim—to grasp the whole of a place lost in time or in the process of disappearing. Loren Eiseley, prowling about his own past as if with a flashlight in the dark, briefly recalled a few places where life went on almost unnoticed before something happened to cut it off abruptly—before the elevated railway in Philadelphia was dismantled, for instance. Other authors dwelled longer on a place known in their childhood or later in life, a place that had always seemed to be fixed, permanent, perhaps a bit confining, but secure.

Some authors were satisfied to have moved on. They grew up in small towns with trees arching over the streets, proper sidewalks, bandstands on the common, trolleys that ran to the next town, and trains that led to the nearest city—amenities that planners try to include in new towns today. Yet planners may ignore other things once remembered with affection, the vacant lots and open fields, the margins of a town or a streambed, and little in-between places, where older and newer buildings happen to meet. Children often take those places for granted. But if they find them gone years later, covered by buildings or freeways or the riprap that lines a flood-control channel, they may regret the loss of a whole world of wonder and discovery, a paradise.

The writings considered here—memoirs, essays, some travel writing—resist neat categories and yet tend toward one of two ways of depicting a lost place. The first seems more objective. Withholding judgment, the writer recalls people, events, and things, colored by some prevailing mood or aura. In reading, we can become immersed in the dense texture of that place, for it has been brought back to life more or less whole. Other writers tend to be partial, recalling some facet or quality of a place now lost. They may be more openly critical than their neighbors. "That's progress," someone remarks, as trees are felled and the bulldozers move in. "Where there's muck, there's money," chuckles another, as the city's air and water remain polluted. But these writers are moved by other voices, other values. And, with a fine economy, some can make the merest fragment of a place stand for the whole.

✳ ✳ ✳

On a return visit to Salisbury, Connecticut, in 1952, one unfamiliar item that Christopher Rand noticed in the landscape was a movable electric fence. A flimsy thing, it signified that a way of life was changing. Within its confines, dairy cows would graze in some area of a grassy field that had already been mowed once and might yield two more crops of hay before the year's end. By pulling up stakes and moving the fence from time to time, the farmer could keep the field from being overgrazed. No longer would cows have to be driven out every morning to some distant pasture, where the land was too poor to cultivate, then be driven back to the barn in the evening. Instead, cows would be kept closer to the farmyard, where their diets and their movements could be carefully monitored. "The whole idea now," Rand's brother Jake explained, "is to get the most milk per acre."[3]

A lot had changed in that northwestern corner of Connecticut since the 1920s and early 1930s. As a young boy and later, in his teens, Rand had spent summers and weekends there, working on his father's farm alongside the hired hands—men who worked mainly in the cow barn or with teams of horses. Back then, men took pride in scything the edges of fields, cutting around rocks and trees, where the mowing machines couldn't reach. Rand remembered, too, what it took to get the hay in the barn in those days, working three teams of horses: two or three men back in the loft, two or three men in the field, three teamsters, three wagons, sometimes a half-hour journey between loft and field. A couple of men with a truck and a wagon did the work more efficiently now—in 1952.

Rand's essay on farming in Salisbury, and others on the town, the woods, the county fair, the lake fish, and other aspects of the place, were

THE DOMAIN

all published in the *New Yorker* from 1952 to 1966, then collected in Rand's book *The Changing Landscape* (1968). Read together, the essays reveal changes from the town's early-eighteenth-century beginnings, through its nineteenth-century industrial development (with ironworks that preceded those of Pittsburgh and Gary), to the period between two world wars and the mid-twentieth century.

Some advances in agriculture struck Rand as revolutionary in 1952. Farmers have access to more knowledge, he noticed. They have more sophisticated machines; there is less hand labor. Like technicians and white-collar workers in town, farmers take an occasional vacation. But there is more paperwork, more worry over costs, production figures, and mortgages. "Half the pleasure has gone out of farming," Rand's brother admits. Meanwhile, Rand seems to withhold judgment.

But he looks intently, with the freshness of one who has been away a long time and with the sharp eye of one who has worked the land he sees. The landscape used to appear as a neat patchwork of greens and yellows: oats, corn, clover, timothy, each growing in separate fields. Now, in 1952, there was less variety, often just a wide sweep of mixed grasses. Some stone walls had been dismantled or buried for the convenience of machines for planting and harvesting. Cows used to graze in a *permanent* pasture. After giving birth, a cow was sometimes allowed to run wild with her calf in a distant woodland for a while. Barns used to have high gambrel roofs, and it took skill to fill those great lofts with hay. Now lower, modern barns were built so that a man could drive in with a truck and let heavy bales roll off, to be stored in ground-level sheds. Apples used to keep well, stored in cellars with dirt floors. Trees in the orchards were pruned, but rarely sprayed; there were fewer blights back then—or so Rand recalled. Now, in 1952, the unpruned, unsprayed trees, full of woodpecker holes, had masses of new growth shooting straight up from old branches. More country roads were paved now, but when you walked on them, the asphalt would overwhelm the smells of woods and fields.

In a brief note to *The Changing Landscape,* Rand admitted that, in 1952, he had found many of these changes disturbing. By 1966 he was more tolerant. "I had come to see change itself as an enduring, reliable quality in the town," he wrote. By then, dairy farming in northwestern Connecticut was waning. The old farms were not being passed on to sons and daughters—who often had jobs and houses in a city or a suburb. People from away, with other sources of income, were buying those farms and keeping up the rural character of the place, living there intermittently or year-round, sometimes as "hobby" farmers. As urban sprawl moved up from New York and the Connecticut coast and along the Hudson and the Housatonic rivers, Salisbury, with its new powers of zoning, was holding the metropolis at bay. Or rather, Salisbury was becoming a special part of it—"a sanctuary for those megalopolitans who needn't embrace the grime and clatter themselves."[4]

By 1964 Salisbury was no longer a fairly self-contained place of self-reliant farmers. Nor was it merely a rural enclave for people of independent means, or for their sons, attending the local boarding schools. Salisbury's lakes, regularly stocked with sockeye salmon (from the Pacific Northwest) and brown and rainbow trout, attracted weekend fishermen from Bridgeport and Waterbury. Its woods, affected by gypsy moth, would not be heavily sprayed; the town's first selectman quoted Rachel Carson and others when he was questioned at town meeting. Salisbury's connection to Boston by passenger rail ceased in 1927, but the tracks remained—a quiet place for winter walks—until they were pulled up in 1967. By then, most people got around by car.

The Changing Landscape is more than an affectionate backward glance and not quite an elegy. Rand holds up no ideal pattern for zoning, conservation, or other creative measures for land use in rural towns. He simply studies one small corner of a southern New England state and tries to see the land and the people clearly, through a couple of centuries at most, mainly since the 1920s. He notices an increasing tameness in the life around him—in cows, in fish, in people everywhere, grown "more abstract and mechanical." He weighs certain losses and gains as new labor-saving, money-saving, time-saving devices come into being. And, despite traces of wistfulness, he seems reconciled to the changed character of a place he once knew. What is lost—although he doesn't quite identify it as such—is *time,* slow time. It was the kind of time that elapsed during the long journey up into the hills to Judge and Mrs. Warner's camp on Upper Riga Lake, getting there on foot, by horse-drawn carriage or horse-drawn sleigh. Or the time of one remembered afternoon in the barn, when a competent old teamster declined the offer of a plug of tobacco, explaining the reasons why, slowly, between forkfuls of hay that he was carefully storing in the loft, beneath the beams.

Slow time—time needed to cut, saw, and haul timber with simple tools and vehicles—may have left smaller scars on the landscape than loggers with modern equipment and tight schedules leave today. Certainly, slow time enhanced young Christopher Rand's anticipation of a trip to Upper Riga Lake in summer or winter, an event that was "almost unbearably exciting." But the mature Rand expressed no regret for loss of that kind of time. He left a great deal unsaid, between the lines.

❊ ❊ ❊

Seated at breakfast, looking out through a wall of glass, Bernardine Kielty Scherman and her husband, Harry, used to see the East River and, often, feel morning sunlight pouring down. Since 1938 they had lived in that apartment building, in the vicinity of Fifty-seventh Street and Second Avenue, several stories up, with a splendid view of towers—the Chrysler, the Empire State, sometimes even the towers and bridges of downtown. By 1964, taller, plainer buildings had risen, blocking out their views and the morning sun. Some of the "old enchantment" was gone, but Scherman's New York was not really lost. She had lived there half a century, since 1913, and absorbed the city's changes gradually. New York was home. Her hometown was something else, as depicted in her memoir *Girl from Fitchburg* (1964).[5]

Fitchburg, Massachusetts, a mill town some fifty miles northwest of Boston, had once seemed permanent, as if it would go on as it always had, forever. Growing up there in the 1890s and 1900s, an only child with friends from all over town, Scherman had felt "free as the wind," yet disciplined, grounded by certain expectations. Children were taught to respect their elders and figures in authority. "Nested among her hills she lies, / The city of our love," they sang of Fitchburg, back in school. On Main Street was Monument Square, a place to remember the Fitchburg men who had died in battle. Facing the square were the courthouse, the library, and the Episcopal church. North of Main Street was the best part of town; the wrong side of the tracks was south of Main. We don't learn where Scherman's family lived; but after college, when she was in her early twenties, her parents died and her ties to Fitchburg were severed.

When Scherman returned in 1962, a few modernized buildings on Main Street seemed like an "architect's nightmare," with their glass-walled additions and false fronts. The old Fitchburg had been a sociologist's dream, a place where people got along—Protestants, Catholics, Jews; immigrants like her grandfather Kielty, from Ireland; old Yankees like her mother's people, the Whitneys and the Pillsburys, who had given their names to country roads north of Fitchburg; the lone African American family and the many Swedish, Finnish, French Canadian, and German families who found work in the mills and machine shops of Fitchburg. Scherman's best friends had been girls with Swedish, English, and Irish surnames. Although brought up Catholic, she sometimes went with her grandmother Whitney to the Calvinistic Congregational church on Sundays. Her parents would take her to the hill country of her mother's forebears, where Finnish people worked some of the old farms. Near Mount Watatic (elevation, 1,832 feet) was the cellar hole of the old Whitney place. And the brick farmhouse of the Pillsburys was still standing in the early 1900s, still lived in by Pillsburys, who always made room for more relatives around the dinner table.

These memories came back to Scherman like "slow magic," after a life spent mainly in New York with her husband, a writer and publisher (who was Jewish), her two children, her own work as a writer and reviewer of books, and a wide circle of friends. The years in Fitchburg absorbed perhaps a quarter of her lifetime—and less than that in her memoir. When it appeared, some readers may have been more curious about her husband, a founder of the Book-of-the-Month Club and author of *The Promises Men Live By: A New Approach to Economics* (1938). Readers would have enjoyed her memories of Greenwich Village before the First World War, the Armory Show, Marsden Hartley, Walter Lippmann, and other acquaintances, and they may have read a lovely book by her daughter, Katharine, *Spring on an Arctic Island* (1956).[6] Today, when planners and designers are trying to avoid urban sprawl and build compact, neo-traditional communities, *Girl from Fitchburg* may have something more to offer.

Around 1900 Fitchburg was a town of about thirty thousand people, with a fairly wide range of industries, institutions, shops, and places of amusement. Scherman recalled the districts where different ethnic groups lived—the Irish at the southern end of town, in the Patch; the Swedes near the mills, in three-story wooden apartment buildings with porches and outside staircases; and the French Canadians in West Fitchburg, near the Cleghorn mill. At one end of Main Street was the Common, with shade trees, gravel paths, a fountain, a bandstand. Along Main Street were shops and houses, the opera house, and Monument Square. Here and there were remnants of the town's colonial past, houses with fine proportions and low ceilings. Their owners—intellectuals, a few artists, a poet—"made no perceptible impression on the life of the town," Scherman recalled. She and her friends were more drawn to a lakeside park on the eastern edge of town, accessible by trolley, for swimming, skating, canoeing, and summer theater. To the north and west were wooded hills, low mountains, and old homesteads. In late spring, roadsides were lined with mountain laurel. Earlier, mayflowers blossomed beneath withered leaves and patches of snow.

As details accumulate, the textures and tone of the place come through. Patterns emerge. Looking back, Scherman realized that the people who had lived in those old colonial houses (people she never knew) must have been responsible for the occasional appearance of a noted string quartet and the fine organ in one of the churches. She could not explain Fitchburg's religious tolerance, the lack of animosity between Yankees and Irish Catholics or between Christians and Jews. But most people sent their children to public schools—which had reputedly high standards. Most people walked, bicycled, or rode the trolleys. You could get from the Common to open country in twenty minutes. The view from nearby Flat Rock Hill showed the whole town and Wachusett Mountain (elevation, 2,006 feet) beyond.

The town and the setting were much the same in *Innocence under the Elms* (1955), a memoir of life in turn-of-the-century Bridgewater, Massachusetts, by Louise Dickinson Rich. The hills around Bridgewater were lower, however. Boston was closer. And the time period was a bit later. Born in 1903, Rich moved to Bridgewater at age two, with her parents and younger sister, Alice. There is no mention of Rich's life as a teacher, writer, wilderness guide, wife, and mother, for the memoir ends when she was about seventeen. Later, while living in Vermont, New Jersey, the Maine woods, and the coast of Maine, Rich would return now and again—often enough to accept small incremental changes in her hometown. But by 1983 she felt something fundamental was missing. She saw parking lots and shopping malls covering the meadows where she and her friends used to gather flowers for Decoration Day. The forests around the old skating pond had disappeared. Pesticides and acid rain, Dutch elm disease and child molesters, all contributed to her awareness of loss.[7]

In any event, *Innocence under the Elms* remained a product of the 1950s, a time when changes in the town were not so striking. Evidently Bridgewater was smaller than Fitchburg—although large enough to have a state college, a few shoe factories, an ice, coal, and coke company, a movie theater, and a bandstand on Central Square. It was also old enough to have a few dilapidated colonial and Federal-era houses, as in Fitchburg, and Rich's family rented one of them for a while. Her parents were somewhat eccentric. Whereas most pillars of the community in Bridgewater were Republican, Rich's father, the owner-editor of a weekly newspaper and a deacon at one of the churches, was a Democrat. Both of Rich's parents came from rural areas in the state. One grandfather was a minister, one, a deacon. Emily Dickinson had been a distant relation. But in Bridgewater, the Dickinsons were simply hard-working upstanding people who lived in rented houses and moved often.

Early on, while their parents worked together on the newspaper, the Dickinson girls were free to roam as long as they stayed within the sound of their mother's old school bell. Each newly rented place had things to discover—not only closets and attics, but barns, henhouses, hedges to hide in, maybe fruit trees, a tree for climbing, or a nearby vacant lot with wildflowers. Each place had been lived in, and every one had a garden with something interesting or edible left behind. With each move, there were also new friends to make; yet, as the town had only one school system, the new friends were not entirely strangers. Most neighborhoods were "good," and in one, near the edge of town, Rich developed a lifelong interest in plants and wildlife. In another, just off Central Square, Rich found that work and play could be inseparable.

Today, you couldn't build a neighborhood like that one on Broad Street, off Central Square; zoning laws would probably not allow it. The Dickinsons moved into an old colonial house with bricked-up fireplaces and a few elegant features, mostly deteriorating. The cramped little backyard looked out onto a large field with trees and a stream—a good place to build huts out of packing cases from the dairy products shop next door. Down the street, toward the river, were shoe factories and the railroad depot. Up the street, toward Central Square, were more shops, offices, and a theater. Sitting by the theater's rear exit, the Dickinson girls could hear the piano player adding sound to the silent movies. Nearby was their father's newspaper office, in a building that fronted on Central Square.

The windows of the *Bridgewater Independent*'s office faced the rear, looking out onto the livery stables and a "little lost green island," once a formal garden, where Mr. Dickinson had laid out a vegetable garden. After school the two girls could work in the garden, vaguely aware of the "surflike" sounds of unseen traffic and their own privileged place, in a secret garden. Or they could sweep the floors of the *Independent*'s office, where only a counter and a gate separated the editorial desk from the three printing presses, the cases of type, the potbellied stove, a cupboard, a sink, and the two flat stones, six inches thick—essential items in that shop. Mr. Dickinson, the editor-printer, would set the type and lock it into a form, resting on one of the stones. Before transferring the form to the press, he would make a "stone proof" to check for typographical errors. And the whole process was connected to the earth, Rich reflected— a connection severed when stainless steel replaced stone. "Working over a stone, a real stone, keeps you constantly reminded of the good earth beneath your feet," she wrote. "It keeps you in touch with fundamental things."[8]

In the office of the *Independent,* Rich and her sister acquired certain skills that would become obsolete, such as "learning the case," or knowing where to reach for each piece of uppercase or lowercase type; composing type on a stick (from right to left); and folding sheets as they came off the press. They also learned from people who would regularly drop by the office. An elderly Englishman would come to read their father's copy of the *Manchester Guardian.* The Chinese man from the laundry downstairs would come up to use the office telephone. Miss Hermann, the milliner below, would put aside a hat she was making and come up for some tea that Mr. Dickinson kept brewing on the potbellied stove. She might stop by the house, too, before dawn, to take the girls bird-watching on the edge of town. In spring, the tramp would arrive— a skilled itinerant printer who would sober up, work for a while in their father's shop, then move on.

Hovering about these recollections was a hint of genteel poverty—no trips to Brockton to buy fabrics for the girls' homemade dresses, no electricity, no bathrooms, nothing but a tin tub in the kitchen for weekly baths. The family would spend a few years in yet another rented house before the owner died or decided to sell, letting the next owner demolish the place for a new school or a parking lot. In 1955, Rich could not say whether things were better when she was young or merely different. In 1983, she was convinced that she and Alice did well to grow up in that small New England village, a world now gone forever.

✳ ✳ ✳

Henry James would not quite fit in either of the groups of writers mentioned earlier—those who aspired to objectivity and wholeness, withholding judgment while evoking the texture and mood of a lost place; and those who were partial, sometimes bitterly opposed to the transformation of a place. James absorbed all these aims and passions, particularly in *The American Scene* (1907), his ruminations on a journey late in life. No one created denser textures to reclaim places once known and loved, then somehow lost. And no one was more persistent, trying to reconstruct the drama of economic and social forces that had (in his absence) devastated the American land. "How grimly . . . the world, for the most part, waits to be less ugly again, less despoiled of interest, less abandoned to monotony," James brooded toward the end of *The American Scene*, recalling his feelings for the conquered land as seen through the window of a Pullman railway car.[9]

During his ten-month sojourn in 1904–5, traveling from New York as far north as New Hampshire, south to Florida, and west to California, James saw more of his native land than he had ever seen before and gathered more impressions than he could distill in a single volume. Having spent the previous two decades abroad, living and writing mainly in England but also in Italy and in France, he was struck by the vast scale of the American land, its flat expanses offering up little resistance to steel rails, Pullman cars, and the forces behind them. In Florida, returning to Palm Beach at sunset after a day's excursion, James studied the tall black palms standing out against a golden sky tinged with red. And he had a vision of a place older than the land of pyramids, with all of human history yet to be written. Such vastness, in time and space, suggested boundless opportunities for the imprint of civilization. But James was troubled by what he had seen all over the American land, evidence of arrogant conquest, indifference, complacency, and waste.

In New York City, where new skyscrapers were continually changing the skyline, James mulled over the buildings they had replaced or would replace before long. The house where he was born in 1843, in Washington Place, had been torn down, as well as the nearby castellated, gabled home of New York University. On the summit of Beacon Hill, in Boston, was the house where James, living with his parents and siblings in 1864–66, had begun his literary career. By 1904–5, that sturdy red-brick house had lasted long enough for James to see it once; a month later, he found it leveled, a casualty of an expansion project for the nearby State House. These losses were painful and personal. But James dwelled longer on a few lost *landscapes*—places no one in his family had ever owned or occupied, yet accessible to anyone with the ability and inclination to walk.

These were not public parks but stretches of unbuilt, more or less wild areas on the fringes of a town. In Cambridge, Massachusetts, the waters of Fresh Pond remained, but their rustic surroundings had been transformed. Once the scene of James's solitary walks and of literary conversations with his friend William Dean Howells, Fresh Pond was now a much more gregarious place, bordered by park roads and a country club, "all tea and ices and self-consciousness." In Newport, Rhode Island, the cliff walk above the shore remained accessible, but some changes to the wilder margins of the unpretentious old town were so startling that James devoted pages of reflection to the opulent new conditions. Huge summer homes, staring out to sea from high ground, had consumed the margins; "the face of nature was now as much obliterated as possible." And some of the mystery had slipped away, some possibility of adventure while walking or riding over rough ground out to the headlands and rocky shores.[10]

Ever the spectator or "restless analyst," James did not reveal to readers of *The American Scene* much of his *own* experience of old Newport or even mention when he first arrived there (in the summer of 1858, at age fifteen). It is as if any place he had known intimately and loved could be described only from a discreet distance. A few years later, however, after the death of his old friend and mentor John La Farge in 1910, James attended a retrospective in Boston of La Farge's lifework, including paintings and drawings of the Newport landscapes where the two had often gone with their easels, paints, palettes, and stools, back in the late 1850s and 1860s. The impact of those works, reassembled, was powerful—apart from any question of artistic achievement. La Farge's paintings and studies brought back to James, a man approaching seventy, the tremendous feeling of possession he had known at age sixteen or twenty-two.[11]

What he and La Farge had possessed was *scenery,* or landscape: views over the pastures and headlands, ponds and shores, that they had cher-

Landscape, Newport, *John La Farge, 1865 (*Paradise Rocks, Looking South*).*
(Pencil on paper; courtesy of Avery Architectural and Fine Arts Library, Colum-
bia University)

ished along with a few companions, mainly Henry's brother William
and a close friend, Thomas Sargeant Perry. Back then, the land beyond
the town of Newport was practically roadless, as Henry James recalled in
his *Notes of a Son and Brother* (1914). One morning he and La Farge
drove a horse and buggy for miles out to the Glen, had breakfast at an
inn, then settled on a spot from which to draw and paint. But more often
they simply walked, craving the longest possible walk. And, as there were
usually no other walkers in sight, they came to feel that they alone possessed what no one else seemed to care about. They recognized the "wise
economy" with which nature had treated a few elements—the sea, the
rocks, a pasture. They could not anticipate the impact of future roads,
scenic drives, and palatial summer houses that James would later characterize as "all cry and no wool, all house and no garden." But even as
young walkers over rough ground, they sensed that Newport was spe-

THE LOST PLACE

cial. "We knew already," James recalled, "that no such range of airs would ever again be played for us on but two or three silver strings."[12]

These themes are familiar by now—the beauty and simplicity of a few natural elements; the feeling of possession, enjoying a place in relative isolation, having arrived by walking, hiking, riding horses, paddling a canoe, rowing a boat, or sailing. And there were other means of moving without motors through a landscape. Walter Prichard Eaton recalled winter afternoons when he was a boy, skating on the frozen pond of Birch Meadow, near a little town north of Boston. Playing hockey with homemade sticks, without adults to organize or supervise the game, with nothing but two piles of boys' overcoats for each goal, he and his friends learned about sportsmanship. On winter evenings, while others skated by the light of a great bonfire near the shore, Eaton would venture out far beyond the radius of the fire's light, skating in darkness pierced by the light of stars and planets that shone in the night sky and on the black surface of the ice. Then a sudden crack, a boom, something to warn of danger, would send him dashing back toward the bonfire, toward solid ground, warmth, friends.

That was in the 1880s, when a meadow on the outskirts of a small country town (Reading, Massachusetts) could be a magical place for people, young and old, as well as a functioning part of the local economy. As Eaton recalled in his essay "Lament for Birch Meadow" (1953), that meadow, a clearing in a woodland of conifers and birches, was perhaps a mile long, with a brook coursing through it and a milldam at one end. In autumn, after the meadow was mowed, the brook would be dammed and the meadow flooded to create a pond. As ice on the pond gave way in spring, flashboards in the dam would be gradually removed to release water to power the sawmill—which was fed by timber from the local farmers' woodlots. In those days, although a few men in town commuted to the city, others still made their living by farming. Classes in the public schools were not very inspiring, Eaton recalled. He and a friend read books on the side, but the happiest, most stimulating times of his youth were spent out-of-doors, in places like Birch Meadow.[13]

Sixty years later, metropolitan Boston had reached little backwaters like Reading. Educational standards had risen. Suddenly Birch Meadow was about to be drained, its low spots filled in, for a new high school. Dismayed, living at the other end of the state, Eaton reflected that the meadow had taught him and his friends more than they ever learned in class. They had built their own boats and kayaks, and capsized once or twice. They had tramped through swampy places, looking for wildflowers, and returned home, walking through woodlands as sunsets glowed through the pines. At one point, the town had declined the chance to purchase the woodlands around the meadow. Trees were felled, the mill was shut down, houses were built. By the early 1950s, the town was ready to spend $1.4 million for a new high school. It's a familiar story. Eaton imagined the facilities that the new school would provide, but he wondered, "Where are the woodland and water ways that once led boys and girls to mystery and wonder? . . . Once we have destroyed our Birch Meadows, they are lost forever, and with them is lost something more precious than algebra, or even than basketball."[14]

Each succeeding generation, each individual, can tote up a different sum of losses. Eaton, born in 1878, was disturbed by the loss of a place that could have nurtured the sense of wonder, some poetic response, whether to lines of poetry (he quoted Wordsworth) or simply to a bit of wetland and wildland. Thomas Barbour, born in 1884, was nearly of the same generation. But when he assessed the loss of certain wetlands and wildlands, he wrote as a naturalist.

In *That Vanishing Eden* (1944) Barbour ranged over the entire state of Florida, blending natural history and human history with reminiscences dating back to the 1890s. The director of Harvard's Museum of Comparative Zoology and a veteran world traveler, Barbour wrote about Florida with authority and ease. He relished a good story, but his words could be sobering. "A large part of Florida is now so devastated," Barbour wrote, "that many of her friends are disinclined to believe that she ever could have been the Paradise which I know once existed."[15]

One place Barbour had known well was Walden, the winter home of his grandmother at Eau Gallie, on the Indian River. In 1898, the year he first visited there, the fish in the Indian River were abundant. By the

1940s, commercial fishing with nets had reduced the size and numbers of fish, Barbour's grandmother had died, and her little palm-shaded Walden Cottage lay in ruins. But Barbour did not dwell on personal losses; he had much more to tell about paleontology, the ancient Native people of Florida, botanists such as John and William Bartram, contemporary Seminole tribes, and changes in the land, ancient and modern. Some of the most devastating changes—soil erosion and depletion, flooding, increasing dryness—were the results of draining the land and burning the forests. It was a global problem. Barbour knew that Colombia, the Dutch East Indies, and many parts of Africa had been wastefully exploited as well; but the treatment of Florida may have been even more callous.

Barbour did not live to see the creation of Everglades National Park—he died in 1946—but he knew that the park project had been approved and funds to purchase private lands were still needed. He knew about the oil fields just north of the proposed park boundary, and warned, "You cannot have drilling and oil production carried on in a natural preserve." And he underscored the need to keep the proposed park's two thousand square miles of wetlands a functioning hydrological system. He knew of the links between large-scale drainage, the slow burning of "muck" or peat below ground, and the action of once-quiescent bacteria on drained land, which caused oxidation and further loss of soil. Then, too, the local climate was changing through human intervention. "Frost follows drainage," he noted—with obvious implications for the region's citrus crops.[16]

That Vanishing Eden includes photos and descriptions of the Florida home of David Fairchild, once the chief agricultural explorer for the U.S. Department of Agriculture. Teeming with flora and fauna, that place also included Barbour's home-away-from-home, the guest house. Another photo shows egrets and jackdaws feeding in a "drainage runoff from the drying Glades." Barbour reported that some wells around Miami were running salt water: "This means that water from the ocean, which is, of course, under pressure, has invaded the deep subterranean drainage systems where previously there was sufficient pressure of fresh water derived from the seepage from the wet Glades to hold the salt water where it belonged." The implication was clear: Miami's water supply might someday be salt water.[17]

Despite the damage already done, Barbour held out a vision of Florida as a real homeland—not merely an expanse of lowland to exploit or a place for carefree vacations. He imagined Miami as the home of a great university and a great institute for tropical research, linked with other institutes in Central and South America. No longer treated as a colony of the United States, Florida could become "a vital, integral part of the American Union."[18] It was inevitable, Barbour asserted. What Floridians needed was a sense of shared responsibility for the land. Interestingly, Barbour's book sold well. Published in November 1944, it went through five more printings by June 1945.

Twenty years later, the wildland ecologist Raymond F. Dasmann tried to do for California what Barbour had done for Florida; he wrote a book that was both an appreciation and a warning, *The Destruction of California* (1965). It, too, sold well. Years later Dasmann recalled that it was "the most publicized and, in paperback, the biggest seller of my books." There were some differences in tone; although engaging, Dasmann was not quite the storyteller that Barbour was. Barbour was not a Florida native. Dasmann was born in San Francisco, in 1919, and he freely confessed his love of cities, especially large cities. But both writers had a professional interest in the fauna and flora of a state that people thought of as a kind of paradise—even as postwar populations swelled and those idyllic lands became increasingly "developed." And both books ended with a vision. Dasmann's California would be a place of great diversity, of human freedom in the midst of natural and manmade beauty, "a place where technology is made to work for the interests of humanity, and man is not forced into a warped mold to suit the requirements of the computer."[19]

Writing long before personal computers became commonplace, Dasmann knew only their predecessors—bulky old mainframe computers, which he may have relied on for data. As a zoologist, biologist, and chairman of the Division of Natural Resources at Humboldt State College, in northern California, he was surely in no position to disparage the tools and techniques of science. And yet he was wary of a civilization too deeply dependent on machines. With perhaps an unconscious echo of Jane Jacobs's now classic work on American cities, he also emphasized the interdependence between cities and their hinterlands. "We cannot have a satisfactory life in a city without having wild country and wildlife accessible on the horizon," he wrote, alluding to Aldo Leopold's feeling for wildland in A Sand County Almanac (1949). "When we chain and confine all our wild country, eliminate the free-roaming animal life, then there will be no space left for that last wild thing, the free human spirit. The machine civilization we have built will have triumphed over us." People would become numbers. Computers, or those who manipulated them, would be in charge.[20]

These reflections follow chapters that dwell on loss and degradation—in Native American ways of life, among farm fields and orchards, in the forested mountains, in habitats for migrating fish and waterfowl, in the air quality of cities and suburbs—all with abundant facts, figures, and stark black-and-white photographs to support Dasmann's arguments. Glimpses of San Francisco are colored by his own memories of the city in the 1920s and '30s. Before the Bay Bridge was built, people rode ferries between San Francisco and Oakland. Before traffic streamed off that bridge, onto a loop of freeway that cordoned off the Ferry Building, San Francisco was a more beautiful city. Dasmann's high school in the city's Western Addition was racially and ethnically "integrated" long before the term was ever used. Then, too, the rapid buildup of wartime industries and postwar suburban growth were in part responsible for the decline of urban life that Dasmann had once enjoyed. And soaring rates of increase in the state's population seemed to be one of the most important problems to tackle in 1965.

Today another problem is at least equally daunting, and Dasmann nearly identified it when he touched on two related developments without quite linking them. On the one hand, he noticed a vast increase in personal mobility. People in California might "live in one place, work someplace else, play in a third place, and feel no community responsibility toward any of the areas concerned." In effect, they might think of San Francisco as home, but freeways, autos, and affordable fuel effectively extend the boundaries of where they really live, to the Big Sur coast, the north coast, the mountains, the deserts, and places in between. On the other hand, when a nuclear power plant is proposed for an earthquake-prone area rich in marine life and scenic beauty such as Bodega Head, or when a new dam is planned for the Trinity River, all Californians should be concerned, Dasmann argued. When a freeway extension in San Francisco is proposed, Californians everywhere should consider the impact. "Conservation is everybody's business," he wrote.[21] It was a variation on Thomas Barbour's theme, the need to feel responsible for the land where we live, work, and play.

Dasmann did not propose limits to people's mobility. His own work in wildlife biology and conservation had given him opportunities to travel through much of California, and soon after his book *The Destruction of California* appeared, he accepted a job with the Conservation Foundation, in Washington, D.C.[22] Still, the challenge he did not quite identify in 1965 remains in the twenty-first century: how to balance the freedoms of mobility with a sense of responsibility for place.

✳ ✳ ✳

In a *New Yorker* essay that later appeared in her memoir *Among Friends* (1971), M. F. K. Fisher contrasted two visions of an ideal community. One, described by a bishop and friend of the family, was of the Heavenly City, where streets were paved with gold, and war and illness were unknown. The other, cherished by Fisher's little sister, Anne, was of a town in miniature, with blue skies, white houses, red roofs, green shutters, a church on the village square, and children with voices like silver bells. As a child, Fisher (then Mary Frances Kennedy) had no comparable visions. It was enough for her that the Quaker town of Whittier, California, where her family (of non-Quakers) settled in 1912, had sidewalks good enough for roller skating and streets quiet enough for bike riding. By the late 1960s, the Whittier she knew was not lost but simply "Old Town," its larger houses converted to apartments and doctors' offices and its fringes, part of suburban Los Angeles.[23]

M. F. K. Fisher, best known for her writing about food, was aware of wider contexts: places where she learned to cook and to eat well, people, and the kinds of hunger they longed to satisfy, their struggles for warmth, security, and power. "It is all one," she wrote.[24] And that sense of the whole is evident in her memory of one lost place, somewhere along a narrow road in a winding canyon between Palmdale and Los Angeles. On a drive from a great-aunt's desert ranch back to Whittier one afternoon in August 1918, she and her father and her little sister stopped for a picnic supper. They ate something later forgotten, and then a memorable, warm, freshly baked peach pie with cream. Aged ten, Mary Frances absorbed the scene by a few details: her father and her sister, seen clearly as individuals; the golden hills, the live oaks, the Royal Alberta peaches in the pie, and the whole meal, "something beautiful to be shared with people instead of . . . a thrice-daily necessity."[25]

In 1943, looking back on that supper, one of the best meals she ever ate, Fisher could not recall which winding canyon her father had taken. Since then, freeways had been built through the San Gabriel Mountains, reducing the journey of nearly a day to perhaps two hours. In any case, that meal was a rare gift—an epiphany—something Loren Eiseley always seemed to be poised for, mulling over chance events in his more somber moods.

Eiseley's essay "The Brown Wasps," written in the mid-1950s, links his own search for a lost place with the searches of wasps, pigeons, and a single, desperate mouse. All those living beings, Eiseley included, seemed to need a certain orientation in the universe, an "attachment to a place." Eiseley needed something more as well, but the common need was what held the odd fragments of his essay together.[26]

The pigeons used to hover about the nut-vending machines at a station of the old elevated railway in Philadelphia. When that El was torn down and the pigeons were deprived of their gleanings, they kept returning to the empty stations anyway, waiting for a food source that had suddenly vanished. The mouse was about to be evicted; a new Wanamaker store would be built on a field near Eiseley's apartment building in suburban Philadelphia. And so, night after night, when Eiseley came home to a scene of potted ferns in disarray, their soil spilled onto the floor, he sensed a mouse in exile. It was a mouse dreaming of his own field, he thought, with a longing no more strange than Eiseley's own.

One day Eiseley went to a small town in Nebraska, to look for a cottonwood tree that he and his father had planted many years earlier in their backyard. When he arrived, the house was standing but the tree had been cut down. A boy on a tricycle asked Eiseley if he lived there. "I do," Eiseley replied. In a sense, he and the field mouse and the pigeons were all "out of touch." Yet there was something permanent about them—a few living beings, holding on, even though the world had changed.[27]

TEN

The Explored Place

If any photographer ever expressed the spirit of Yosemite National Park, Ansel Adams did, exploring it in all seasons, at different times of the day, beneath clearing storms and above timberline. Having seen his photographs, we may never see the place as if for the first time, but that's how he hoped we would explore Yosemite. "Do not be content to stop at the popular viewpoints," he advised in 1949; "walk in the cool forests . . . [;] watch the great rocks and waterfalls reveal themselves in endless and varied character." Leave the roads and buildings; study the "living things of earth and air." Adams believed that the spirit and beauty of Yosemite were not contained in its grandeur and vast scale alone; little things mattered. And, as most people would be struck first by the grandeur, he called attention to nature's minutiae. Only in time, through direct experience, would people notice the subtleties—the mist rising at daybreak, grooves in a granite cliff, and flowers on the valley floor.[1]

Writing of a less spectacular place, half sky, half water and watery land, Marjorie Kinnan Rawlings also noticed little things—drifting hyacinths on the Saint John's River, a mockingbird's song at sunrise, morning dew-drops on mosquito netting, and casual talk of those who loved the river life. "Now a man may learn a deal of the general from studying the specific," she wrote in *Cross Creek* (1942), "whereas it is impossible to know the specific by studying the general." It was not the South, then, or southerners, or Florida that she wrote about in the 1930s and '40s—but some specific people in north-central Florida, their quirks, loyalties, and flashes of wisdom; and their land, *her* land, the land of redbirds, quail, mockingbirds, and whippoorwills. A memoir of sorts, *Cross Creek* is also a love story about land, a specific place.[2]

And so it is with many writers in these pages, people who wanted to make some small part of the world better known and appreciated for what it is—not as a model or standard, but as a wonderful place, unique in the world. This might, incidentally, seem like barren ground for those seeking clues to rebuild or reclaim an entirely different sort of place, or to build a new place from the ground up. Some designers and planners are more drawn to models, methods, prototypes, something a bit more generalized. But others are picking up on people's yearning for something real and specific, connected to the past, with perhaps a layering of the old and the new to enrich a community, a city, a park, or a garden.

We have already noticed Henry Beston's disappointment with sumptuous gardens, where large blooms and superb horticultural displays seemed to be ends in themselves. He described the living connections between a few garden herbs and the history of nations and cultures, wars, trade routes, and the poetry of the ages. He saw how the shadowed, deeply veined leaf of balm was flattened to a pattern of lines beneath the midday sun. And he described the human journey toward peace with the earth, accomplished with "the sun to our right hand," the moon wheeling overhead, the sound of rain, and the sight of lengthening furrows in spring. Ideally, no motorized vehicles pulled the plow that dug those furrows—only horses.[3]

But Christopher Alexander wanted it both ways. Using the latest technology, he wanted to recapture the spirit and beauty of traditional places—the mud huts of African tribesmen; stone houses, or *trulli,* in southern Italy; Egyptian houses of the Nile; Navaho hogans; thatched cottages in South Wales—all products of an unselfconscious culture of building, refined over centuries of trial and error, corrections, and common consent. Rather than try to imitate those places, Alexander would use the tools of his own self-conscious culture to devise new methods that would approximate older, much slower processes of design. Working with an IBM 7090 computer in the early 1960s, he wrote programs to help him sort through potential misfits in a given design problem.[4] The mathematical problems are explained in his *Notes on the Synthesis of Form* (1964), but more compelling for a nonmathematician was one example of unselfconscious design in that book—the traditional Slovakian peasant's shawl. A small thing of great beauty, the shawl expressed what Alexander longed to find in built environments of his own time.

Weaving yarns colored by homemade dyes, those peasants made shawls well known for their lovely colors and patterns—that is, until the early twentieth century, when new aniline dyes with a wider range of brilliant colors became available to them. As Alexander reasoned, the beautiful old shawls were products of a long tradition, gradually refined. Then the advent of too much choice, too quickly, had led to a product without interest. The peasants' mastery—like that of many contemporary architects and designers—had slipped away. For the next few decades, then, Alexander would explore new ways to determine patterns of building that might yield something deeply satisfying, like a traditional Slovakian peasant's shawl or the smile on a person's face. His aim was not beauty, exactly, but conditions of order, peace, a sense of rightness and relaxation. As he remarked to the architect Stephen Grabow, "When someone smiles it is as though the fabric of the universe seems to melt. . . . And it can happen in a million different ways."[5]

Such a little thing, a smile! Like drifting hyacinths, a groove in granite, or the vein of a leaf. The following pages, tracing journeys to places across the continent, from west to east, open onto vistas of some of the most impressive places on the globe—impressive for vast scale, but also for small, revealing details.

✳ ✳ ✳

Shortly before the Wilderness Act was passed, in 1964, William O. Douglas brought out two volumes, *My Wilderness: The Pacific West* (1960) and *My Wilderness: East to Katahdin* (1961). There, in a series of personal essays, Justice Douglas wrote of treks along rivers and canals and up mountain trails, camping for days, sometimes fly fishing. Douglas and his companions might get around on horseback or by canoe, rubber raft, or a wooden boat with a small engine. Occasionally a Cessna plane or a jeep would bring them to a spot where the real journey would begin, on foot. A good storyteller, Douglas could have dwelled on what Ansel Adams considered "external events," such as the heroic adventures of the early American pioneers and mountain climbers. But like Adams, Douglas was more intrigued by internal events, moments of spiritual and emotional intensity when he felt deeply connected to the world around him.[6]

It happened that Douglas and Adams were featured speakers at the Sierra Club's Seventh Biennial Wilderness Conference, held in San Francisco on April 7 and 8, 1961. At issue was the preservation of wilderness and wildlands—which Justice Douglas viewed as both a *new frontier* and a matter of human rights. He saw people's rights to clean air and water, dignity in their work, quiet retreats, and beauty and wildness in the landscape all increasingly threatened by the products of science and technology—including automation, industrialization, and rampant exploitation of natural resources. Interestingly, he spoke not as a man in black robes, citing legal precedents, but as an occasional hiker and amateur botanist, alert to the intricacies of sphagnum moss and the sounds of a whippoorwill at dawn. Ansel Adams spoke as an artist. He hoped that photography, combined with the written word, would be able to reach the hearts and minds of people, inspiring them to defend the wilderness—and avert disaster.[7]

At that time the Sierra Club's president, David Brower, had already begun his prizewinning Exhibit Format series of books on the American environment, with photographs by Adams and others.[8] In a few years the Wilderness Act of September 3, 1964, would be seen as one victory in the continuing fight to defend places "where the earth and its community of life are untrammeled by man, where man himself is a visitor who does not remain."[9] And yet, just as a great photograph could leave many things unsaid, so an act of Congress, encumbered by sections, provisions, and restrictions of all kinds, subject to revision years later, could not represent the last word or the finest expression of wilderness ideals. Artists and writers had a continuing challenge to express what it was, exactly, that moved them, beyond the most commonly recognized values of natural resources—as raw materials, perhaps, or as background scenery.

Douglas's writing in *My Wilderness* is accessible, often lyrical, with narrative descriptions that shade almost imperceptibly into discussions of ecology, diversity in plant and animal life, and threats to human and environmental well-being. These essays effectively crisscross the United States, from Alaska to the Everglades and from southern California to Mount Katahdin, in Maine. The flora and fauna vary widely, yet Douglas seems to know them. "There are many starting points for one who enters the wilderness," he told his San Francisco audience in 1961. "Mine was botany."[10] Douglas also had knowledgeable traveling companions, including Harvey and Anne Broome in the Great Smokies of Tennessee, Olaus and Margaret Murie in the Brooks Range of Alaska, and Sigurd Olson in the Quetico-Superior border lakes country of Minnesota. And he seemed to make himself at home anywhere—for a while.

Although Douglas had lived on the East Coast for most of his adult life and served as a justice of the Supreme Court since 1939, he knew the West more intimately. Born in the little town of Maine, Minnesota, in 1898, he lived from the age of four through his early twenties mainly in Yakima, Washington. From his family's front porch on the outskirts of Yakima, looking west, he could see Mount Adams, third-highest peak in the Cascade Range, rising up over twelve thousand feet. Covered with snow the year round, flanked by meadows, lakes, and trails, Mount Adams was a favorite destination on weekends, an escape from chores and part-time jobs, where he could fish, hike, pick blueberries, and stalk wildlife. That country was an "old familiar friend," Douglas wrote in *My Wilderness: The Pacific West.* Years later he elaborated. When his father was laid in his grave in the Yakima cemetery, William O. Douglas, aged five, stood by, sobbing, until he looked up and saw Mount Adams on the west, a calm, unperturbed friend, "symbol of stability and strength."[11]

When Douglas wrote of the Brooks Range in Alaska, however, in the region that now contains the Arctic National Wildlife Refuge, he dwelled not on any towering peaks but on the interrelations of many smaller things, on the tundra, in the streams, and within the white spruce forests. Having joined the Muries and their fellow scientists, Douglas apparently went off on his own for stretches of time to watch whatever creatures came along—a ground squirrel, a willow ptarmigan, a flock of cliff swallows, a pin-tailed duck, two Pacific loons. Hiking in the knolls above the tundra, he would pause to study tiny lichens, heather, patches of anemones, yellow saxifrage, and ground-hugging kinnikinnick. Some hillsides were covered with a brilliant cerise azalea, *Rhododendron lapponicum*. Caribou would pass by, in a herd of forty or by the thousands. Unseen grizzly bears had left tracks and scat. Once Douglas spied a gray wolf heading for a pass in the mountains. At that time a hunter could claim a fifty-dollar bounty on the wolf's carcass. But alive, slipping through a landscape, the wolf was "as moving as a symphony."[12]

In *My Wilderness* Douglas omitted many dates, names, and the facts of a conservation battle won or lost. It would be left to historians to determine his place in environmental history. He himself was more interested in physical places, especially wild places, their sights and sounds and smells, and the webs of plant and animal life that made a place not only interesting but vitally important in the long run. Having wandered among the rain forests and glacial peaks of the Olympics, west of Puget Sound, he reflected that such places are "essential to our long-time welfare and well-being as a nation. The wilderness area is the norm." Without it, we could not fully appreciate the difference between good health and decline in the environment.[13]

In each volume of *My Wilderness,* the high-contrast black-and-white drawings of Francis Lee Jaques (who had illustrated Louis Halle's *Spring in Washington*) are as understated and confident as the writing of Justice Douglas. Some images are like poems in themselves, while the text reveals other layers of meaning. Early one morning in winter, walking along the Chesapeake and Ohio Canal toward the pond of Widewater, Douglas became aware of a great sweep of land and sky, a bald eagle, flocks of other birds, snow, and silence—"the immense northland stretching to the Arctic Circle and beyond," or so it seemed. And yet Washington, D.C., was less than twelve miles away. Hardly wilderness, some might say. But Douglas believed cities needed that—"a wilderness at their back door, where a man can go and once more find harmony and peace in his inner being."[14]

Ann Zwinger found such a place for her family among the foothills and mountains west of Colorado Springs. From some spots on their forty-acre property, the granite summit of Pike's Peak (elevation, 14,110 feet) was visible. Other areas of the land were sheltered and inward-looking, defined by slopes and streambeds, young aspen groves, a meadow rising to 8,400 feet, and a tiny lake with a bit of granite rising a few feet above its surface—not high, but high enough to establish a point of order and stability. "From here I can reach out to my less orderly world beyond," Zwinger wrote in *Beyond the Aspen Grove* (1970). "From here I can see the seasons chain together in a continuity that runs through our lives."[15]

By the definition in the Wilderness Act of 1964, the Zwingers' land was not "wilderness." A campsite on the property, intended as a week-end and seasonal retreat from their home in Colorado Springs, eventually yielded to a wooden shelter that became a cabin, with an old wood-stove, a deck, bunks, and accommodations for a couple, three daughters, pets, and friends. Evidently man was something more than a visitor at "Constant Friendship," the Zwingers' name for the place. The preexisting dam that held back the waters of two streams, forming the tiny lake, would never be mistaken for the work of beavers. In the aspen grove in summer, slender trunks and rustling leaves could not quite hide the cabin. But the Zwingers planted no garden; they considered no living green thing a weed. As nonnatives, they simply wanted to explore the land and share their little discoveries, including favorite places. In time they came to feel that they didn't so much own the land as belong to it,

THE DOMAIN

through experience and growing understanding. "It is its own reason for being," Zwinger admitted. "The life of the wood, meadow, and lake go on with or without us."[16]

One way Zwinger came to know that life was to help survey the land. Long before global positioning systems, global imaging systems, and other sophisticated technologies were available, she worked with two friends over a period of about six weeks, wielding a transit, survey chain, rod, plumb bob, stakes, and laths tied with orange surveyor's tape, in order to get accurate readings on one-hundred-foot grid intersections over forty acres of wildly uneven ground. There were hazards involved, thunder and lightning storms to weather, aching muscles to soothe, but also discoveries among the wildflowers and birds, in places Zwinger might otherwise have missed. In the end she acquired what all students of civil engineering and landscape architecture used to acquire through surveying, an "immediate physical awareness" of the land that came back to her as she interpolated spot readings and drew the contours on what would always be an abstraction—a map.

Much less abstract, yet removed from reality in their greatly reduced or enlarged forms on a page, are Zwinger's fine pencil drawings of trees, leaves, flowering plants and grasses, insects, and minute creatures of water and air. She spent hours peering through a microscope, and many professionals helped her in some way, including a soil scientist, a geologist, a botanist, a forester, and several biologists. Still, the drawings in *Beyond the Aspen Grove* are more than technical illustrations; they are delicate, expressive products of her own very personal explorations.

Attending to little things, Zwinger writes with affection and admiration for liverworts (*Marchantia polymorpha*) growing on a rock down by the watercress. She crouches down to draw the tiny wild candytuft (*Thlaspi alpestre*) that grows in the lee of a grass clump in a windy meadow. She hears a stream flowing, its rhythm "just slower than the heartbeat." On the Fourth of July, as her children and those of friends race through the aspens and pines, they become part of a pattern, "at home in a world of wind and light." They seem to belong to the land. Later, seedpods break open and announce the "shattering of summer."[17]

As the wife of a military man, Zwinger was used to packing up and moving on. Before coming to Colorado, she and her family had lived near the ocean in Florida, on an Arkansas farm, in a city, in a small town. She had grown up in Muncie, Indiana. Now, she and her family had a house with a garden and a carefully tended lawn in Colorado Springs; and a tract of land in the mountains, meant to remain as wild and unaltered as possible. "My interest in the vast world of nature began when we came to this land," Zwinger explained, "with the finding of a new world, a sense of discovery, a sharing."[18]

In *Beyond the Aspen Grove* Zwinger looks so intently at her immediate world of hills and mountains that highways, cities, and her city garden, mentioned now and again, seem far away. Stars and planets, brilliant in the dark sky, are mainly distant reminders of what is precious on earth. "Looking upward, I wonder if any of those other worlds can possibly match this one," she writes.[19] In the end, she returns to the land and a feeling of responsibility for it. Myriad life forms are everywhere, such that two inanimate objects stand out—the lake rock, made of "Pike's Peak granite," tough, yet susceptible to crumbling; and the old woodstove that Zwinger lights before making supper.

❋ ❋ ❋

In the late 1950s the editor of the *New York Times* travel section asked Joseph Wood Krutch how much of the celebrated landscape of the Old Southwest was still intact. Krutch, a longtime New Yorker, formerly a professor of English at Columbia and drama critic for the *Nation,* had made automobile trips to the Southwest since 1937. Having settled there, in Tucson, in the early 1950s, Krutch could report that some remote, quiet stretches remained, but they were rapidly disappearing. "Help Tucson Grow," read the posters of the Chamber of Commerce, while new residential subdivisions opened week after week. Cities in the Southwest were beginning to look like cities everywhere, while Disneyland in California had an imitation Grand Canyon. Soon, Krutch mused, "simulacra will be all that is left to remind us of what a vanished world, which some still find interesting, was like. All the plants will be in gardens and greenhouses, all the animals in cages, and all the scenery in stage sets."[20]

Then in his late sixties, Krutch was concluding his autobiography with glimpses of the increasingly mechanized world about him. In 1961 a commencement speaker at the University of New Mexico had told how new electronic devices with memory would soon store information, translate texts from Russian into English, and in many ways liberate people from "mechanical drudgery." Some scientists, including two Nobel laureates, had appeared on television, talking about mail to be delivered by satellite, recreational resorts to be built in outer space, and other wonders. The military wanted to surround the city of Tucson with bases of Titan missiles. Meanwhile demographers were predicting that Tucson and Phoenix, 125 miles apart, would grow into a continuous settlement within twenty-five years. If so, one place in the path of that development would have to be carefully defended—the Arizona–Sonora Desert Museum, of which Krutch was a trustee. Not that this outdoor museum of flora and fauna could make up for the loss of much more extensive wildlands beyond, but it might be all that people could preserve.

In his biography of Thoreau, published in 1948, Krutch had recognized the value of small stretches of wildland near a town. The woods of Walden, he noted, were "not very wild and not very remote," for Thoreau could easily walk to the heart of Concord. "Thousands now living in cities are more isolated from other human beings than he ever was," Krutch added.[21] A century after Thoreau's time, living 2,500 miles from Concord, Krutch was not likely to draw many comparisons between Walden and Tucson's desert museum. But Thoreau's appreciation of wildland near a town, some broader and wilder margin for the lives of urban dwellers, remained intriguing to Krutch, even as he looked out onto a dry land hardly imaginable in the wooded fringes of Concord.

Krutch informed regional and national audiences about the many values of southwestern deserts, as places to explore and as biotic communities where living things had learned to adapt and endure. In *The Voice of the Desert* (1955) he singled out small things—ground squirrels, jackrabbits, toads, roadrunners, doves, mule deer, yucca moths, saguaro cactus, paloverde trees, prickly pears—and suggested the human's place among them, much as Aldo Leopold had done in his posthumous *Sand*

County Almanac (1949). Scientific education and conservation law were not enough, Krutch wrote, echoing Leopold. There had to be affection, love, "some feeling for, as well as understanding of, the inclusive community of rocks and soils, plants and animals, of which we are a part."[22]

Krutch, who outlived Leopold by more than twenty years (long enough to see the first Earth Day, in 1970), could introduce Leopold's environmental values to a much wider public. In 1963 NBC aired a special one-hour television program in which Krutch read selections from his own writings on the Southwest, while images of desert fauna and flora appeared on the screen, in color. Among those selections may have been passages from Krutch's book *Grand Canyon: Today and All Its Yesterdays* (1958). There, his journeys into vast chasms of space and time are offset by his attention to smaller things—chipmunks, lizards, gopher snakes, swallows, ravens, a cliff-dwelling juniper, a red penstemon—all familiar signs of life in a place that might otherwise seem alien. And he moves on, ultimately to reflect on national parks, conservation, and wilderness preservation in a wider context. "The wilderness and the idea of the wilderness is one of the permanent homes of the human spirit," he asserts—in words that would be quoted long after his time. Those who knew its source might assume that Krutch had somehow managed to feel at home in the Grand Canyon—which was not exactly the case.[23]

Krutch would always remain somewhat distanced from the Grand Canyon, a place he found fascinating but ultimately inhospitable to human life. On the rim, he and other visitors depended on a network of roads, hotels, restaurants, shops, and other services catering to their short-term needs. Beyond the reach of those services, visitors could find solitude, beauty, and spiritual renewal for a while, but not indefinitely. And so, for all his ventures below the rim, in different seasons, for all his research into the Grand Canyon's human and natural history, Krutch could not explore the place with the casual intimacy and daily familiarity evident in his earlier nature writings, set in rural Connecticut.

Krutch and his wife did, however, explore less-dramatic parts of the Southwest before they settled in Tucson. While still based in New York, they spent an extended sabbatical year in 1950–51, living near Tucson

Section of the Colorado River in the Cañon. *(Image from John L. Stoddard, Lectures, vol. 10:* Grand Cañon of the Colorado River *[1905]; photographer unknown)*

and traveling often. On one journey, described in *The Desert Year* (1952), Krutch and a native of the Southwest ventured into a country of snow-clad mountain peaks, aspen-covered slopes, high plateaus, sandstone buttes, and desert on the valley floor. In the heat of early summer—in June—wandering through that valley, they saw no other humans, although for years, the guide explained, a local rancher had been turning his cattle loose in the valley for winter pasture. Krutch was intrigued; he found the place strangely beautiful, thrilling to move through, yet inaccessible, somehow unreal. "Only a country which one has both lived in and contemplated can assume in the mind that special sort of solidity which no amount of mere sight-seeing can give it," he wrote. "Really to possess the Valley I should need both the cowboy's doing and my own looking."[24]

And so a Tennessee-born New Yorker who had once had no interest in landscape scenery or rural life came to be an articulate spokesman for both wilderness and the more accessible, half-wild places that some people call home. It was an evolutionary process, not to be accounted for by a single experience—writing about Thoreau; spending long weekends in rural Connecticut with Mark and Carl Van Doren, Lewis Gannett, and other friends from the city; listening to spring peepers in the marsh in April, or brooding over Charles Darwin's legacy in November. Writing as a thoughtful companion, not as a confidant, Krutch revealed the development of his own feeling for land and place, especially in the Southwest. He responded to the region's dry, warm sunlight and the hard, austere forms of a desert extending from northern Mexico into southern Arizona. He explained why he preferred a land less spectacular, more livable, than the canyon-and-monument country farther north. But until late in life, he seems to have withheld from readers one personal reason why he was so drawn to the desert. Having long suffered from asthma, he found that in the desert he could at last breathe freely.[25]

* * *

Spring in the desert of the American Southwest is legendary. After the normal rains of winter, the desert in bloom can seem like a miracle, especially to strangers. But "there is no spring in Florida," wrote the poet Wallace Stevens. And Marjorie Kinnan Rawlings reflected, "He came as a stranger, a traveller, to Florida. . . . He did not know when the red-bird begins to sing again, and when the cypress bursts from gray bareness into a dress of soft needles and the swamp maple puts out young passionate red leaves." Evidently the poet did not know a little portion of north-central Florida, where Rawlings tended her citrus orchards, confident that, even blindfolded, she would know the month of spring by the particular fragrance of bloom—first orange blossoms, then grapefruit, then tangerine.[26]

A northerner, Rawlings had come to that region in Florida on a whim, with her husband, Charles, in the spring of 1928. Fourteen years later, she had written four books set in that land of creeks and marshes, lakes, woods, groves, worn-out fields, and "hammocks," made of dark, rich soil and covered mainly with live oaks, palms, or sweet gums, or perhaps

THE DOMAIN

hollies and magnolias. It was not a conventionally scenic land, but Rawlings had found it enchanting and conveyed something of its magic to a wide audience. A few of Rawlings's books were picked up by the Book-of-the-Month Club. Her third, *The Yearling* (1938), won the Pulitzer Prize, and the movie rights to the book were sold. But those details are absent from her partly autobiographical *Cross Creek* (1942), where her abiding interest lay in the people of the creek, a few families, some white, some African American; in their relations with one another, through hard times and calamities, memorable meals and returned favors; and in their relations to the land.[27]

Those relations may have varied a great deal, but Rawlings wrote of no callous exploitation, no hostility or indifference to the land. To endure the daily struggles and squabbles of a remote, loosely knit community, the isolation from old friends and periods of loneliness, along with the hazards of raising crops in a zone not entirely temperate or tropical, was a challenge. People either found the environment congenial or drifted away. Rawlings's husband couldn't take it. She stayed on, captivated by the place. It was not only the physical beauty of the land that held her there, a land where she could walk from glaring brightness to the dark, cool, sheltering aisles of an orange grove pierced by shafts of sunlight; or the sense of rediscovering the "mystic loveliness of childhood" in an utterly strange place that felt like home. It was not only the comfort of one African American neighbor, Martha Mickens, who moved freely among her neighbors, passing on gossip and wisdom and maintaining, along with her husband, Old Boss, standards of dignity that the worldly would find old-fashioned. What kept Rawlings at Cross Creek was in part its familiarity. She came to know what to expect of the place and its people, just as she came to recognize signs of the changing seasons. "Spring is beautiful because it is familiar," she wrote. "Its coming is as important as the smile across a beloved face."[28]

Cross Creek and its environs are not extensive—a few square miles loosely defined by two lakes, a country road, and the creek. One chapter, however, the previously published essay "Hyacinth Drift," expands the book's geographical range and, by introducing the unknown, serves as a foil for what has come to be familiar. There Rawlings tells of her journey down the Saint John's River, at a time when some unidentified hardships in her life had become unbearable. (As biographers later explained, Rawlings's husband had just made his final departure.)[29] From the original article and the chapter, we know only that something has marred her happiness at Cross Creek. A woman friend, Dess, has offered sympathy and suggested a journey of several hundred miles in an open boat with an outboard motor, down the river, south to north, toward Jacksonville. Men warn them of dangers but reveal a twinge of envy at the thought of such an adventure. After recent droughts, the main channel of the river, clogged with water hyacinths, would be difficult to distinguish from false leads into endless grassy margins. Despite their maps, river charts, and compass, they'd get lost.

In fact they were never lost for very long. Attentive to small things like water hyacinths, all drifting slowly downriver but some drifting slightly faster than others, they detected the main channel and followed it, absorbing along the way adventures and impressions delightful in the retelling. Readers would think of Huckleberry Finn. Rawlings thought of Cross Creek; could she ever be happy on land again?

She could. "Because I had known intimately a river, the earth pulsed under me. The Creek was home." It was a "forgotten loveliness" that she possessed, but only for a brief time on earth.[30] Her final thoughts about the dubious nature of private property, land ownership, love, and mastery are echoed in many works considered in these pages. In the end Rawlings conceded ownership of the creek to wind and rain, sun and seasons, seeds, time—that is, to no living beings, except for a few winged creatures, the redbirds, whippoorwills, blue-jays, and ground doves, to whom mortgage payments and deeds were irrelevant.

✳ ✳ ✳

William Beebe once had a vision of two worlds, about a mile apart, each functioning without the faintest awareness of the other. He was on the deck of a tugboat in the Atlantic, about a hundred miles southeast of the Statue of Liberty. On board were fifty-five species of deep-sea fish that had been netted from the depths of the Hudson River Gorge, a crevice on the continental shelf. The day's catch had yielded five species new to science and of great interest to Beebe, a naturalist. As the tug headed back to New York, he happened to see a speck on the horizon—an ocean liner—and he thought of the comings and goings of those people on board. What did they know of the sea creatures swimming a mile beneath their keel?[31]

It was to draw connections between those two worlds, human and nonhuman, that Beebe wrote *Unseen Life of New York* (1953). He invited readers to imagine a sphere with a radius of a hundred miles centered on New York City—perhaps at the Statue of Liberty. Within that sphere—reaching up into the sky, down to the ocean floor, northeast to Hartford, Connecticut, southwest to Philadelphia—were ordinary living things amazing to contemplate. There, with senses alerted and with common notions of time and space stretched a bit, people could begin to perceive creatures ordinarily unseen because they were too old, too young, too small, too clear, too high, too dark, too deep, or too familiar. Some tiny creatures could be scooped up from a bit of water in Central Park and admired under a microscope. There were furry things running wild, uncaged and untended, in and around the Bronx Zoo. On well-worn steps of brownstone houses in New York and Brooklyn people might find fossilized footprints of huge reptiles—remains of the area's former life.

Dr. Beebe, born in Brooklyn in 1877, was for many years director of tropical research at the New York Zoological Society. He was also a pioneer oceanographer, popular lecturer, and prolific author, writing scientific monographs and books of natural history for the general public. From his small studio on West Sixty-seventh Street and his laboratory at the Bronx Zoo, he set out on expeditions to Mexico, Bermuda, the Galapagos, the Andes, the Himalayas, and beyond. Interestingly, a trustee of the Zoological Society once observed that Beebe liked to work intensively on a limited area, such as a single square kilometer of cloud jungle, centered on his Rancho Grande Laboratory in the Venezuelan Andes.[32] In *Unseen Life in New York,* the hundred-mile radius of his study area took in a much wider zone of human and nonhuman life. But the idea of a central focus, some familiar building or monument from which to explore, was apparently congenial to him.

Surveying the great range of New York life within a few miles of Manhattan and nearby towns, Beebe singled out both the exotic and the commonplace. He trapped a few mink along the Bronx River and knew of wild beavers and a few wild black bears living within thirty miles of City Hall. Walking in a woodland near New York, he might flush a well-camouflaged woodcock or spot a lichen-colored moth on the trunk of a tree. Near Fort Lee, on the Palisades along the Hudson River, someone had uncovered the remains of a twelve-foot-long reptile, *Rutiodon manhattanensis*, the "first Triassic New Yorker." But also intriguing were the comings and goings of bats, fireflies, earthworms, and pollen grains—those marvelously diverse carriers of the continuity of life on earth.

Some of Beebe's explorations were beyond the reach of most readers. He recalled one memorable night in May 1904, spent on top of the Statue of Liberty to get a closer look at migrating birds. With permission, he and a friend had used the crown of the statue as a base camp; and after his friend retired for the night, Beebe remained high up on the torch, enduring the wind, the cold, and the statue's swaying. A few creatures collided against his coat as they flew toward the fog-shrouded, well-lighted torch, and the more fortunate among them continued on. "For the period of a few hours I was permitted to share the feelings and activities of birds on migration," Beebe wrote, "sensing altitude, isolation, darkness, wind, speed, and the awful confusion and dangers of light-in-fog."[33] By their cries, he recognized several birds—sandpipers, warblers, sparrows, a red-eyed vireo, a goldfinch, possibly a green heron. The next morning, he and his friend picked up 271 dead birds near the statue's base. Nearly fifty years later, however, Beebe reported that the protests of bird lovers and disoriented pilots in the harbor had led to a less dazzling and dangerous lighting of the Statue of Liberty. Thereafter fewer birds perished on their night flights.

Within his hundred-mile compass, Beebe noticed traces of all kinds of life—including the mastodons that once roamed the now submerged

THE DOMAIN

Hudson Gorge and left their bones at the corner of Broadway and 141st Street. The region's hidden beauty and drama could be seen, once enlarged, uncovered, or simply detected within the commonplace, like sounds of crickets on a summer night. Above all it was the wonder and magic of familiar things that needed to be rediscovered. In 1944 Beebe imagined the fear of a Stone Age child, watching leaves fall and birds disappear in autumn, not knowing if they would ever return. Even the sun's rising after nightfall was not a certainty, yet there were compensating rewards for that child of a prehistoric age: "everything in nature fresh, a continual surprise, nothing named." A kindred experience, Beebe knew, awaited any modern child who would look around him (or her) with keen senses and an open mind.[34]

A decade later a younger friend of Beebe's, Rachel Carson, took up that same theme—a child's delight in things that are fresh and new, before their beauty has been dulled and their mystery explained away. Writing an article for *Women's Home Companion,* in 1956, Carson had in mind those parents who knew very little about birds, stars, trees, fish, and other things of the natural world. They did not need to know the name of a single star or creature, she wrote. More important was to keep alive the feeling of wonder, gazing up at a splendid display in the night sky, or bending down to see what lay in a tide pool. For a child, names and facts were much less important than curiosity and a sense of wonder. Although not a mother herself, Carson had often explored her own nearby woods and shores with her grandnephew, Roger. She knew how he responded to booming waves on the beach in a night storm and to springy, wet reindeer moss beneath his bare feet.[35]

Carson's 1956 article was brought out as a book, *The Sense of Wonder,* in 1965, the year after her death. Augmented by new color and black-and-white photographs, the slim book became a classic. It also revealed some of Carson's haunts on the Maine coast—although the precise location of the photographs was not disclosed. Most had been taken on Southport Island, in Sheepscot Bay. In 1953 Carson had had a cabin built there, and her explorations of that meeting place of land and water continued to inform her books, including *The Edge of the Sea* (1955). As her editor Paul

Brooks later noted, she had had to rewrite certain parts of the manu-script-in-progress for that book, since her perspective had changed. "For the first time, I'm writing about something while it is right under my nose, and it gives me a very different feeling about it," she explained.[36]

One chapter in *The Edge of the Sea,* "The Rocky Shores," gives another glimpse of Carson's home territory in Maine. Early in the morning, a favorite path through an evergreen forest leads to a scene so diffused by fog, gray water, and mist that it might seem "a world of creation, stirring with new life." This scene of vague, strange newness is, in fact, a relatively new place, when viewed from the perspective of geological time. Sketch-ing in the contours and compositions of the rocky North Atlantic shores as they changed over eons, Carson describes the sea, rising and falling over millions of years, yet gives no time frames. It is as if she wants to awaken among adult readers something of the sense of wonder that might lie dormant in their own remote pasts.[37]

Carson, Beebe, and other naturalists at the midcentury, including Henry Beston, Joseph Wood Krutch, Donald Culross Peattie, and Edwin Way Teale, could take readers on journeys of exploration and perhaps express misgivings about past or present misuses of lands and waters without necessarily sounding an alarm about threats to the whole web of life, human and nonhuman. Carson's *Silent Spring* (1962), however, an explicit warning about the devastating effects of DDT and other poisons and pesticides, represented a sharp departure in the tone and purposes of her own writing for the general public. And that controversial, exceed-ingly influential book was a catalyst for other warnings that followed, from the lyrical and yet darkly contemplative later works of Loren Eise-ley to the more pragmatic, even blunt, writings of Barry Commoner, Paul Ehrlich, Ian McHarg, and many others, during the years just before and after the first Earth Day, in 1970.[38]

If that Earth Day can be seen as a divide of sorts, marking a new, much more widespread awareness of environmental dangers and opportuni-ties in the modern Western world, then Beebe, who died in 1962, and Car-son, who lived only two years longer, represent the other side of the divide. That is one convenient way of organizing events in time—taking

THE DOMAIN

the metaphor of a great chain of mountains from which waters flow to one ocean or another. And yet William Beebe, once famous for explorations of ocean depths in his "bathysphere," and Rachel Carson, who also ventured undersea, might prefer to be associated not with divides but with connections, by waters that circle the globe.

One glimpse of Manhattan in *Unseen Life in New York* is from Beebe's studio on West Sixty-seventh Street. By leaning out his window, he can just make out a glimmer of the Hudson River—which could be a theoretical starting point, he muses, for an uninterrupted journey, by boat, around the world. Streams, rivers, seas, and oceans connect us all. And there are other connections, to be traced not in space but in time. While specialists in evolutionary biology might disagree on specific lines of ascent from simpler forms of life to human life, Beebe underscores an area of consensus: "Of an unbroken ascent from Amoeba to ourselves there is not the slightest doubt."[39]

In *The Book of Naturalists* (1944), an anthology, Beebe let Rachel Carson have the last word. Although working under the usual constraints of space limitations—and under wartime conservation measures—Beebe chose two entire chapters from Carson's *Under the Sea Wind* (1941) to complete his selections on natural history from Aristotle to the present. His sole illustrations were reproductions of three magnificent creatures, a bison, a wild horse, and a wild boar, from prehistoric cave paintings in Spain and France. And if those images represented the finest expressions of a human response to the environment before language was invented, Rachel Carson's chapters represented something comparable, in words alone: the story of an eel, one creature among countless others of her kind, migrating from a pond, some two hundred miles downstream to the Atlantic and to her distant spawning place, south of Bermuda and east of Florida. In the end that story transcends the death of a single eel, in the continuity of generations coursing through oceans and estuaries, upstream and downstream. What begins as a journey in space becomes an odyssey in time, barely sketched in, spanning geological ages from the rise of mountains (and of the land beneath coastal cities and towns) to their eventual erosion and return to the sea.[40]

There is of course a hint of foreboding in these stories of natural history, reaching backward and forward in vast sweeps of time. Both Carson and Beebe wrote of places on earth as seen in an endless process of change. Meanwhile they were aware of imminent threats to the life forms that they studied. As Carson wrote to Beebe in 1948, alluding to humans' profound dependence on the waters around the globe, "We will become even more dependent upon the ocean as we destroy the land."[41] And yet in their well-known writings at midcentury, no single note of fear or foreboding can overwhelm the greater, splendid whole. Lands and waters are not reduced to mere abstractions. They are particular places: unique in the world, increasingly understood by scientists, and still looked upon with wonder and delight.

THE DOMAIN

Epilogue

In these divisive times, it's good to be reminded of things that unite us all. A half century ago, as we have seen, William Beebe and Rachel Carson wrote of waters that flow along streams and rivers to mingle in the oceans round the world. Pointing to our common descent from the amoeba, Beebe reminded us of the continuity among all living beings. To a pond full of exuberant spring peepers (*Hyla crucifer*), Joseph Wood Krutch whispered, "Don't forget, we are all in this together."[1]

Today we may be more aware of other connections, via the Internet, satellite, cable, cell phones, voice mail, laptops, Palm Pilots, fax and telephone answering machines, and other devices. A half century ago, television, commercial jet planes, and interstate highways offered new connections. Radios and telephones had appeared earlier, allowing us to transcend distances in space and time and to stay in touch. Still, the old connections essential to biological life—our dependence on water, air, light, heat—remained as critical as ever in the 1950s. The old yearnings for stability, security, a place to call home, were hardly diminished. At midcentury you could pick up a shelter magazine or a Sunday supplement to the local newspaper and see those yearnings reflected in the feature stories, the little poems used as fillers, the ads. . . .

But look more closely at the ads. Not long ago *Sierra* magazine reproduced a selection from popular magazines at midcentury. "We Came. We Sawed. We Conquered," announced one ad in 1949 for a chain-saw manufacturer, over a color photograph of two men in hard hats, cutting into a redwood tree perhaps eleven feet in diameter. "Free flowing for instant protection," proclaimed another ad in 1956, beneath an eerie colored drawing. It's winter. A lime-green late-model car is parked above a stream. Nearby, wedged into the snow, is a giant can of Mobiloil Special, adorned with the red flying horse that lovers of poetry and painting know as Pegasus, the legendary Greek horse that kicked open a fountain of inspiration—a stream—on Mount Helicon, home of the Muses. But the red horse is a red herring; the important thing, from Mobil's point of view, is that the oil can is punctured and tipped so that golden oil pours freely into the stream—even in "sub-zero cold."[2]

Only one other ad, from Union Carbide in 1962, is more chilling. Above the words "Science helps build a new India," a plowman and his team of oxen labor by a placid river. Beyond are the gleaming towers and pipes of a pesticide plant. From the sky a giant hand pours a red liquid from a test tube into the soil and onto the panel of text. The place is Bhopal, scene of the disastrous poison-gas leak in 1984.[3]

The year 1984 was, of course, long after the first Earth Day celebrations that mark a divide between the literature of place considered in these pages and any writings that followed. Just as data from the 1890 U.S. Census alerted Frederick Jackson Turner to the closing of the western frontier, so Earth Day 1970 can be considered the opening of another frontier—a whole planet, on which the fine webs of interconnection among living organisms were only beginning to be understood. In 1984, as the biologist Barry Commoner pointed out, *Time* magazine assessed the damage at Bhopal—more than 2,000 people killed—as part of the cost of providing jobs and pesticides. "There is no avoiding that hazard, and no point in trying," the writer argued in *Time;* "one only trusts that the gods in the machines will give a good deal more than they take away."[4]

Allowing for poetic license, we may still wonder about that writer's trust in machines—not only in certain technologies but in a whole mindset, the acquiescence to what Paul R. Josephson has recently called "Industrialized Nature."[5] Most of the writers considered in *Literature of Place* were trying to make sense of environments shaped and managed on smaller scales—not the giant dams, massive clear-cut forests, vast ranches, and widespread industrial agriculture that Josephson studied. These writers focused on family farms, small towns, urban neighborhoods, or some desirable balance of city and country, cultivation and wildness. And, whatever their technological links to other people, they tended not to lose sight of age-old social and biological connections to people, places, and living things. The desert recluse Edward Abbey could look forward to subway crowds and the clatter of clamshells on the floor of a bar in Hoboken, New Jersey. Louise Beebe Wilder could be gardening in Bronxville, New York, content to know that Grand Central Station was only a half hour away by train. Raymond F. Dasmann loved San Francisco, in part because wildlands were never too far away.

An unexpected pleasure of working on *Literature of Place* has been to recognize, again and again, how some writers managed to make peace with a world changing beneath their feet even as it does today. Some forces, not all, were beyond their control. Places and situations were never perfect, but some of the inner strength and resilience of these authors seemed to come from their attachment to a physical place. Or, to put it a bit differently, their sense of who they were was somehow connected with a clear sense of *where* they were, in space and time. It's difficult to generalize, for often what mattered was the particular texture or aura of the place.

It could be that the abundance of connections now made possible through technology, along with the accelerated pace of our lives and the multiple realities we may be aware of at any one time, both virtual and actual, near and far, will tend to distance us from writings that date from the other side of that divide, 1969–70. And yet many individuals, aside from those mentioned in my opening pages, are now dwelling on the same or similar concerns. Here I'll add a few more to the group, men and women who are still trying to show us what it is to be human, living in a real place, in real time.

After weighing the opinions of many informed individuals, from the molecular biologist and Nobel laureate James D. Watson to the Sun Microsystems scientist Bill Joy, Bill McKibben has drawn a line beyond which humans should not go in pursuit of ever smarter, stronger, more beautiful, creative, and longer-living progeny. However elusive the distinction, McKibben wants to separate somatic gene therapy, or efforts to cure human ills, from "germline" genetic engineering, in which fertilized human embryos would be manipulated so as to create a better "product," a human being with particular traits programmed by other humans. The prospects can be dazzling, but McKibben thinks the price would be too high. He would not give up what it is to be human—to struggle, often to fail, sometimes to succeed, knowing that whatever we achieve has not been preconceived and cleverly programmed before we were born. He would not sever the ties between our human past and present, so as to let some of our progeny—"designer children"—live forever in the future. He would not "give up our citizenship in the land of the finite, which is the place that humans have known, and trade it for a passport to the infinite." That's one place—the land of the finite—that McKibben would not abandon.[6]

Designed places pose different issues, but not entirely, in the eyes of architects, planners, and landscape architects now engaged in New Urbanism, Traditional Neighborhood Development, Transit-Oriented Development, and other movements toward the building of livable and sustainable communities. Many of these professionals were born at or around the midcentury (as McKibben was), and they too do not want to sever the ties between our human past and present, despite the design theories they may have absorbed in school decades ago and the incredibly sophisticated technologies at their disposal today.

Among this group are two architects based in Miami, Andres Duany and Elizabeth Plater-Zyberk, who have designed many well-publicized new communities since the early 1980s, from Seaside, Florida, to Cornell, in Markham, Ontario.[7] Often they are contacted by strangers who are drawn to these walkable, likable (and photogenic) places, with front porches, small lots, picket fences, gridded streets, and shared amenities. Looking for community, these people say they would move "almost anywhere" to live in such a place. And the architects' response is illuminating.

"Why live in Seaside instead of Key West, or Kentlands instead of Georgetown?" Duany and Plater-Zyberk ask. Residents of older communities themselves, these architects appreciate the maturity, layered history, diversity, and beauty of older places. Their livelihoods may depend on commissions for designing new communities on open land, yet they have recommended infill projects for the inner city and older suburbs, temporary halts on greenfield development, and other measures to resist market forces that lead to more sprawl. Then, too, these architects have tried, sometimes without success, to provide physical connections in the form of streets that would link their own new projects with neighboring ones, new or old. Detractors can always find flaws, but as more people are drawn to New Urbanist communities like Kentlands, Maryland, mayors of older towns can continue to point to these new communities in support of their own efforts to revitalize Main Street.[8]

And what of the rest of us, caught somewhere between real places and virtual ones, not only between the hours of 8 AM and 5 PM but almost anytime? With all the Web sites and links, with the near infinity of information available, who has time to—who wants to—*read*? Not simply ingest information, but read with undivided attention and penetration—who will do that? These are the sorts of questions that Sven Birkerts persists in asking, brushing aside all the simple, unsatisfying answers. Like many others in these pages, he is troubled by a widening rift between us and the natural world. And as technology brings us all closer together, he wonders about "the breaching of our essential solitude" and the "dissolved interconnectedness" that may come in time.[9] Some years ago he reflected, "Through language, which makes of the page a place of focus and immersion, the writer gives the reader the deeper picture of things,

John Deere tractor and future housing site near Interstate 80, Stuart, Iowa

the picture he might assemble for himself if only he had the time, the concentration, and the imaginative penetration."[10]

Stephen L. Talbott has struggled with the reciprocal questions, about how to *write*, to communicate, now that long hours before the computer screen leave many of us with eyestrain, neck aches and backaches, and mental fatigue. Once an organic farmer, Talbott spent some eighteen years working on software and technical writing in the computer industry and in publishing before his own physical ailments led him, in 1998, to begin writing on a yellow notepad. (He would eventually type his text into a computer, but limit his daily hours on the screen to half a workday.) By then a published author, he was also known for his online newsletter, *NetFuture*, begun in 1995.[11]

Subtitled "Technology and Human Responsibility," this newsletter has been a wide window to me, an outsider with nose pressed against one of the panes, looking in on the thoughts of those who not only navigate with ease in cyberspace; many of them helped to design the vessel! More important, their discussions are often broadly humanistic, not technical.

But as my allegiance is to the book, and print media in general, I would like to close with a word about Talbott's *The Future Does Not Compute: Transcending the Machines in Our Midst* (1995). This book is so dense with ideas that it must be read and reread, slowly. It is as if Talbott were staying up late at night, trying to find deeper levels of agreement among old friends (and friends on the shelf), such as Stewart Brand, founder of the Whole Earth 'Lectronic Link, or WELL, and author of *The Clock of the Long Now* (1999); Howard Rheingold, author of *The Virtual Community* (1993); Goethe, Rousseau, Freud, Jung; and the British luminary Owen Barfield, whose works have led Talbott to reconsider his own notions of virtual reality and the other, heavier, more tangible reality that we grew up with.

Thinking of photographs, models of atoms, a television screen, a painting, Talbott can conceive of "no *final* distinction between the virtual and the real." All these things are constructs, to some extent abstractions, invested with meanings we give them. Could the appeal of virtual reality be a sign, he wonders, that we have become unaware of how we already participate (or once did participate) in the world? And he suggests that we may respond in one of two ways. We could become more consciously, creatively involved in the world, without mediation by anything programmed or manipulated. Or we could let our world continue in the direction it has been moving for some time, from the real to the virtual. Eventually we would inhabit an entirely artificial world.[12]

And what would that world look like, feel like? Talbott includes no images in *The Future Does Not Compute*, but we can imagine it. We have seen it already, in fragments. Now, if Talbott is correct—if there is no clear line dividing the virtual place from the real place—we should at least be conscious of which end of the spectrum we are heading toward, and why.

Notes

PREFACE

1. Wallace Stegner, *Wolf Willow* (1962; rpt., New York: Penguin, 1990), 23.
2. See Charles Frankel, "The Year of the Moon," and Thomas O. Paine, "NASA Prepares for the Future," in *Americana Annual 1970: Encyclopedia of Events of 1969. Yearbook of Encyclopedia Americana,* 15–19, 36–38.
3. William J. Mitchell, *City of Bits* (Cambridge: MIT Press, 1995), 107.
4. See, for instance, Paul Hawken, Amory Lovins, and L. Hunter Lovins, *Natural Capitalism: Creating the Next Industrial Revolution* (Boston: Back Bay Books/Little, Brown, 1999); Peter Calthorpe, *The Next American Metropolis: Ecology, Community, and the American Dream* (New York: Princeton Architectural Press, 1993); Sim Van der Ryn and Peter Calthorpe, *Sustainable Communities: A New Design Synthesis for Cities, Suburbs, and Towns* (San Francisco: Sierra Club Books, 1986); and Peter Katz, *The New Urbanism: Toward an Architecture of Community* (New York: McGraw-Hill, 1994).
5. James Howard Kunstler, *The Geography of Nowhere: The Rise and Decline of America's Man-Made Landscape* (New York: Simon & Schuster, 1993); and Clifford Stoll, *Silicon Snake Oil: Second Thoughts on the Information Highway* (1995; rpt., New York: Anchor/Doubleday, 1996), 235.
6. William J. Mitchell, *E-topia* (Cambridge: MIT Press, 1999), 8, 80. See also Jane Jacobs, *The Death and Life of Great American Cities* (New York: Random House, 1961); and Stephen Doheny-Farina, *The Wired Neighborhood* (New Haven, Conn.: Yale University Press, 1996).

1. Walter Prichard Eaton, "Literature of Place," *Bookman* (September 1918): 13–20.
2. Christopher Alexander, *The Timeless Way of Building* (New York: Oxford University Press, 1979); and Stephen Grabow, *Christopher Alexander: The Search for a New Paradigm in Architecture* (Stocksfield, Northumberland, UK: Oriel Press, 1983).
3. Henry Beston, *Herbs and the Earth* (Garden City, N.Y.: Doubleday, Doran, 1935), 6–7.
4. Van Wyck Brooks, *Letters and Leadership* (1918), in Brooks, *America's Coming of Age* (1934; rpt., Garden City, N.Y.: Doubleday/Anchor, 1958), 154.
5. Cheryl Weber, "Continuing Education," *Residential Architect* (November–December 2003): 24–26. See also Jill Stoner, ed., *Poems for Architects: An Anthology* (San Francisco: William Stout Publishers, 2001).
6. John R. Stilgoe, "J. B. Jackson: A Literary Appreciation," in *Land Forum* (Summer/Fall 1997): 8–10. See also "John Brinckerhoff Jackson, 1909–1996," in *Landscape Journal* 16 (Spring 1997): 1–26; and Ernie Pyle, *Brave Men* (New York: Henry Holt, 1944), 409–10.
7. John Brinckerhoff Jackson, *American Space: The Centennial Years, 1865–1876* (New York: W. W. Norton, 1972).
8. Aldo Leopold, "The Role of Wildlife in a Liberal Education" (1942), in Leopold, *The River of the Mother of God and Other Essays*, ed. Susan L. Flader and J. Baird Callicott (Madison: University of Wisconsin Press, 1991), 303; and Melanie L. Simo, *Forest and Garden: Traces of Wildness in a Modernizing Land, 1897–1949* (Charlottesville: University of Virginia Press, 2003).
9. See, for example, "Walter Prichard Eaton Deplores Turning New England Roadsides into Offensive Slums," in *American City* (February 1928): 90; and Walter Prichard Eaton, "Saving New England," *Atlantic* (May 1930): 614–21.
10. Malcolm Cowley, *Exile's Return* (1951; rpt., New York: Penguin, 1976), 9–10, 27.
11. Ibid., 221–22, 292.
12. Sarah Orne Jewett, quoted in *Willa Cather: Stories, Poems, and Other Writings*, ed. Sharon O'Brien (New York: Library of America, 1992), 854.
13. Sarah Orne Jewett, *The Country of the Pointed Firs* (Boston: Houghton Mifflin, 1896), 71.
14. Loren Eiseley, *The Invisible Pyramid* (New York: Scribner's, 1970), 149–50.
15. Ibid., 153.
16. Ibid., 155.
17. Leon Edel, *Henry James: The Treacherous Years, 1895–1901* (Philadelphia: J. B. Lippincott, 1969), 174–75. Edel notes that the typewriter became widely used in the 1880s; and that, in 1896, James suffered increasing pains in his right wrist—"writer's cramp," Edel imagined.
18. Christopher Alexander, Sara Ishikawa, Murray Silverstein, et al., *A Pattern Language* (New York: Oxford University Press, 1977), 55–56.
19. A photograph of Christopher Alexander at work on *Notes on the Synthesis of Form*

(Cambridge: Harvard University Press, 1964) appears in Grabow, *Christopher Alexander*, 290.

20. Elizabeth Coatsworth, *Personal Geography: Almost an Autobiography* (Brattleboro, Vt.: Stephen Greene Press, 1976), 118–19.

21. Sven Birkerts, *Readings* (St. Paul, Minn.: Graywolf, 1999), 113–18.

22. Kevin Lynch, *What Time Is This Place?* (1972; rpt., Cambridge: MIT Press, 1995).

23. Elizabeth Coatsworth, *Country Neighborhood* (New York: Macmillan, 1944), 181.

ONE NEW ENGLAND

1. Louise Dickinson Rich, *The Peninsula* (Philadelphia: J. B. Lippincott, 1958), 24–26.

2. Ibid., 30–32.

3. Ibid., 281.

4. Walter Prichard Eaton, *Green Trails and Upland Pastures* (Garden City, N.Y.: Doubleday, Page, 1917), 10.

5. Robert P. Tristram Coffin, *Yankee Coast* (New York: Macmillan, 1947), 22, 179; and Walter Prichard Eaton, *On Yankee Hilltops* (Boston: W. A. Wilde, 1933), 98.

6. Gerald Warner Brace, *Between Wind and Water* (New York: W. W. Norton, 1966), 209–10.

7. Ibid., 166.

8. See, for example, Gerald Warner Brace, *The World of Carrick's Cove* (New York: W. W. Norton, 1957) and *Light on a Mountain* (New York: G. P. Putnam's, 1941). See also Charlotte Holt Lindgren, *Gerald Warner Brace: Writer, Sailor, Teacher* (Hollis, N.H.: Hollis, 1998); and Joseph Lovering, *Gerald Warner Brace* (Boston: Twayne/G. K. Hall, 1981).

9. Brace, *Between Wind and Water*, 32–35; and Gerald Warner Brace, *Days That Were* (New York: W. W. Norton, 1976), 61–77.

10. Brace, *Between Wind and Water*, 207–8.

11. Ibid., 101.

12. Lindgren, *Gerald Warner Brace*, 3. See also Charles C. McLaughlin and Charles E. Beveridge, eds., *The Papers of Frederick Law Olmsted*, vol. 1: *The Formative Years, 1822–1852* (Baltimore: Johns Hopkins University Press, 1977).

13. Rich, *Peninsula*, 80.

14. See, for example, Louise Dickinson Rich, *We Took to The Woods* (Philadelphia: J. B. Lippincott, 1942) and *Happy the Land* (Philadelphia: J. B. Lippincott, 1946). Alice Arlen's biography of Rich, *She Took to The Woods* (Rockport, Maine: Down East Books, 2000), includes articles by Rich and excerpts from her diaries.

15. Rich, *Peninsula*, 94.

16. Ibid., 96.

17. Mary Ellen Chase, *The Edge of Darkness* (New York: W. W. Norton, 1957), 223.

18. Mary Ellen Chase, *The White Gate* (New York: W. W. Norton, 1954), 153–65. See also Mary Ellen Chase, *A Goodly Heritage* (New York: Henry Holt, 1932), 43.

19. Robert P. Tristram Coffin, *Lost Paradise* (New York: Macmillan, 1934), 284. See also Annie Coffin Sanborn, *The Life of Robert Peter Tristram Coffin and Family* (Alton, N.H.: privately printed, 1963).

20. Robert P. Tristram Coffin, *Strange Holiness* (New York: Macmillan, 1935). See also Raymond C. Swain, *A Breath of Maine: Portrait of Robert P. Tristram Coffin* (Boston: Branden, 1967). Coffin taught at Bowdoin College from 1934 to 1955. Chase taught at Smith College from 1926 to 1955.

21. Sarah Orne Jewett, *The Country of The Pointed Firs* (1896; rpt., New York: W. W. Norton, 1981), 96.

22. Mary Ellen Chase, introduction to *The Country of the Pointed Firs,* by Sarah Orne Jewett (New York: W. W. Norton, 1981), xxv.

23. Sarah Orne Jewett, "The White Rose Road" (1889), in Jewett, *Strangers and Wayfarers* (Boston: Houghton Mifflin, 1890), 278–79. See also Jewett, "The White Heron" (1886) and "The Gray Mills of Farley" (1898), in *Sarah Orne Jewett: Novels and Stories* (New York: Library of America, 1994); Jewett, "A Neighbor's Landmark," in Jewett, *The Life of Nancy* (Boston: Houghton Mifflin, 1895); and George Held, "Heart to Heart with Nature: Ways of Looking at 'A White Heron,'" in *Critical Essays on Sarah Orne Jewett,* ed. Gwen L. Nagel (Boston: G. K. Hall, 1984).

24. Sarah Orne Jewett to Bradford Torrey, 21 January [1890], in Sarah Orne Jewett, "Letters, 1873–1900," Dartmouth College, Special Collection, MS-271, folder "1890, Jan. 21." On the relations between Jewett and Fields, see Sarah Way Sherman, *Sarah Orne Jewett, an American Persephone* (Hanover, N.H.: University Press of New England, 1989); and Judith A. Roman, *Annie Adams Fields: The Spirit of Charles Street* (Bloomington: Indiana University Press, 1990).

25. Bradford Torrey, *A Rambler's Lease* (Boston: Houghton Mifflin, 1889), 195.

26. The original manuscript of *Land of the Lingering Snow* includes several clipped newspaper columns, with Bolles's handwritten alterations; see the Frank Bolles Papers, Dartmouth College Library, Special Collections, MS-724. See also the Papers of Frank and Elizabeth Bolles, 1994:07, Tamworth (N.H.) Historical Society; Stephen F. Ells, "From *Boston's Hills* to *Chocorua's Heights*: Frank Bolles Wrote from the Land," *Appalachia* (December 2002): 92–112; and Stephen F. Ells, "Franks Bolles Biography, Writings, and Research" (http://homepage.mac.com/sfe/henry/frank_bolles/bolles .html).

27. Bradford Torrey, *Footing It in Franconia* (Boston: Houghton Mifflin, 1901), 39; and Frank Bolles, *Land of the Lingering Snow: Chronicles of a Stroller in New England from January to June* (Boston: Houghton Mifflin, 1891), 222.

28. Bolles, *Land of the Lingering Snow,* 60. See also *Dictionary of American Biography,* s.v. "Bolles, Frank," and *National Cyclopaedia of American Biography,* s.v. "Torrey, Bradford." Torrey, a Thoreau scholar, was also an editor of the *Youth's Companion.* Bolles was secretary to Charles W. Eliot, president of Harvard University, before becoming secretary of the university in 1887.

29. Bolles, *Land of the Lingering Snow,* 211–12.

30. Torrey, *Footing It in Franconia,* 5–7.

31. On the naming of the Bolles Trail (by the U.S. Forest Service) and the gift of the Bolles Nature Preserve, see the obituary of Evelyn B. Phenix (1976), in the Frank Bolles Papers, Dartmouth College Library, Special Collections, MS-724, folder, "Miscellaneous." See also Frank Bolles, *At the North of Bearcamp Water: Chronicles of a Stroller in New England from July to December* (Boston: Houghton Mifflin, 1893), 43–61.

32. Torrey, *Footing It in Franconia,* 46.

33. Bolles, *Bearcamp Water,* 291–93.

34. Ibid., 80–81.

35. Walter Prichard Eaton, "Literature of Place," *Bookman* 48 (September 1918): 13–20; Allen Chamberlain, *Vacation Tramps in New England Highlands* (Boston: Houghton Mifflin, 1919); and Appalachian Mountain Club, *AMC White Mountain Guide,* 25th ed. (Boston: Appalachian Mountain Club, 1992), 351–52.

36. Walter Prichard Eaton, "What Are the Berkshire Hills?" in *The Berkshires: The Purple Hills,* ed. Roderick Peattie (New York: Vanguard, 1948), 21. See also *National Cyclopaedia of American Biography,* s.v. "Eaton, Walter Prichard."

37. Eaton, *Green Trails and Upland Pastures;* Walter Prichard Eaton, *In Berkshire Fields* (New York: Harper & Bros., 1920) and *Wild Gardens of New England* (Boston: W. A. Wilde, 1936).

38. Walter Prichard Eaton, *Barn Doors and Byways* (Boston: Small, Maynard, 1913), 8.

39. Walter Prichard Eaton, "Upland Pastures" (1914), in Eaton, *Green Trails and Upland Pastures,* 3–20.

40. Walter Prichard Eaton, "Nature and the Psalmist" (1915), in Eaton, *Green Trails and Upland Pastures,* 277, 290–91.

41. Chamberlain, *Vacation Tramps,* 34.

42. Katharine Toll, "Winter Sports in the Four Ranges," in *The Friendly Mountains,* ed. Roderick Peattie (New York: Vanguard, 1942), 275–301; Louise Closser Hale, *We Discover New England* (New York: Dodd, Mead, 1915); and Charles Hanson Towne, *Jogging Around New England* (New York: D. Appleton-Century, 1939). Several WPA guides of the 1930s, part of the Federal Writers Project of the Works Progress Administration, were reprinted by Pantheon Books, New York, in the 1980s.

43. Dorothy Canfield Fisher, "Hiker's Philosophy," in *Footpath in the Wilderness: The Long Trail in the Green Mountains of Vermont,* ed. W. Storrs Lee (Middlebury, Vt.: Middlebury College Press, 1941), 2, 4. See also Elizabeth Yates, *The Lady from Vermont: Dorothy Canfield Fisher's Life and World* (1958; rpt., Brattleboro, Vt.: Stephen Greene Press, 1971); and Ida H. Washington, *Dorothy Canfield Fisher: A Biography* (Shelburne, Vt.: New England Press, 1982).

44. Esther Edwards, quoted in Eaton, "What Are the Berkshire Hills?" 30.

45. John Hay, *In Defense of Nature* (Boston: Atlantic Monthly Press/Little Brown, 1969), 165–66. See also John Hay, *The Run* (Garden City, N.Y.: Doubleday, 1959).

46. John Hay, *Nature's Year: The Seasons of Cape Cod* (Garden City, N.Y.: Doubleday, 1961), 13–16, 198–99.

47. Hay, *In Defense of Nature,* 36, x, 94–112.

48. Ibid., 151.

TWO THE SOUTHERN HIGHLANDS

1. Horace Kephart, *Our Southern Highlanders* (New York: Outing Pub. Co., 1913), 11–27.

2. Ibid., 27. See also George Ellison, introduction to *Our Southern Highlanders: A Narrative of Adventure in the Southern Appalachians and a Study of Life among the Mountaineers,* rev. ed., by Horace Kephart (1922; rpt., Knoxville: University of Tennessee Press, 1984).

3. Bradford Torrey, *A World of Green Hills: Observations of Nature and Human Nature in the Blue Ridge* (Boston: Houghton Mifflin, 1898).

4. Ibid., 168–77.

5. Ibid., 83–87, 38.

6. *Dictionary of American Biography,* s.v. "Morley, Margaret Warner."

7. Margaret W. Morley, *The Carolina Mountains* (Boston: Houghton Mifflin, 1913), 33–34. See also her study of flora and fauna, *A Song of Life* (Chicago: A. C. McClurg, 1894).

8. Morley, *Carolina Mountains,* 75.

9. Ibid., 193–97.

10. Ibid., 187–89.

11. Kephart, *Southern Highlanders* (1913 ed.), 383.

12. Morley, *Carolina Mountains,* 154. On Biltmore, see also Gifford Pinchot, *Biltmore Forest: The Property of Mr. George W. Vanderbilt: An Account of Its Treatment and the Results of the First Year's Work* (Chicago: Lakeside Press/R. R. Donnelley, 1893); Laura Wood Roper, *FLO: A Biography of Frederick Law Olmsted* (Baltimore: Johns Hopkins University Press, 1973), 414–24; Charles E. Beveridge and Paul Rocheleau, *Frederick Law Olmsted: Designing the American Landscape* (New York: Rizzoli, 1995); and Alan Ward, *American Designed Landscapes: A Photographic Interpretation* (Washington, D.C.: Spacemaker Press, 1998).

13. Kephart, *Southern Highlanders* (1913 ed.), 254, 395.

14. Ibid., 210, 206–7.

15. Ellison, introduction to Kephart, *Southern Highlanders,* ix, xli–xlii.

16. Morley, *Carolina Mountains,* 385.

17. Jean Thomas, *The Traipsin' Woman* (New York: E. P. Dutton, 1933).

18. Details of Thomas's life are found in several of her works, including *Devil's Ditties: Being Stories of the Kentucky Mountain People* (Chicago: W. Wilbur Hatfield, 1931); *Ballad Makin' in the Mountains of Kentucky* (New York: Henry Holt, 1939); *The Sun Shines Bright* (New York: Prentice-Hall, 1940); and *Blue Ridge Country* (New York: Duell, Sloan & Pearce, 1942).

19. Thomas, *Blue Ridge Country,* 42.

20. Thomas, *Sun Shines Bright,* 179–83.

21. A few stanzas of "Down in the Valley" appear in *Traipsin' Woman,* 270–71. For one

version of the complete ballad, see *A Treasury of American Folklore,* ed. B. A. Botkin (New York: Crown, 1944), 902–3.

22. Ted Olson, preface to James Still, *From the Mountain, from the Valley: New and Collected Poems,* ed. Ted Olson (Lexington: University Press of Kentucky, 2001), 2–3. See also Jeff Biggers, "His Side of the Mountains: The Enduring Legacy of Southern Poet James Still: An Interview with Editor Ted Olson," *Bloomsbury Review* 22 (July/August 2002): 17–18.

23. James Still, *River of Earth* (1940; Lexington: University Press of Kentucky, 1978), 240.

24. Ibid., 134.

25. Ibid., 76–77.

26. James Still, "A Man Singing to Himself: An Autobiographical Essay," in *From the Mountain,* 13. See also *I'll Take My Stand: The South and the Agrarian Tradition,* by *Twelve Southerners* (1930; rpt., New York: Harper, 1962).

27. Still, *River of Earth,* 103.

28. Harvey Broome, *Out Under the Sky of the Great Smokies: A Personal Journal* (1975; rpt., Knoxville: University of Tennessee Press, 2001), 39.

29. Ibid., 3–17.

30. Kephart, *Our Southern Highlanders* (1913 ed.), 29–30; Still, "Man Singing to Himself," 5–6, 10; and James Still, "Interview" (with Laura Lee), in Still, *The Wolfpen Notebooks: A Record of Appalachian Life* (Lexington: University Press of Kentucky, 1991), 35.

31. Broome, *Out Under the Sky,* 124, 37.

32. See, for instance, Loren Eiseley, *The Immense Journey* (New York: Random House, 1957) and *The Invisible Pyramid* (New York: Scribner's, 1970).

33. Broome, *Out Under the Sky,* 143–44. See also William O. Douglas, *My Wilderness: East to Katahdin* (Garden City, N.Y.: Doubleday, 1961), 181–211; and chapter 10, below.

34. Michael Frome, foreword to Broome, *Out Under the Sky,* xiii–xxvii. See also Wilma Dykeman, review of Broome, *Out Under the Sky of the Great Smokies: A Personal Journal* (Knoxville: Greenbrier, 1975), in *Living Wilderness* 40 (April/June 1976): 47–48; and Stephen Fox, "'We Want No Straddlers,'" *Wilderness* (Winter 1984): 5–19.

35. Broome, *Out Under the Sky* (2001 ed.), 184–88.

36. Ibid., 43, 252.

THREE PACIFIC SHORES

1. Theodora Kroeber, *Ishi in Two Worlds: A Biography of the Last Wild Indian in North America* (Berkeley: University of California Press, 1961).

2. On the writing and publishing of *Ishi in Two Worlds,* see August Frugé, *A Skeptic among Scholars: August Frugé on University Publishing* (Berkeley: University of California Press, 1993), 137–56. In 1993 Frugé was director emeritus of the University of California Press.

3. Saxton Pope, quoted in Kroeber, *Ishi,* 237.

4. By 1976 a half-million copies of the paperback edition, published by the University of California Press, were in print; see Frugé, *Skeptic among Scholars,* 145.

5. Ernest C. Peixotto, *Romantic California* (New York: Scribner's, 1910); and Charles Dudley Warner, *Our Italy* (New York: Harper, 1891).

6. Ernest C. Peixotto, *By Italian Seas* (New York: Scribner's, 1906).

7. *National Cyclopaedia of American Biography*, s.v. "Peixotto, Ernest Clifford"; and Ernest C. Peixotto, *Through the French Provinces* (1909). Peixotto was made an officer in the French Legion of Honor in 1924.

8. On the word "gringo": During the Mexican War, a favorite song of American soldiers was "Green Grow the Rushes, Oh!" Thereafter "gringo" became an epithet for any American of that time; see Peixotto, *Romantic California*, 45, 93–94.

9. On the Bohemian Club of San Francisco and its rural retreat, Bohemian Grove, see Kevin Starr, *Americans and the California Dream, 1850–1915* (New York: Oxford University Press, 1973), 246–49, 282–83, 380–82. In 1903 Bernard Maybeck designed the clubhouse at Bohemian Grove; see Kenneth H. Cardwell, *Bernard Maybeck: Artisan, Architect, Artist* (Santa Barbara: Peregrine Smith, 1977), 82–85. Peixotto was also a Bohemian Club member.

10. Mary Austin, *California: The Land of the Sun* (New York: Macmillan; London: Adam & Charles Black, 1914), 3–9. This was the first American edition, printed in Edinburgh; see also Mary Austin, *Earth Horizon* (New York: Literary Guild, 1932), 337.

11. Augusta Fink, *I-Mary: A Biography of Mary Austin* (Tucson: University of Arizona Press, 1983), 170. See also T. M. Pearce, *The Beloved House* (Caldwell, Idaho: Caxton Printers, 1940); and Esther Lanigan Stineman, *Mary Austin: Song of a Maverick* (New Haven, Conn.: Yale University Press, 1989.

12. Austin, *California*, 17.

13. Ibid., 20–22.

14. Ibid., 113. In 1909 the North Farallon Islands were designated a national wildlife refuge, but the South Farallon Islands were not included in the refuge until 1969; see Allan A. Schoenherr, C. Robert Feldmeth, and Michael J. Emerson, *Natural History of the Islands of California* (Berkeley: University of California Press, 1999), 366–76.

15. Austin, *California*, 110, 65.

16. Ibid., 84.

17. Austin, *Earth Horizon*, 337; Augusta Fink, *I-Mary*, 170; and note 10, above.

18. John Steinbeck, *The Pastures of Heaven* (1932; rpt., New York: Penguin, 1982); John Steinbeck to Amasa (Ted) Miller, May 1931, quoted in Jackson J. Benson, *The True Adventures of John Steinbeck, Writer* (New York: Viking, 1984), 210; and John Steinbeck to Amasa (Ted) Miller, [December 1931], in Elaine Steinbeck and Robert Wallsten, eds., *Steinbeck: A Life in Letters* (New York: Viking, 1975), 51–52.

19. Steinbeck, *Pastures of Heaven*, 104.

20. Ibid., 64–84. On Steinbeck's gardening, see Benson, *True Adventures of John Steinbeck*, 177–78; Jackson J. Benson, *Looking for Steinbeck's Ghost* (Norman: University of Oklahoma Press, 1988), 8–10, 57–59, 64; and Jay Parini, *John Steinbeck: A Biography* (New York: Henry Holt, 1995), 130. See also Susan F. Beegel, Susan Shillinglaw, and Wesley

N. Tiffney Jr., eds., *Steinbeck and the Environment: Interdisciplinary Approaches* (Tuscaloosa: University of Alabama Press, 1997).

21. John Steinbeck, *The Long Valley* (1938; rpt., New York: Compass/Viking, 1966), 27–42.

22. Steinbeck, *Pastures of Heaven*, 102.

23. Steinbeck, *Long Valley*, 238–56.

24. Ibid., 302.

25. Armine von Tempski, *Born in Paradise* (New York: Literary Guild, 1940), 3–5. The original publisher was Duell, Sloan and Pearce, New York.

26. Ibid., 292; and Hassoldt Davis, review of *Born in Paradise*, in *Saturday Review of Literature*, 26 October 1940, 14.

27. On sugar cane production in the Hawaiian Islands, see Gavan Daws, *Shoal of Time: A History of the Hawaiian Islands* (1968; Honolulu: University Press of Hawaii, 1974), 311–17.

28. Von Tempski, *Born in Paradise*, 55, 212–22, 9–12.

29. Ibid., 258–68, 66–68.

30. Armine von Tempski, *Aloha: The Story of One Who Was Born in Paradise* (New York: Duell, Sloan & Pearce, 1946), 121–23. See also Armine von Tempski, *Hawaiian Harvest* (New York: Frederick A. Stokes, 1933).

31. The first of the Exhibit Format books, *This Is the American Earth* (1960), by Ansel Adams and Nancy Newhall, won an award from the American Institute of Graphic Arts; see David Brower, *Work in Progress* (Salt Lake City: Peregrine Smith, 1991), 11–15.

32. David Brower, ed., *Not Man Apart* (San Francisco: Sierra Club, 1965), 20. The quotation is from Jeffers's poem "The Answer," in *The Selected Poetry of Robinson Jeffers* (New York: Random House, 1938), 594. On the Owings's home at Big Sur and the freeway controversy, see also Nathaniel Alexander Owings, *The Spaces In Between: An Architect's Journey* (Boston: Houghton Mifflin, 1973), 185–212.

33. On the publishing of the Sierra Club Exhibit Format books and their paperback editions (by Ballantine Books), see Brower, *Work in Progress*, 11–26.

FOUR THE ARID WEST

1. Mary Austin, *The Land of Little Rain* (1903; rpt., Albuquerque: University of New Mexico Press, 1974), 8–9.

2. Christopher Lasch, *The True and Only Heaven: Progress and Its Critics* (New York: W. W. Norton, 1991), 82–83, 117–19.

3. J. B. Jackson, *Landscapes: Selected Writings*, ed. Ervin H. Zube (Amherst: University of Massachusetts Press, 1970); and Robert Venturi, Denise Scott Brown, and Steven Izenour, *Learning from Las Vegas* (1972; rev. ed., Cambridge: MIT Press, 1977). Jackson was the founder-editor of *Landscape* magazine from 1951 to 1968; see Helaine Kaplan Prentice, "John Brinckerhoff Jackson," *Landscape Architecture* (November 1981): 740–46.

4. John R. Stilgoe, "J. B. Jackson: A Literary Appreciation," *Land Forum* (Summer/Fall

1997): 8–10; Andrea Oppenheimer Dean, "Riding into the Future," *Landscape Architecture* (January 1996): 58–63; and Prentice, "John Brinckerhoff Jackson."

5. J. B. Jackson, "The Public Landscape" (1966), in Jackson, *Landscapes: Selected Writings*, 153–60. On Jackson and environmentalism, see also his "Learning about Landscapes," in J. B. Jackson, *The Necessity for Ruins* (Amherst: University of Massachusetts Press, 1980), 1–2, 16; and Marc Treib's contribution to "John Brinckerhoff Jackson, 1909–1996," *Landscape Journal* 16 (Spring 1997): 6.

6. Stilgoe, "J. B. Jackson," 10.

7. J. B. Jackson, "The Four Corners Country" (Autumn 1960), in *Changing Rural Landscapes*, ed. Ervin H. Zube and Margaret J. Zube (Amherst: University of Massachusetts Press, 1977), 88–101.

8. J. B. Jackson, "First Comes the House" (Winter 1959–60), in Jackson, *The Essential Landscape: The New Mexico Photographic Survey with Essays by J. B. Jackson* (Albuquerque: University of New Mexico Press, 1985), 13–22.

9. J. B. Jackson, "Two Street Scenes" (Spring 1954), in Jackson, *Landscapes: Selected Writings*, 107–12.

10. J. B. Jackson, "Pueblo Dwellings and Our Own," in Jackson, *A Sense of Place, A Sense of Time* (New Haven, Conn.: Yale University Press, 1994), 29–37. This essay, originally published as "Pueblo Architecture and Our Own" in *Landscape* (Winter 1953–54), was revised for inclusion in Jackson, *Essential Landscape*.

11. Jackson, "Pueblo Dwellings and Our Own," 32–34.

12. J. B. Jackson, Harvard College *Class Record* (Class of 1932), Twenty-fifth Anniversary Report (1957), in Harvard University Archives; and Stilgoe, "J. B. Jackson."

13. Mary Austin, *The Land of Journey's Ending* (1924; Tucson: University of Arizona Press, 1983), 437. See also T. M. Pearce, *The Beloved House* (Caldwell, Idaho: Caxton Printers, 1940).

14. Larry Evers, introductory essay in Austin, *Land of Journey's Ending*, xv–xxi.

15. Austin, *Land of Journey's Ending*, 72–73.

16. Ibid., 70, 73, 77–78.

17. Ibid., 86–116. See also Mary Austin, *Earth Horizon: Autobiography* (New York: Literary Guild, 1932), 349–54; Augusta Fink, *I-Mary: A Biography of Mary Austin* (Tucson: University of Arizona Press, 1983), 223–27; and Evers, introductory essay.

18. Willa Cather, *The Professor's House* (1925; rpt., New York: Vintage, 1990).

19. See especially Bernice Slote, ed., *The Kingdom of Art: Willa Cather's First Principles and Critical Statements, 1893–1896* (Lincoln: University of Nebraska Press, 1966); and Hermione Lee, *Willa Cather: A Life Saved Up* (1989; London: Virago, 1997), 244–48. See also David Harrell, *From Mesa Verde to* The Professor's House (Albuquerque: University of New Mexico Press, 1992); and Janis P. Stout, *Willa Cather: The Writer and Her World* (Charlottesville: University Press of Virginia, 2000).

20. Virgil, *The Aeneid*, trans. Robert Fitzgerald (New York: Random House, 1983), 8.314–29, 6.791–95. See also A. Bartlett Giamatti, *The Earthly Paradise and the Renaissance Epic* (1966; New York: W. W. Norton, 1989), 25.

21. Willa Cather, *The Song of the Lark* (1915; rpt., Boston: Houghton Mifflin, 1937), 367–76. See also Sharon O'Brien, *Willa Cather: The Emerging Voice* (New York: Oxford University Press, 1987), 403–20; and James Woodress, *Willa Cather: A Literary Life* (Lincoln: University of Nebraska Press, 1987), 3–11.

22. Cather, *Song of the Lark*, 378, 408, 564.

23. See Stout, *Willa Cather*, 184–219; and Edward W. Said, *Culture and Imperialism* (New York: Alfred A. Knopf, 1993).

24. Emerson Hough, *The Passing of the Frontier: A Chronicle of the Old West* (1918; rpt., New Haven, Conn.: Yale University Press, 1921), 168–72.

25. Wallace Stegner, *Wolf Willow: A History, A Story, and a Memory of the Last Plains Frontier* (1962; rpt., Lincoln: University of Nebraska Press, 1980), 306, 29. See also Dick Harrison, "Frontiers and Borders: Wallace Stegner in Canada," in *Wallace Stegner: Man and Writer*, ed. Charles E. Rankin (Albuquerque: University of New Mexico Press, 1996), 181–204.

26. Wallace Stegner, "At Home in the Fields of the Lord" (1950), in Stegner, *The Sound of Mountain Water* (1969; rpt., New York: E. P. Dutton, 1980), 161.

27. Jackson Benson, *Wallace Stegner: His Life and Work* (New York: Viking, 1996), 34–38.

28. Stegner, "At Home in the Fields of the Lord," 169. Stegner's second thoughts in 1979 are footnoted here, p. 160.

29. Ann Woodin, *Home Is the Desert* (1964; rpt., Tucson: University of Arizona Press, 1984), 3–4, 237–38.

30. Ibid., 241.

31. Wallace Stegner, *Beyond the Hundredth Meridian: John Wesley Powell and the Second Opening of the West* (1954; rpt., New York: Penguin, 1992).

32. Wallace Stegner, "San Juan and Glen Canyon" (1948), in Stegner, *Sound of Mountain Water*, 120. This essay was reprinted as "Back Roads River" in Stegner, *Marking the Sparrow's Fall: Wallace Stegner's American West*, ed. Page Stegner (New York: Henry Holt, 1998), 68–81.

33. Stephen J. Pyne, *How the Canyon Became Grand: A Short History* (1998; New York: Penguin, 1999), 140–41.

34. On Stegner, Brower, and Glen Canyon Dam, see Wallace Stegner and Richard W. Etulain, *Conversations with Wallace Stegner on Western History and Literature* (Salt Lake City: University of Utah Press, 1983), 168–69; David Brower, *For Earth's Sake: The Life and Times of David Brower* (Salt Lake City: Peregrine Smith, 1990), 341–51; John McPhee, *Encounters with the Archdruid* (New York: Farrar, Straus & Giroux, 1971), 161–63, 196–208; Benson, *Wallace Stegner*, 227–28; and Dan Flores, "Citizen of a Larger Country: Wallace Stegner, the Environment and the West," in *Wallace Stegner*, ed. Rankin, 73–86.

35. Woodin, *Home Is the Desert*, 163, 166–67; and Joseph Wood Krutch, *Grand Canyon: Today and All Its Yesterdays* (New York: William Sloane, 1958), 275.

36. Wallace Stegner, "Glen Canyon Submersus" (1965), in Stegner, *Sound of Mountain*

Water, 121–36. Revised, this essay appeared in *Holiday,* in 1966, and was reprinted in Stegner, *Marking the Sparrow's Fall;* see Benson, *Wallace Stegner,* 304–5.

37. Stegner, "Glen Canyon Submersus," 136. See also Eliot Porter, *The Place No One Knew: Glen Canyon on the Colorado* (1963; rev. ed., San Francisco: Sierra Club, 1966); and Edward Abbey, *Desert Solitaire* (1968; rpt., New York: Touchstone/Simon & Schuster, 1990).

38. Stegner, "Glen Canyon Submersus," 134 note.

39. Wallace Stegner, "Wilderness Letter" (1960), in Stegner, *Sound of Mountain Water,* 145–53.

FIVE THE HEART OF THE COUNTRY

1. Josephine Johnson, *Now in November* (New York: Simon & Schuster, 1934); and John H. Davis and Kenneth Hinshaw, *Farmer in a Business Suit* (New York: Simon & Schuster, 1957).

2. Davis and Hinshaw, *Farmer in a Business Suit,* 133.

3. On pioneering research behind the development of genetic engineering, see James D. Watson, *The Double Helix: A Personal Account of the Discovery of the Structure of DNA* (New York: Atheneum, 1968); and Francis Crick, *What Mad Pursuit: A Personal View of Scientific Discovery* (New York: Basic Books, 1988). See also John Fraser Hart, *The Land That Feeds Us: The Story of American Farming* (New York: W. W. Norton, 1991); and Daniel E. Vasey, *An Ecological History of Agriculture, 10,000 B.C.–A.D. 10,000* (Ames: Iowa State University Press, 1992).

4. Jeremy Rifkin, with Nicanor Perlas, *Algeny* (New York: Viking, 1983), 18, 252–55.

5. Robert West Howard, *The Vanishing Land* (New York: Villard, 1985), 237.

6. On negative impacts, see Debi Barker, "Globalization and Industrial Agriculture," in *The Fatal Harvest Reader: The Tragedy of Industrial Agriculture,* ed. Andrew Kimbrell (Washington, D.C.: Island Press, 2002), 249–63. For positive arguments, see International Food Information Council, "Food Biotechnology and the Environment" (1998), in Theodore D. Goldfarb, ed., *Taking Sides: Clashing Views on Controversial Environmental Issues,* 8th ed. (Guildford, Conn.: Dushkin/McGraw-Hill, 1999), 128–34. Bill McKibben broadens the debate in *The End of Nature* (New York: Random House, 1989), 160–66; and *Enough: Staying Human in an Engineered Age* (New York: Times Books/Henry Holt, 2003), 137–43.

7. Rachel Peden, *Rural Free: A Farmwife's Almanac of Country Living* (New York: Knopf, 1961), 35–37.

8. Wendell Berry, "A Native Hill" (1969), in *Recollected Essays, 1965–1980* (San Francisco: North Point, 1981), 101.

9. Hamlin Garland, *Boy Life on the Prairie* (1899; rpt., Lincoln: University of Nebraska Press, 1961) and *Main-Travelled Roads* (1891; rpt., New York: Harper, 1930).

10. In *Boy Life on the Prairie* Garland wrote of the "coolly," a typical Wisconsin valley formed by a stream. In *A Son of the Middle Border* (New York: Macmillan, 1917), he used the term "coolee."

11. Hamlin Garland, introduction to the 1926 Allyn and Bacon school ed. of *Boy Life on the Prairie*, reprinted in the 1961 ed., 425–27. On Garland's life, see also Joseph B. McCullough, *Hamlin Garland* (Boston: Twayne/G. K. Hall, 1978); B. R. McElderry Jr., introduction to *Boy Life on the Prairie* (1961 ed.); Hamlin Garland's 1922 foreword and W. D. Howells's introduction to *Main-Travelled Roads* (1930 ed.); and "Hamlin Garland," in *Living Authors: A Book of Biographies*, ed. D. Tante (New York: H. W. Wilson, 1935), 141–42.

12. Garland, *Boy Life on the Prairie*, 80.

13. Ibid., 29.

14. Maginel Wright Barney, *The Valley of the God-Almighty Joneses* (New York: Appleton-Century, 1965). On Wright and the Taliesin landscape, see Walter L. Creese, *The Crowning of the American Landscape: Eight Great Spaces and Their Buildings* (Princeton, N.J.: Princeton University Press, 1985), 241–65; and Anne Whiston Spirn, "Frank Lloyd Wright: Architect of Landscape," in *Frank Lloyd Wright: Designs for an American Landscape, 1922–1932*, ed. David G. De Long (New York: Abrams, 1996), 135–69.

15. It is not clear which version of *The Sower* Enos had in reproduction. After Millet exhibited the painting at the Paris Salon of 1850–51, he returned to this subject repeatedly, in different media, for the next twenty years; see Alexandra R. Murphy, Richard Rand, Brian T. Allen, et al., *Jean-François Millet: Drawn into the Light* (Williamstown, Mass.: Sterling and Francine Clark Art Institute, 1999), 49–51, cat. 14–16.

16. Noting some previous farming and manufacturing in the Lloyd-Joneses' valley, Anne Spirn writes that the Lloyd-Joneses were *not* pioneers; see Spirn, "Frank Lloyd Wright: Architect of Landscape," 137. My discussion of pioneering refers to the Lloyd-Joneses' prior experience in America.

17. Barney, *Valley of the God-Almighty Joneses*, 49, 109.

18. Meryle Secrest, *Frank Lloyd Wright* (New York: Knopf, 1993), 197–98.

19. Some dates in Barney's memoir do not coincide with those in Secrest's *Frank Lloyd Wright*, a well-documented biography.

20. Mary Ellen Chase, *A Goodly Fellowship* (New York: Macmillan, 1939), 89–92.

21. Secrest, *Frank Lloyd Wright*, 198; and Chase, *Goodly Fellowship*, 114.

22. Frank Lloyd Wright, quoted in Barney, *Valley of the God-Almighty Joneses*, 13. See also Edgar Tafel, *Years with Frank Lloyd Wright: Apprentice to Genius* (1979; rpt., New York: Dover, 1985).

23. Florence Fifer Bohrer, "The Unitarian Hillside Home School," *Wisconsin Magazine of History* 38, no. 3 (Spring 1955): 151–55. See also Perry D. Westbrook, *Mary Ellen Chase* (New York: Twayne, 1965).

24. Carl Van Doren, *Three Worlds* (New York: Harper, 1936), 1.

25. Ibid., 27.

26. Ibid., 56–57, 22.

27. Johnson, *Now in November*, 119.

28. Josephine Johnson, *Seven Houses* (New York: Simon & Schuster, 1973); and Nancy Hoffman, afterword to Johnson, *Now in November* (1934; rpt., New York: Feminist

Press at The City University of New York, 1991). See also James Still, *River of Earth* (1940; rpt., Lexington: University Press of Kentucky, 1978); and Robert Frost, "The Death of the Hired Man," in Frost, *North of Boston* (New York: Henry Holt, 1914).

29. Johnson, *Now in November* (1934 ed.), 230–31.

30. Nancy Hoffman, afterword to *Now in November,* 267. Hoffman notes that *Now in November* won the Pulitzer Prize in 1935.

31. Rachel Peden, *The Land, the People* (New York: Knopf, 1966), 216, 292.

32. Ibid., 332.

33. Ibid, 6.

34. On Johnson's life, see John Fleischman, foreword to Josephine Johnson, *The Inland Island* (1969; rpt., Cincinnati: Story Press, 1996); and Hoffman, afterword to Johnson, *Now in November.* See also Andrew J. Angyal, *Wendell Berry* (New York: Twayne/Prentice Hall, 1995); and Paul Merchant, ed., *Wendell Berry* (Lewiston, Idaho: Confluence Press, 1991).

35. Wendell Berry, "The Long-Legged House" (1969), in Berry, *Recollected Essays, 1965–1980,* 17–72. See also Scott Slovic, *Seeking Awareness in American Nature Writing: Henry Thoreau, Annie Dillard, Edward Abbey, Wendell Berry, Barry Lopez* (Salt Lake City: University of Utah Press, 1992).

36. Wendell Berry, "A Native Hill" (1969), in Berry, *Recollected Essays,* 98.

37. Josephine Johnson, *The Inland Island* (New York: Simon & Schuster, 1969), 138.

38. Ibid., 159.

SIX   THE SMALL PLACE AND THE LITTLE GARDEN

1. Fletcher Steele, *Design in the Little Garden* (Boston: Atlantic Monthly Press, 1924), 115–16.

2. Mrs. Edward Harding, *Peonies in the Little Garden* (Boston: Atlantic Monthly Press, 1923), 4–5, and photograph facing p. 4.

3. Childe Hassam, *Celia Thaxter in Her Garden,* in Ella M. Foshay, *Reflections of Nature: Flowers in American Art* (New York: Knopf/Whitney Museum of American Art, 1984), pl. 47.

4. Reproductions of Hassam's *Celia Thaxter in Her Garden* appear in David Park Curry, *Childe Hassam: An Island Garden Revisited* (Denver and New York: Denver Art Museum/W. W. Norton, 1990); Deborah Nevins, "Poet's Garden, Painter's Eye," *House and Garden* (August 1984): 92; and Susan Rayfield, "Blossoms by a Summer Sea," *Americana* (June 1990): 32.

5. Childe Hassam, *Gathering Flowers in a French Garden,* in Foshay, *Reflections of Nature,* pl. 46; and Steele, *Design in the Little Garden,* 121.

6. Celia Thaxter to Sarah Orne Jewett, 28 September 1893, in Rosamond Thaxter, *Sandpiper: The Life and Letters of Celia Thaxter* (1963; rpt., Hampton, N.H.: Peter E. Randall, 1982), 238; and Celia Thaxter, *An Island Garden* (1894; rpt., Boston: Houghton Mifflin, 1988), 2.

7. Thaxter, *Island Garden*, 75.

8. See, for instance, Van Wyck Brooks, *New England: Indian Summer, 1865–1915* (New York: E. P. Dutton, 1940); Jane E. Vallier, *Poet on Demand: The Life, Letters and Works of Celia Thaxter*, 2d ed. (Portsmouth, N.H.: P. E. Randall, 1994); Sharon Paiva Stephan, *One Woman's Work: The Visual Art of Celia Laighton Thaxter* (Portsmouth, N.H.: P. E. Randall, 2001); and Doreen Bolger Burke, Jonathan Freedman, Alice Cooney Frelinghuysen, et al., *In Pursuit of Beauty: Americans and the Aesthetic Movement* (New York: Metropolitan Museum of Art/Rizzoli, 1986).

9. Thaxter, *Sandpiper*, 243. See also *Letters of Celia Thaxter*, ed. A[nnie] F[ields] and R[ose] L[amb] (Boston: Houghton Mifflin, 1895); and *By This Wing: Letters by Celia Thaxter to Bradford Torrey about Birds at the Isles of Shoals, 1888–1894*, ed. Donna Marion Titus (Manchester, N.H.: J. Palmer, 1999).

10. Caleb Mason, *Isles of Shoals Remembered: A Legacy from America's First Musicians' and Artists' Colony* (Rutland, Vt.: Charles E. Tuttle, 1992).

11. Alan Emmet, *So Fine a Prospect: Historic New England Gardens* (Hanover, N.H.: University Press of New England, 1996).

12. Vera Norwood, *Made from This Earth: American Women and Nature* (Chapel Hill: University of North Carolina Press, 1993).

13. Celia Thaxter, *Among the Isles of Shoals* (1873; rpt., Bowie, Md.: Heritage Books, 1978), 14, 99, 133.

14. Celia Thaxter to Annie Fields [1881], and Celia Thaxter to Mary Cowden Clarke [1894], in *Letters of Celia Thaxter*, 129, 219.

15. Chris Robarge and John M. Kingsbury, quoted in Rayfield, "Blossoms by a Summer Sea," 33.

16. Celia Thaxter to Sarah Orne Jewett [undated], and Thaxter to Jewett, 5 February 1893, in *Letters of Celia Thaxter*, 198–200; Thaxter to Jewett, 28 September 1893, in Thaxter, *Sandpiper*, 238; and Sarah Orne Jewett, *The Country of the Pointed Firs* (Boston: Houghton Mifflin, 1896).

17. Mabel Osgood Wright, *The Garden, You, and I* (New York: Macmillan, 1906). See also Virginia Lopez Begg, "Mabel Osgood Wright: The Friendship of Nature and the Commuter's Wife," *Journal of the New England Garden History Society* 5 (Fall 1997): 35–41; and Beverly Seaton, "Gardening Books for the Commuter's Wife, 1900–1937," *Landscape* 28, no. 2 (1985): 41–47.

18. Wright, *Garden, You, and I*, 60.

19. Ibid., 223.

20. *Who Was Who in America*, s.v. "Mitchell, Sydney Bancroft."

21. Sydney B. Mitchell, *Gardening in California* (Garden City, N.Y.: Doubleday, Page, 1923), 6.

22. Ibid., 37–58; and Sydney B. Mitchell, *Your California Garden and Mine* (New York: M. Barrows, 1947), xiii.

23. *Who Was Who in America*, s.v. "Mitchell, Sydney Bancroft."

24. Steele, *Design in the Little Garden,* 33–34.

25. Robin Karson, *Fletcher Steele, Landscape Architect: An Account of the Gardenmaker's Life, 1885–1971* (New York: Abrams/Sagapress, 1989).

26. See Fletcher Steele, "New Styles in Gardening," *House Beautiful* 65 (March 1929): 317, 352–54; and Fletcher Steele, "New Pioneering in Gardening Design," *Landscape Architecture* 20 (April 1930): 159–77.

27. George B. Tobey, quoted in Karson, *Fletcher Steele,* 68.

28. Steele, *Design in the Little Garden,* 87.

29. Ibid., 34.

30. Mrs. Francis King, *The Little Garden* (Boston: Atlantic Monthly Press, 1921), vii–viii.

31. Ibid., 26–27.

32. Virginia Lopez Begg, "Louisa Yeomans King (1863–1948)," in *Pioneers of American Landscape Design,* ed. Charles A. Birnbaum and Robin Karson (New York: McGraw-Hill, 2000), 216–17; and King, *Little Garden,* 67.

33. Frances Edge McIlvaine, *Spring in the Little Garden* (Boston: Little, Brown, 1928).

34. Kate L. Brewster, *The Little Garden for Little Money* (Boston: Atlantic Monthly Press, 1924), 4.

35. Harding, *Peonies in the Little Garden,* 86–90.

36. Mrs. Francis King, *Variety in the Little Garden* (Boston: Atlantic Monthly Press, 1923), 115–16.

37. Herbert Durand, *My Wild Flower Garden* (New York: Putnam's, 1927).

38. Ibid., 193–94. See also Herbert Durand, *Taming the Wildings* (1923), and its second edition, retitled *Wild Flowers and Ferns: In Their Homes and in Our Gardens* (New York: Putnam's, 1925).

39. Louise Beebe Wilder, *Adventures in a Suburban Garden* (New York: Macmillan, 1931), ix; and *Who Was Who in America,* s.v. "Wilder, Louise Beebe." See also Virginia Lopez Begg, "Louise Beebe Wilder (1878–1938)," in *Pioneers of American Landscape Design,* 453–54; Lynden B. Miller, introduction to Louise Beebe Wilder, *Color in My Garden* (1918; rpt., New York: Atlantic Monthly Press, 1990); and Charles Elliott, foreword to Louise Beebe Wilder, *Adventures with Hardy Bulbs* (1936; rpt., New York: Lyons Press, 1998).

40. Louise Beebe Wilder, *Adventures in My Garden and Rock Garden* (1923; rpt., New York: Macmillan, 1929), 1–7, 16, 24.

41. Louise Beebe Wilder, *Pleasures and Problems of a Rock Garden* (Garden City, N.Y.: Doubleday, Doran, 1928), 57.

42. Wilder, *Adventures in My Garden and Rock Garden,* 3.

43. Wilder, *Adventures in a Suburban Garden,* 93.

44. Henry Beston, *Herbs and the Earth* (Garden City, N.Y.: Doubleday, Doran, 1935), 112–15.

45. Ibid., 9.

46. Ibid., 87, 30.

47. Wright, *The Garden, You, and I,* 289–95; and Louise Beebe Wilder, *The Fragrant Garden: A Book about Sweet Scented Flowers and Leaves* (1932; rpt., New York: Dover, 1974). On medicinal plants, see Ann Leighton, *Early American Gardens: "For Meate or Medicine"* (Boston: Houghton Mifflin, 1970).
48. Beston, *Herbs and the Earth,* 33–34.
49. Ibid., 4.
50. Ibid., 5, 17.

SEVEN THE ABANDONED PLACE

1. Elizabeth Coatsworth, *Country Neighborhood* (New York: Macmillan, 1944), 140–44.
2. Robert Frost, "The Black Cottage," in Frost, *Collected Poems, Prose, and Plays,* ed. Richard Poirier and Mark Richardson (New York: Library of America, 1995), 59–62.
3. "What This Magazine Stands For," *Country Life in America* 1 (November 1901): 24–25. See also Philip Dorf, *Liberty Hyde Bailey: An Informal Biography* (Ithaca, N.Y.: Cornell University Press, 1956).
4. "The Abandoned Farms," *Country Life in America* 1 (November 1901): 3–8.
5. "What This Magazine Stands For," 25.
6. Walter Prichard Eaton, "The Abandoned Farm" (1911), in Eaton, *Barn Doors and Byways* (Boston: Small, Maynard, 1913), 210–37.
7. Eaton, "Abandoned Farm," 225, 236–37.
8. Robert Frost to Walter Prichard Eaton, 15 July 1915, in *Selected Letters of Robert Frost,* ed. Lawrance Thompson (New York: Holt, Rinehart & Winston, 1964), 182–83.
9. Robert Frost, *Mountain Interval* (New York: Henry Holt, 1916), copy inscribed "For Walter Eaton," with Frost's handwritten transcription of his poem "Lodged," in Special Collections, Dartmouth College Library.
10. Robert Frost to Walter Prichard Eaton, 15 July 1915, and 18 September 1915 (excerpt), in *Selected Letters,* ed. Thompson, 182–83, 191–92. For the complete letter of 18 September 1915, see Frost, *Collected Poems, Prose, and Plays,* 690–91. See also Peter J. Schmitt, *Back to Nature: The Arcadian Myth in Urban America* (New York: Oxford University Press, 1969), 25.
11. Robert Frost, quoted in "Robert Frost on Poetic Drama" (1925), in *Interviews with Robert Frost,* ed. Edward Connery Lathem (New York: Holt, Rinehart & Winston, 1966), 61. See also Walter Prichard Eaton, *American Stage of Today* (Boston: Small, Maynard, 1908) and *The Actor's Heritage: Scenes from the Theatre of Yesterday and the Day Before* (Boston: Atlantic Monthly Press, 1924).
12. Between 1897 and 1899, both Frost and Eaton were studying philosophy and English literature at Harvard. By 1910, both had also visited the Dismal Swamp, on the border between Virginia and North Carolina. See Jay Parini, *Robert Frost: A Life* (New York: Henry Holt, 1999), 48–51, 59–66; "Eaton, Walter Prichard, 1900," folder, Harvard University Archives, HUD 300.505, box 617; and Walter Prichard Eaton, "The Dismal Swamp," in Eaton, *Barn Doors and Byways,* 178–209.

13. Robert Frost, "Ghost House," in *Collected Poems, Prose, and Plays,* 15–16. On the dating of this poem, see Edward Connery Lathem, ed., *The Poetry of Robert Frost* (New York: Holt, Rinehart & Winston, 1969), 531.

14. Robert Frost, "The Wood-Pile," in *Collected Poems, Prose, and Plays,* 100–101. See also Robert Bernard Hass, *Going by Contraries: Robert Frost's Conflict with Science* (Charlottesville: University Press of Virginia, 2002).

15. Robert Frost, quoted in Paul Waitt, "A Visit in South Shaftsbury" (1921), in *Interviews with Robert Frost,* 35.

16. Jay Parini, *Robert Frost,* 441. See also William Prichard, *Frost: A Literary Life Reconsidered,* 2d ed. (Amherst: University of Massachusetts Press, 1993); and Reginald L. Cook, *The Dimensions of Robert Frost* (New York: Rinehart & Co., 1958).

17. Robert Frost, "A Brook in the City" and "The Need of Being Versed in Country Things," in Frost, *New Hampshire* (New York: Henry Holt, 1923), 98, 113; and Frost, "The Birthplace," in *Collected Poems, Prose, and Plays,* 243. On the dating of "The Birthplace," see *Poetry of Robert Frost,* 556.

18. Robert Frost, "The Last Mowing," in *Collected Poems, Prose, and Plays,* 242–43.

19. Robert Frost to Louis Untermeyer, 13 May 1932, in *The Letters of Robert Frost to Louis Untermeyer* (New York: Holt, Rinehart & Winston, 1963), 222–23.

20. In an interview with Benson Y. Landis, published in 1931, Frost spoke of his need to be "almost wastefully alone." See *Interviews with Robert Frost,* 76.

21. Robert Frost, "Directive," in *Collected Poems, Prose, and Plays,* 341–42. On the dating of this poem, see *Poetry of Robert Frost,* 569. On the poem's local context, see John Elder, *Reading the Mountains of Home* (Cambridge: Harvard University Press, 1998).

22. Walter Prichard Eaton, "Cellar Holes" (1921), in Eaton, *On Yankee Hilltops* (Boston: W. A. Wilde, 1933), 9–28.

23. Walter Prichard Eaton, "Sweets for Squirrels" (1932), in Eaton, *On Yankee Hilltops,* 111–28.

24. Elizabeth Coatsworth, "Houses without People," in Coatsworth, *Maine Ways* (New York: Macmillan, 1947), 87–90.

25. William Graves, *Hawaii* (Washington, D.C.: National Geographic Society, 1970), 169, 172.

26. Armine von Tempski, *Dust: A Novel of Hawaii* (New York: Frederick A. Stokes Co., 1928); *Born in Paradise* (New York: Literary Guild, 1940); and *Aloha: The Story of One Who Was Born in Paradise* (New York: Duell, Sloan & Pearce, 1946), 167–69. See also chapter 3, above.

27. Von Tempski, *Dust,* 31, 258, 168.

28. Ibid., 81; and von Tempski, *Aloha,* 26.

29. Von Tempski, *Aloha,* 12; and von Tempski, *Dust,* 241.

30. Edward Abbey, *Desert Solitaire* (1968; rpt., New York: Touchstone/Simon & Schuster, 1990), 268.

31. Devereux Butcher, *Exploring Our National Parks and Monuments,* 9th ed. (Boulder,

Colo.: Roberts Rinehart; Washington, D.C.: National Parks and Conservation Association, 1995), 9.

32. Abbey, *Desert Solitaire*, 34–37.

33. See Wallace Stegner, "San Juan and Glen Canyon" (1948), in Stegner, *The Sound of Mountain Water* (1969; rpt., New York: E. P. Dutton, 1980); Ann Woodin, *Home Is the Desert* (1964; rpt., Tucson: University of Arizona Press, 1984); and chapter 4, above.

34. Abbey, *Desert Solitaire*, 265.

35. Aldo Leopold, quoted in Luna B. Leopold, preface to Aldo Leopold, *Round River: From the Journals of Aldo Leopold* (1953; rpt., Minocqua, Wisc.: NorthWord Press, 1991), vii.

36. Sigurd Olson, *The Singing Wilderness* (New York: Alfred A. Knopf, 1956), 206.

37. Aldo Leopold, *Round River*, 191, 93–101.

38. David Backes, *A Wilderness Within: The Life of Sigurd F. Olson* (Minneapolis: University of Minnesota Press, 1997), 85–90, 96–98.

39. Sigurd Olson, *Singing Wilderness*, 204–8.

39. Backes, *Wilderness Within*, 320–26.

EIGHT   THE REINHABITED PLACE

1. Wolf Von Eckardt, *A Place to Live: The Crisis of the Cities* (1967; rpt., New York: Delta/Dell, 1969), 308.

2. Ibid., 388–403.

3. Kevin Lynch, *The Image of the City* (Cambridge: MIT Press, 1960); and Jane Jacobs, *The Death and Life of Great American Cities* (New York: Random House, 1961). Other classics of urban life and planning from the 1960s include Charles Abrams, *The City Is the Frontier* (New York: Harper & Row, 1965); and Herbert J. Gans, *The Urban Villagers: Group and Class in the Life of Italian-Americans* (1962; rpt., New York: Free Press, 1965).

4. Von Eckardt, *Place to Live*, 52, 311.

5. Jacobs, *Death and Life of Great American Cities*, 190–91.

6. Ibid., 14, 150–51, 447.

7. Alan Dunn, *East of Fifth: The Story of an Apartment House* (New York: Simon & Schuster, 1948).

8. On New York's historic zoning law of 1916, see William H. Jordy, *American Buildings and Their Architects: The Impact of European Modernism in the Mid-Twentieth Century* (1972; rpt., Garden City, N.Y.: Anchor/Doubleday, 1976), 40–44; and M. Christine Boyer, *Dreaming the Rational City: The Myth of American City Planning* (Cambridge: MIT Press, 1983), 93–95, 158–63.

9. Brendan Gill, *Here at the New Yorker* (New York: Random House, 1975), 241; and E. B. White, *Here Is New York* (New York: Harper, 1949).

10. Gill, *Here at the New Yorker*, 242.

11. Dunn, *East of Fifth*, 168.

12. Margaret Hard, *A Memory of Vermont: Our Life in the Johnny Appleseed Bookshop* (New York: Harcourt, Brace & World, 1967), 5.

13. Walter and Margaret Hard, *This Is Vermont* (Brattleboro, Vt.: Stephen Daye Press, 1936), 43–50.

14. David Grayson, *Adventures in Contentment* (New York: Doubleday, Page, 1907).

15. Hard, *Memory of Vermont*, 24–25, 58–59.

16. Ibid., 21–23.

17. Ibid., 175.

18. Walter Hard, *A Mountain Township* (New York: Harcourt, Brace, 1933), 10.

19. Hard, *Memory of Vermont*, 202. Walter Hard Jr. became editor-in-chief of *Vermont Life* in 1950. His sister, Ruth Hard Bonner, became a columnist for the Brattleboro (Vermont) *Reformer* and, later, a reference librarian in Watertown, New York.

20. Margaret and Walter Hard sold the Johnny Appleseed Bookshop to Frederick F. Taylor, who owned it for three decades, until the bookshop was closed in 1994. See Margaret Hard, *A Memory of Vermont* (1967; rpt., Tarrytown, N.Y.: Booksellers House, 1995). Margaret's poem "O Singing Greenness" concludes the book.

21. Lewis Gannett, *Cream Hill: Discoveries of a Weekend Countryman* (New York: Viking, 1949). On New Yorkers' weekend and seasonal migrations to northwestern Connecticut, see also Malcolm Cowley, *Exile's Return* (1951; rpt., New York: Penguin, 1982), 206–14.

22. Gannett, *Cream Hill*, 176–83; and *Who Was Who in America*, s.v. "Gannett, Lewis Stiles."

23. Gannett, *Cream Hill*, 153–56. On myths and realities of town meetings, see Howard Mansfield, *In the Memory House* (Golden, Colo.: Fulcrum, 1993), 81–111.

24. Gannett, *Cream Hill*, 140–43.

25. Elizabeth Coatsworth, *Country Neighborhood* (New York: Macmillan, 1944), 11.

26. Elizabeth Coatsworth, *Maine Ways* (New York: Macmillan, 1947), 12. Parts of *Country Neighborhood* and *Maine Ways* were reprinted, with slight changes, in Elizabeth Coatsworth, *Maine Memories* (Brattleboro, Vt.: Stephen Greene Press, 1968).

27. Henry Beston, *Northern Farm* (New York: Rinehart, 1948), 19.

28. Henry Beston, quoted in Larry Willard, "The Bestons of Chimney Farm," *Yankee* (September 1950): 33–34, 39.

29. Coatsworth, *Country Neighborhood*, 55. See also Roger Swain, introduction to Henry Beston, *Herbs and the Earth* (1935; rpt., Boston: David R. Godine, 1990). On MacDonald's drawings for *Northern Farm*, see Thoreau MacDonald, *Notebooks* (Moonbeam, Ontario: Penumbra Press, 1980), 129–34.

30. Ibid., 50–55; Coatsworth, *Maine Ways*, 7; Coatsworth, "The Farm," in *Country Poems* (New York: Macmillan, 1942), 12–13. I am indebted to Kate Barnes for introducing me to this poem.

31. Beston, *Northern Farm*, 17, 44–45.

32. Coatsworth, *Personal Geography: Almost an Autobiography* (Brattleboro, Vt.: Stephen Greene Press, 1976), 115–16; and Beston's report in Harvard College *Class Records*,

Class of 1909, Twenty-fifth Anniversary Report (1934), 566–71; and Thirtieth Anniversary Report (1939), 105–6; Harvard University Archives.

33. Beston, *Northern Farm*, 135.

34. Coatsworth, *Personal Geography*, 110–11. See also Elizabeth Coatsworth, "I Am an Old Woman Now . . . ," *Yankee* (October 1976): 6–7.

35. On suburban development in history, see John R. Stilgoe, *Borderlands: Origins of the American Suburb, 1820–1939* (New Haven, Conn.: Yale University Press, 1988); James Howard Kunstler, *The Geography of Nowhere: The Rise and Decline of America's Man-Made Landscape* (New York: Simon & Schuster, 1993); and Dolores Hayden, *Building Suburbia: Green Fields and Urban Growth, 1820–2000* (New York: Pantheon, 2003).

36. George Woodbury, *John Goffe's Mill* (New York: W. W. Norton, 1948), 17–27; and George Woodbury, *John Goffe's Legacy* (New York: W. W. Norton, 1955), 254–72.

37. Woodbury, *John Goffe's Legacy*, 256, 255. On Manchester's millworkers, see also Tamara K. Hareven and Randolph Langenbach, *Amoskeag: Life and Work in an American Factory-City* (New York: Pantheon, 1978).

38. Woodbury, *John Goffe's Mill*, 239.

39. Woodbury, *John Goffe's Legacy*, 272.

NINE THE LOST PLACE

1. Marjory Stoneman Douglas, *The Everglades: River of Grass* (New York: Rinehart, 1947), 385.

2. Ibid., 8. See also Marjory Stoneman Douglas, *Voice of the River: An Autobiography*, with John Rothchild (Sarasota, Fla.: Pineapple Press, 1987).

3. Christopher Rand, "The Farming" (1952), in Rand, *The Changing Landscape* (New York: Oxford University Press, 1968), 5.

4. Rand, "The Town" (1964), in Rand, *Changing Landscape*, 146. Rand's note on change appears at the beginning, unpaginated.

5. Bernardine Kielty Scherman, *Girl from Fitchburg* (New York: Random House, 1964).

6. Ibid., 165–81, 153–54. See also *National Cyclopaedia of American Biography*, s.v. "Scherman, Harry"; and Katharine Scherman, *Spring on an Arctic Island* (Boston: Little, Brown, 1956).

7. Louise Dickinson Rich, preface to the 1983 ed., *Innocence under the Elms* (1955; rpt., Orleans, Mass.: Parnassus Imprints, 1983). See also Louise Dickinson Rich, *We Took to the Woods* (Philadelphia: Lippincott, 1942) and *Happy the Land* (Philadelphia: Lippincott, 1946); and the biography by Alice Arlen, *She Took to the Woods* (Rockport, Maine: Down East Books, 2000), 2–7, 111–12.

8. Rich, *Innocence under the Elms*, 241.

9. Henry James, *The American Scene* (1907; rpt., Bloomington: Indiana University Press, 1968), 462. In the introduction to this reprint, James's biographer Leon Edel notes that the first American edition of *The American Scene* did not contain James's last few pages, from which this quotation is taken. Later American editions included these pages, which had appeared in the first English edition, of 1907.

10. Ibid., 71, 211.

11. Henry James, *Notes of a Son and Brother* (1914), in Henry James, *Autobiography*, ed. F. W. Dupee (New York: Criterion, 1956), 296–300. See also Leon Edel, *Henry James: The Untried Years, 1843–1870* (Philadelphia: Lippincott, 1953); and Henry Adams, "The Mind of John La Farge," in Henry Adams, Kathleen A. Foster, Henry A. La Farge, et al., *John La Farge* (New York: Abbeville Press, 1987).

12. James, *American Scene*, 224; and James, *Notes of a Son and Brother*, 299.

13. Walter Prichard Eaton, "Lament for Birch Meadow," *Virginia Quarterly Review* 29, no. 1 (Winter 1953): 93–102.

14. Ibid., 102.

15. Thomas Barbour, *That Vanishing Eden* (Boston: Atlantic–Little, Brown, 1944), 3. See also Thomas Barbour, *Naturalist at Large* (Boston: Atlantic–Little, Brown, 1943); and *Dictionary of American Biography*, s.v. "Barbour, Thomas."

16. Barbour, *Vanishing Eden*, 225, 229.

17. Ibid., 230, and photo opposite p. 148. On efforts to revive the Everglades, see Michael Grunwald's series of four front-page articles in the *Washington Post*, 23–26 June 2002; and Raymond F. Dasmann, *No Further Retreat: The Fight to Save Florida* (New York: Macmillan, 1971). For a social and environmental history, see Mark Derr, *Some Kind of Paradise: A Chronicle of Man and the Land in Florida* (New York: William Morrow, 1989).

18. Barbour, *Vanishing Eden*, 237.

19. Raymond F. Dasmann, *Called by the Wild: The Autobiography of a Conservationist* (Berkeley: University of California Press, 2002), 122; and Raymond F. Dasmann, *The Destruction of California* (New York: Macmillan, 1965), 225.

20. Dasmann, *Destruction of California*, 211, 221. See Aldo Leopold, *A Sand County Almanac* (New York: Oxford University Press, 1949); Jane Jacobs, *The Death and Life of Great American Cities* (New York: Random House, 1961); and chapter 8, above.

21. Dasmann, *Destruction of California*, 220, 175–80, 209.

22. Dasmann, *Called by the Wild*, 118–20.

23. M. F. K. Fisher, "Streets of Gold Forsworn" and "Prologue," in Fisher, *Among Friends* (New York: Knopf, 1971).

24. M. F. K. Fisher, *The Gastronomical Me* (1943), in Fisher, *The Art of Eating* (Cleveland and New York: World Pub. Co., 1954), 353. See also Joan Reardon, *M. F. K. Fisher, Julia Child, and Alice Waters: Celebrating the Pleasures of the Table* (New York: Harmony Books, 1994).

25. Fisher, *Gastronomical Me*, 358.

26. Loren Eiseley, "The Brown Wasps" (ca. 1956), in Eiseley, *The Night Country* (New York: Scribner's, 1971), 235. On the dating of this essay, see Gale E. Christianson, *Fox at the Wood's Edge: A Biography of Loren Eiseley* (New York: Henry Holt, 1990), 294.

27. Eiseley, "Brown Wasps," 236.

1. Ansel Adams, *My Camera in Yosemite Valley: 24 Photographs and an Essay on Mountain Photography* (Boston: Houghton Mifflin, 1949), foreword, reprinted in *Living Wilderness* 14, no. 31 (Winter 1949–50): 1–2. See also Ansel Adams, *Yosemite and the Range of Light* (Boston: Little, Brown/New York Graphic Society, 1979).

2. Marjorie Kinnan Rawlings, *Cross Creek* (New York: Scribner's, 1942), 359; and Gordon E. Bigelow, *Frontier Eden: The Literary Career of Marjorie Kinnan Rawlings* (Gainesville: University of Florida Press, 1966), 43.

3. Henry Beston, *Herbs and the Earth* (Garden City, N.Y.: Doubleday, Doran, 1935), 137–39.

4. Christopher Alexander, *Notes on the Synthesis of Form* (1964; rpt., Cambridge: Harvard University Press, 1971), 216, note 17. In 1962 Christopher Alexander and Marvin Manheim published their computer program "HIDECS 2" as an MIT Civil Engineering Systems Laboratory Publication (no. 160). In "HIDECS 3" (1963) Alexander published four more computer programs.

5. Alexander, *Notes on the Synthesis of Form*, 53–54; and Christopher Alexander, quoted in Stephen Grabow, *Christopher Alexander: The Search for a New Paradigm in Architecture* (Stocksfield, Northumberland, UK: Oriel Press, 1983), 21.

6. William O. Douglas, *My Wilderness: The Pacific West* (Garden City, N.Y.: Doubleday, 1960) and *My Wilderness: East to Katahdin* (Garden City, N.Y.: Doubleday, 1961); and Ansel Adams, "The Artist and the Ideals of Wilderness," in *Wilderness: America's Living Heritage,* ed. David Brower (San Francisco: Sierra Club, 1961), 49–59.

7. William O. Douglas, "Wilderness and Human Rights," in *Wilderness: America's Living Heritage,* 13; and Adams, "Artist and the Ideals of Wilderness," 57–58.

8. The first book in the Sierra Club's Exhibit Format series was *This Is the American Earth* (1960), by Ansel Adams and Nancy Newhall; see David Brower, *Work in Progress* (Salt Lake City: Peregrine Smith, 1991), 11–15; and chapter 3, above.

9. The Wilderness Act of September 3, 1964 (78 Stat. 890; 16 U.S.C. 1131–1136), reprinted in *Selected Federal Public Wildlands Management Law,* vol. 1, compiled by Richard E. Shannon (Missoula: Montana Forest and Conservation Experiment Station, University of Montana, 1983), 191.

10. Douglas, "Wilderness and Human Rights," 11.

11. Douglas, *My Wilderness: The Pacific West,* 82; and William O. Douglas, *Go East, Young Man: The Early Years* (New York: Random House, 1974), 13.

12. Douglas, *My Wilderness: The Pacific West,* 30.

13. Ibid., 116. On Douglas's place in environmental history, see, for instance, Roderick Nash, *Wilderness and the American Mind,* 3d ed. (New Haven, Conn.: Yale University Press, 1982); and Stephen Fox, *The American Conservation Movement: John Muir and His Legacy* (1981; rpt., Madison: University of Wisconsin Press, 1985).

14. Douglas, *My Wilderness: East to Katahdin,* 189–90; and Louis J. Halle Jr., *Spring in Washington* (New York: William Sloane, 1947).

15. Ann Zwinger, *Beyond the Aspen Grove* (New York: Random House, 1970), 305.

16. Ibid., 9. On Zwinger's background, see Scott Slovic, "Ann Haymond Zwinger: A Portrait," in Ann Haymond Zwinger, *Shaped by Wind and Water: Reflections of a Naturalist* (Minneapolis, Minn.: Milkweed Editions, 2000); and *At Home on This Earth: Two Centuries of U.S. Women's Nature Writing,* ed. Lorraine Anderson and Thomas S. Edwards (Hanover, N.H.: University Press of New England, 2002).

17. Zwinger, *Beyond the Aspen Grove,* 85–87, 142, 127, 226, 171. In the paperback edition (1981), the wild candytuft has been renamed *Thlaspi montanum.*

18. Ibid., 304.

19. Ibid., 55.

20. Joseph Wood Krutch, *More Lives Than One* (New York: William Sloane Assoc., 1962), 362.

21. Joseph Wood Krutch, *Henry David Thoreau* (New York: William Sloane Assoc., 1948), 75.

22. Joseph Wood Krutch, *The Voice of the Desert* (New York: William Sloane Assoc., 1955), 193. See also Aldo Leopold, "The Land Ethic," in *A Sand County Almanac and Sketches Here and There* (1949; rpt., New York: Oxford University Press, 1970).

23. *Boston Globe,* "TV Week," title page photograph and text, 18 August 1963; and Joseph Wood Krutch, *Grand Canyon: Today and All Its Yesterdays* (New York: William Sloane Assoc., 1958), 275.

24. Joseph Wood Krutch, *The Desert Year* (1952; rpt., New York: Viking, 1963), 250.

25. Krutch, *More Lives Than One,* 307. See also Joseph Wood Krutch, *The Twelve Seasons* (New York: William Sloane Assoc., 1949); and John D. Margolis, *Joseph Wood Krutch: A Writer's Life* (Knoxville: University of Tennessee Press, 1980).

26. Rawlings, *Cross Creek,* 245–47.

27. See Gordon Bigelow, *Frontier Eden: The Literary Career of Marjorie Kinnan Rawlings* (Gainesville: University of Florida Press, 1966); and Elizabeth Silverthorne, *Marjorie Kinnan Rawlings: Sojourner at Cross Creek* (Woodstock, N.Y.: Overlook Press, 1988).

28. Rawlings, *Cross Creek,* 245.

29. See Bigelow, *Frontier Eden;* Silverthorne, *Marjorie Kinnan Rawlings;* Samuel I. Bellman, *Marjorie Kinnan Rawlings* (New York: Twayne, 1974); and Marjorie Kinnan Rawlings, "Hyacinth Drift," *Scribner's* 94 (September 1933): 169–73.

30. Rawlings, *Cross Creek,* 357–58.

31. William Beebe, *Unseen Life in New York: As a Naturalist Sees It* (New York: Duell, Sloan & Pearce; Boston: Little, Brown, 1953), 155–63.

32. De Forest Grant, foreword to *High Jungle,* by William Beebe (New York: Duell, Sloan & Pearce, 1949), v–vi. See also Paul Brooks, *Speaking for Nature: How Literary Naturalists from Henry Thoreau to Rachel Carson Have Shaped America* (1980; rpt., Sierra Club Books, 1983), 223–29.

33. Beebe, *Unseen Life in New York,* 128.

34. William Beebe, *The Book of Naturalists: An Anthology of the Best Natural History* (New York: Knopf, 1944), 4.

35. Rachel Carson, "Help Your Child to Wonder," *Woman's Home Companion* (July 1956):

25–27, 46–48; and Rachel Carson, *A Sense of Wonder* (New York: Harper & Row, 1965). See also Linda Lear, *Rachel Carson: Witness for Nature* (New York: Henry Holt, 1997).

36. Rachel Carson, quoted in Paul Brooks, *The House of Life: Rachel Carson at Work, with Selections from Her Writings, Published and Unpublished* (Boston: Houghton Mifflin, 1972), 160.

37. Rachel Carson, *The Edge of the Sea* (Boston: Houghton Mifflin, 1955), 41–43.

38. See, for example, Barry Commoner, *Science and Survival* (New York: Viking, 1966); Barry Commoner, *The Closing Circle: Nature, Man, and Technology* (New York: Alfred A. Knopf, 1971); Paul R. Ehrlich, *The Population Bomb* (New York: Ballantine Books, 1968); and Ian McHarg, *Design with Nature* (Garden City, N.Y.: Natural History Press, 1969).

39. Beebe, *Unseen Life in New York,* 101.

40. See Rachel Carson, "Journey to the Sea" and "Return" (1941), reprinted in Beebe, *Book of Naturalists,* 478–95.

41. Rachel Carson to William Beebe, 6 September 1948, quoted in Paul Brooks, *House of Life,* 110.

EPILOGUE

1. Rachel Carson, *Under the Sea-Wind: A Naturalist's Picture of Ocean Life,* 2d ed. (New York: Oxford University Press, 1952); William Beebe, *Unseen Life in New York: As a Naturalist Sees It* (New York: Duell, Sloan and Pearce/Boston: Little, Brown, 1953), 101; and Joseph Wood Krutch, *The Twelve Seasons: A Perpetual Calendar for the Country* (New York: William Sloane Assoc., 1949), 13.

2. Paul Rauber, "New! Improved! Destroys the Environment!" in *Sierra* (May/June 1998): 56–59.

3. Ibid., 59.

4. *Time,* quoted in Barry Commoner, *Making Peace with the Planet* (New York: Pantheon, 1990), 61.

5. Paul R. Josephson, *Industrialized Nature: Brute Force Technology and the Transformation of the Natural World* (Washington, D.C.: Island Press/Shearwater, 2002).

6. Bill McKibben, *Enough: Staying Human in an Engineered Age* (New York: Henry Holt/Times Books, 2003), 224.

7. See Peter Katz, *The New Urbanism: Toward an Architecture of Community* (New York: McGraw-Hill, 1994); and Philip Langdon, "A Good Place to Live," *Atlantic* (March 1988): 39–60.

8. Andres Duany, Elizabeth Plater-Zyberk, and Jeff Speck, *Suburban Nation: The Rise of Sprawl and the Decline of the American Dream* (2000; rpt., New York: North Point Press, 2001), 184–86.

9. Sven Birkerts, *Readings* (St. Paul, Minn.: Graywolf Press, 1999), 20.

10. Sven Birkerts, *The Gutenberg Elegies: The Fate of Reading in an Electronic Age* (Boston: Faber & Faber, 1994), 209.

11. Stephen L. Talbott, ed., *NetFuture: Technology and Human Responsibility* (http://www

.netfuture.org/); and Lisa Guernsey, "Editor Explores Unintended, and Negative, Side of Technology," *New York Times,* "Circuits" section, 25 November 1999.

12. Stephen L. Talbott, *The Future Does Not Compute: Transcending the Machines in Our Midst* (San Francisco: O'Reilly & Assoc., 1995), 420–22. For an extended juxtaposition of the real and the virtual, see Bill McKibben, *The Age of Missing Information* (New York: Random House, 1992).

Index

Italicized page numbers refer to illustrations.

INDEX